Variability is the Rule

A Companion Analysis of K–8 State Mathematics Standards

A volume in
Research in Mathematics Education

Series Editor:
Barbara J. Dougherty, *Iowa State University*

Research in Mathematics Education

Barbara J. Dougherty, Series Editor

*The Intended Mathematics Curriculum as
Represented in State-Level Curriculum Standards* (2006)
edited by Barbara Reys

The Classification of Quadrilaterals: A Study in Definition (2008)
by Zalman Usiskin (2008)

*A Decade of Middle School Mathematics Curriculum Implementation:
Lessons Learned From the Show-Me Project* (2008)
edited by Margaret R. Meyer and Cynthia W. Langrall

The History of the Geometry Curriculum in the United States (2008)
by Nathalie Sinclair

*Mathematics Curriculum in Pacific Rim Countries—China, Japan, Korea, and
Singapore: Proceedings of a Conference* (2008)
edited by Zalman Usiskin and Edwin Willmore

*Future Curricular Trends in School Algebra and Geometry:
Proceedings of a Conference* (2010)
edited by Zalman Usiskin, Kathleen Andersen, and Nicole Zotto

*Variability is the Rule:
A Companion Analysis of K–8 State Mathematics Standards* (2011)
edited by John P. Smith III

Variability is the Rule

A Companion Analysis of K–8 State Mathematics Standards

edited by

John P. Smith III
Michigan State University

Information Age Publishing, Inc.
Charlotte, North Carolina • www.infoagepub.com

Library of Congress Cataloging-in-Publication Data

Smith, John P. III (John Philip), 1952-
  Variability is the rule : a companion analysis of K-8 state mathematics /
John P. Smith. III
     p. cm. -- (Research in mathematics education)
Includes bibliographical references.
ISBN 978-1-61735-198-3 (hardcover) -- ISBN 978-1-61735-197-6 (pbk.) --
ISBN 978-1-61735-199-0 (e-book)
1. Mathematics--Study and teaching (Elementary)--Standards--United States.
2. Curriculum planning--United States. I. Title.
  QA135.6.S565 2010
  372.70973--dc22

                                                              2010041405

Printed in the United States of America

CONTENTS

ACKNOWLEDGMENTS

The research reported in this volume would not have been possible without the wisdom of my colleagues, Chris Hirsch, Glenda Lappan, and Barbara Reys, to create, develop, and maintain the Center for the Study of Mathematics Curriculum (CSMC) and without the foresight of the National Science Foundation to fund that Center (Grant No. ESI-033879). That said, all the approaches, results, interpretations, and judgments expressed in this volume are the authors' and do not necessarily reflect the views of the Foundation.

I wish also to acknowledge that nearly all the data analysis and most all the writing reported in this volume was completed by graduate students working simultaneously to complete their doctoral programs—that typically involved research on other topics and issues in mathematics education. In guiding these students through the research process, special thanks go to Glenda Lappan, Betty Phillips, and James Tarr.

As is generally the case with a volume of this sort, many scholars besides the authors have contributed to the quality of the analysis and exposition. They principally include colleagues who offered their time and expertise to read and review earlier versions of the chapters—Tom Banchoff, Doug Clements, Joan Ferrini-Mundy, Susan Friel, Katherine Halvorsen, Glenda Lappan, Rich Lehrer, Vince Melfi, Betty Phillips, Anna Sfard, Mike Shaughnessy, Nathalie Sinclair, Michelle Stephan, and Zal Usiskin. Their comments and criticisms have contributed substantially to the quality of this work. I also wish to acknowledge and thank Aladar Horvath for his careful reading of the near-to-final drafts of the chapters. Finally, I am grateful to the series Editor, Barbara Dougherty, for her careful editorial eye and support throughout the production process.

Jack Smith
January 2011

CHAPTER 1

INTRODUCTION

Completing the Analysis of
States' K–8 Mathematics Standards

John P. Smith III, Gregory V. Larnell, and James E. Tarr

The contents of this volume extend and deepen the analyses of grade level expectations in state mathematics standards developed in response to the federal No Child Left Behind (NCLB) legislation. Recently, Barbara Reys and her colleagues have reported an analysis of content expectations for number and operation, algebra, and reasoning in the K–8 mathematics standards of 42 states (Reys, 2006a). The focal question they addressed was whether and to what degree the United States had a *de facto* national curriculum based on a strong commonality across states in the content expected of teachers to teach and students to learn. Their analyses emphasized variability over commonality, as they found "a consistent lack of national consensus regarding common learning goals in mathematics at particular grade levels" (p. xxiv).

This volume extends their analysis and central focus of variability across states into additional and complementary mathematical domains. It applies new perspectives for examining and assessing the content of standards. Like the first, this volume reports careful examinations of the

Variability is the Rule: A Companion Analysis of K–8 State Mathematics Standards, pp. 1–11
Copyright © 2011 by Information Age Publishing

mathematical content of standards documents from the same 42 states, here in geometry & measurement and probability & statistics—two important domains of mathematics that often receive little national attention. Four chapters, the bulk of the volume, focus on describing states' choice of and progression through content in spatial measurement (length, area, and volume), congruence and similarity transformations (isometries and dilations), probability, and statistics—to enhance and expand the scope of the first volume. However, the character of two chapters differs from those four and the chapters in the first volume. They present more interpretive cognitive analyses, examining states' geometry & measurement expectations from particular analytic perspectives—the van Hiele hierarchy of geometric thinking and Bloom's taxonomy applied the verbs that structure grade-level learning expectations (GLEs).

The chapters in this volume also call attention to a different central theme. Rather than solely pursuing the question of curricular commonality at the national level, a second focus developed in this volume concerns specific features of GLEs that influence the teaching and learning of K–8 mathematics—their clarity and complexity, continuity across grades, and the capacity to help readers understand the mathematics they target. Despite the challenges raised in these analyses, this volume is optimistically oriented toward the future. Its authors hope to inform the work of future standards writers, who will return to and revise their expectations, and the teachers, students, and other stakeholders whose opportunities to learn mathematics will be influenced by the clarity and content of those standards.

The balance of this Introduction aims to orient readers more fully to the content of the chapters that follow. Before presenting an overview of each content area and chapter, we first briefly describe the national context that has shaped the development of state standards and the general methods that produced these analyses. Readers of the Reys (2006a) volume may find this introductory material familiar and wish to skip ahead.

THE NATIONAL CONTEXT: INFLUENCES ON AND EFFECTS OF STATE MATHEMATICS STANDARDS

A central catalyst for the current national focus on the precollege mathematics education has been the publication of numerous and diverse recommendations from private and professional organizations concerning the content and shape of school mathematics content, instruction, assessment and learning (e.g., Achieve, 2006; The College Board (2006); Franklin et al., 2007; National Council of Teachers of Mathematics [NCTM], 1989, 1991, 1995, 2000). All these "standards" have had a significant impact on the nature of mathematics teaching and mathematics education-oriented policy in the United States.

But NCLB certainly remains the strongest single influence on current K–8 mathematics education through its requirement that each state produce a comprehensive set of learning expectations for Grades 3 through 8 and an annual assessment of students' achievement based on those expectations. Before NCLB, many states organized standards by grade band (e.g., K–2, 3–5, 6–8 or K–5, and 6–8), and assessment took place toward the end of those grade bands, often at Grades 4 and 8. While the merits of NCLB continue to be debated, its impact cannot be questioned. The publication of state standards and the annual state testing programs mandated by the legislation have had a profound effect on what mathematics content is taught and tested in our nation's schools. The relationship, however, between state-level standards and other national-level recommendations has been contentious. More now than ever before, the constitutionally-protected tradition of state control of schooling is being challenged by federal demands for performance accountability (Lott & Nishimura, 2004).

On both sides of the issue, educational researchers, commentators from various academic fields and industries, as well as mathematics teachers and administrators, have contributed to this spirited discussion. One of the more notable assessments of state standards and mathematics curricula resulted from the Third International Mathematics and Science Study (TIMSS), where researchers noted the very wide breadth, lack of depth, and highly repetitive structure of school mathematics content in the United States, especially in Grades K through 8 (Schmidt, McKnight, Valverde, Houang, & Wiley, 1997). Continued attention to the same or similar content over multiple years coupled with relatively shallow coverage in each year led to the now-popular characterization of the U.S. mathematics curriculum as a "mile wide and inch deep" (cited in Reys, 2006a, pp. 4–5).

The publication of state mathematics standards have not only had important state-level effects on teaching and learning, they have also directed attention to their differential content (e.g., the analyses produced in these volumes) and, for some, their differential quality. For example, The Thomas B. Fordham Foundation has published evaluations that grade and rank individual states' standards. Their report, *The State of State Standards 2006*, characterized their orientation as follows:

> We supposed that states would respond constructively to criticisms of their standards, correct their shortcomings, and strive for excellence. We further supposed that the added stakes of the 2001 *No Child Left Behind Act* would cause state leaders to ask themselves, "are our standards up to the task at

hand?" So we supposed. But we also honor the arms-control mantra: Trust but verify. Beginning in 2003 (and culminating this spring) we set out again to see whether such improvement had in fact occurred, whether state academic standards in the *NCLB* era are significantly better than in 2000. (Finn, Julian, & Petrilli, 2006, p. 9)

The "Fordham reports," as they are often called, have attracted a wide array of responses and criticism. One such response, released within a month after the 2006 report was published, addressed the validity of the claims and methods used by the Fordham authors.

These three analyses [of state standards in English/language arts, science, and mathematics] were selectively mined from data gathered by Fordham— data which themselves are flawed and for which there is no evidence of validity. No rationale for Fordham's unorthodox and ad hoc analyses is provided, and those analyses are sorely lacking in methodological rigor. (Howe, 2006, p. 6)

As the debates over both state standards and the responses to standards have intensified, national-level organizations have published their own school mathematics standards as a means to influence thinking and practice at the state level. For example, NCTM has presented its mission as being "a public voice in providing vision and leadership to ensure mathematics learning of the highest quality for all" (NCTM, 2006), and Achieve sees itself leading "the national movement to raise standards, improve teaching and learning, and hold schools more accountable for student success" (Achieve, 2006).

THE CSMC AUTHORS

Like the first volume (Reys, 2006a), the analysts and authors of the chapters in this volume completed their work within the Center for the Study of Mathematics Curriculum (CSMC) as part of its broader effort to understand the role of curriculum in shaping school mathematics. The Center was funded by the National Science Foundation to develop, pursue, and support research on mathematics curriculum and to build national capacity to continue such research in the near-term future. Its work has been primarily carried out at five research institutions, the University of Missouri-Columbia (UM-C), Michigan State University (MSU), Western Michigan University (WMU), Horizon Research, Inc. (HR), and the University of Chicago (UC).

CSMC has understood the term "mathematics curriculum" broadly and intentionally to include what is expected (e.g., in state standards), what is written, organized, and sequenced in textbooks, and what is taught, learned and assessed. Standards that specify what is expected of teachers and students directly shaped, if not completely determine the content of what is written and taught. The Center has been well-positioned to carry out analyses of state standards because of its ability to bring mathematical, educational, and historical expertise to bear in the design, implementation, writing, and revision of those analyses. Relative to its task of building capacity for future research and scholarship on mathematics curricula, it is noteworthy that significant parts of the analyses presented in both volumes have been completed by graduate students working with faculty at three principal CSMC universities (UM-C, MSU, WMU). Their central role in carrying out the research and communicating its results is particularly evident in this volume.

TWO COUPLED DOMAINS OF SCHOOL MATHEMATICS

The mathematical content areas examined in this volume were chosen to complement the analyses completed in the first volume (Reys, 2006a). Where that volume surveyed content expectations for number & operation and algebra, this volume presents analyses of two content domains that are seldom the focus of discussions of school mathematics—geometry & measurement and statistics & probability. We use ampersands in this chapter to emphasize that the content areas in both pairings are rarely mentioned in K–12 education contexts in isolation from each other (for example, probability separate from statistics) and are often taught in deeply connected ways. Measurement, for example, is impossible to teach without considering the geometry of the spatial objects measured. Likewise, intelligent data collection and statistical analysis and inference depend centrally on concepts of probability. These two content domains share this "coupled status" while they live in the shadow of arithmetic, algebra, and calculus—areas that receive much more attention in national discussions of mathematics education (see, for example, the National Mathematics Panel's final report [National Mathematics Advisory Panel, 2008]). But because they are "coupled," it is appropriate to clarify how the authors of these analyses have understood these terms.

Geometry & Measurement

The four chapters that examine geometry & measurement standards are based on analyses conducted jointly by Sarah Kasten (Northern Kentucky University), Gregory Larnell (MSU), Sasha Wang (MSU), and Jill

Newton (Purdue University) using the same set of geometry and measurement GLEs from 42 states.[1] Collectively, they have understood K–8 school geometry to involve the *description* of two- and three-dimensional shapes, their properties (e.g., the regularity of polygons), relationships between them (e.g., congruence and similarity) and hierarchical organization (e.g., within the family of quadrilaterals), and *reasoning* about statements concerning such figures and their properties and relationships. By contrast, measurement is *metric* because spatial units are iterated and enumerated to characterize the features of geometric shapes. To make the measurement analysis both manageable and conceptually coherent, its scope was restricted to spatial measurement, that is, to length, area, and volume. At its core, measurement involves the identification of an attribute of an object or shape and a unit suitable to measure that attribute, the iteration of that unit, and the enumeration of the units (and parts of units) required to exhaust the attribute. It also involves qualitative judgments about length, area, and volume (i.e., judgments of more, less, and equal) that are not numerical (no iteration and enumeration of a unit is involved).

Despite this basic conceptual distinction, even a brief review of the geometry & measurement chapters will show that the states' geometry and measurement GLEs frequently combine descriptive and metric content. Indeed, many such examples can be identified in school mathematics; the Pythagorean Theorem, for example, unites the analysis of triangular shape with the measurement of length (and/or area). The authors of the state standards documents have addressed this coupled distinction in three different ways. Some states have constructed separate geometry and measurement strands with distinct expectations in each; others have offered separate strands but listed some expectations in both strands; still others have combined their expectations into a single "geometry & measurement" strand.

In contrast to the chapters on statistics & probability, the four chapters that address geometry & measurement are, despite their collective length, selective in their coverage. As suggested above, the measurement chapter (Kasten & Newton) does not address weight, time, or angular measure. The chapter on transformations (Wang & Smith) is far from an exhaustive treatment of descriptive geometry, though it "covers" the most central topics of symmetry, congruence, and similarity. Finally, the chapters that apply the van Hiele levels to analyze geometry expectations (Newton) and that use Bloom's taxonomy to analyze the cognitive demand of principal verbs (Larnell & Smith) provide extensive, if not complete "coverage" of descriptive geometry in pursuit of other analytic goals. As a consequence, readers may have to review multiple chapters to locate particular geometry or measurement topics and see how states have framed expectations for them.

Statistics & Probability

The two chapters that focus on statistics and probability are based on analyses of related but separate sets of learning expectations. In the statistics chapter, Jill Newton, Aladar Horvath (MSU), and Leslie Dietiker (MSU) have applied the American Statistical Association (ASA) *Guidelines for Assessment and Instruction in Statistics Education* (GAISE) *Report* to analyze GLEs relative to four components of work in statistics: (1) formulating questions, (2) collecting data, (3) analyzing data, and (4) interpreting results (Franklin et al., 2007). These four process components are both intricately related and central elements in the development of statistical literacy. We note with interest that the *GAISE Report* does not identify probability as a distinctive element in the statistical process but does recognize its importance in the school mathematics curriculum. Its authors assert that, "probability is an essential tool in applied mathematics and mathematical modeling ... [and] is also an essential tool in statistics" (Franklin et al., 2007, p. 8).

In the probability chapter, Shannon Dingman (University of Arkansas) and James E. Tarr (University of Missouri) examine four central constructs in probabilistic reasoning: (1) sample space, (2) theoretical probability, (3) experimental probability, and (4) conditional probability and independence.[2] When probability is viewed as the long-run relative frequency of an event, rich connections can be made between statistics and probability as students use experimental data to draw inferences regarding the theoretical probability of an event. Despite the potential to integrate the study of data and chance, the reader will learn that most states offer separate learning expectations for statistics and probability.

METHODS AND CHARACTER OF THE ANALYSES

The geometry & measurement analyses were jointly conducted on a common "data" set. Standards documents were collected from the 42 "states"—40 actual states, along with the Department of Defense Educational Agency and the District of Columbia—whenever those documents were structured by grade (e.g., Grade 5) rather than grade-band (e.g., K–2). From that set, the authors collectively identified 5,710 GLEs as addressing geometric and/or measurement content. These were placed into a single document with the identifiers of state, grade, and content strand (geometry, measurement, or geometry & measurement). Authors then searched and selected the appropriate expectations for his/her particular analyses, so each chapter reports an analysis of a different subset of the initial aggregate. Methods specific to their individual analyses are described in each chapter.

The analyses reported in the statistics and the probability chapters were pursued separately. Using a similar set of 41 state standards documents,[3] 1,711 GLEs were identified as addressing statistics content and 818 for probability. All statements were grouped by state; ordered by grade; and coded using an analytic framework developed for that chapter.

Appendix A contains the titles and dates of the 42 state standards documents that were used in these analyses. Readers should hold in mind that state standards regularly undergo revision. Thus this analysis represents the "state" of state standards in two content areas at a particular (recent) point in time. That said, the lessons contained in these analyses can be useful in examining current standards and informing their revision. The perspectives used and the issues raised should remain highly relevant for standards' authors and readers for some time.

Consistent with the first volume (Reys, 2006a), the principal analytic focus here has been the careful, accurate, and complete description of the content of GLEs. This stance is consistent with the overall goal of informing the field about how states have articulated expectations in these two important topic areas. Comparisons between states are frequent, but explicit and evaluative "grading" has been avoided. No attempt has been made to identify stronger vs. weaker states, much less "best" states, as a clear and accepted foundation for making such judgments does not yet exist. Authors do raise questions about specific practices (e.g., leaving gaps in the trajectory of topics across grades and repeating the same expectation across grades) and about the expression of specific expectations (e.g., see the Larnell & Smith chapter) in hopes of supporting improvement in the clarity and precision of expectations. As long as state mathematics standards continue to play an important role in determining what mathematics is taught in this country, we expect they will be continuously revised and improved. So we hope the analyses reported here will support that work.

INTRODUCTIONS TO SPECIFIC CHAPTERS

An Analysis of K–8 Measurement Grade-Level Expectations (Kasten & Newton)

The authors address a difficult task: Providing a single analysis of all GLEs that concern spatial measurement. It capitalizes research on the teaching and learning of measurement in two significant ways. First, the authors adapt a developmental framework from the research literature to answer the central questions of what students are expected to learn about measurement and when. Their analyses describe how GLEs targeting specific topics in one-, two-, and three-dimensional measurement are distributed across grade and developmental levels in their framework. They also analyze how well those expectations cover the "big ideas" of measurement that have been emphasized in research. Their results raise serious concerns about the focus of content and teaching of spatial measurement.

The Treatment of Transformations in K–8 Geometry and Measurement Grade-Level Expectations (Wang & Smith)

This chapter traces the role of distance-preserving transformations (isometries) and shape-preserving transformations (dilations) in geometry & measurement GLEs. The concept of transformation is relatively new in school geometry and therefore may be relatively unknown to many K–8 teachers. With this likelihood in mind, the authors analyze how, when, and how often transformations appear in the states' standards and how they are linked to the traditional geometric topics of congruence, similarity, and symmetry. Indeed, the question of *whether* they are explicitly and clearly linked (or not) to those traditional topics is central. The general answer is, "not as regularly as mathematics educators would like."

An Examination of K–8 Geometry State Standards Through the Lens of van Hiele's Levels of Geometric Thinking (Newton)

As the title indicates, this chapter applies a particular interpretive frame for the analysis of geometry GLEs. Newton introduces readers to the influential van Hiele framework of hierarchical levels of geometric thinking and then to research that has used that framework. She applies the framework to sort the states' GLEs according to the character of geometric reasoning each requires. The results point to a serious gap in students' introduction to and preparation for deductive reasoning about properties and relationships (Level 3 in the van Hiele framework). This gap presents serious challenges in high school geometry for teachers' and students' work on formal proof.

Verbs and Cognitive Demand in K–8 Geometry and Measurement Grade-Level Expectations (Larnell & Smith)

This chapter applies Bloom's taxonomy of educational objectives (Bloom, 1956) to assess how strongly the key verbs in GLEs shape the cognitive demand of those expectations. The results generally indicate that verbs associated with lower-levels of cognitive demand dominate the standards. Based on a more detailed examination of three specific verbs, the authors argue that verbs alone cannot be taken as useful indicators of cognitive demand and that pairing verbs with their mathematical "objects" is a more promising approach. Explicit focus is given to the linguistic structure of expectations and to the importance of clarity and explicitness in their expression.

The Statistical Process: A View Across the K–8 State Standards (Newton, Horvath, & Dietiker)

This chapter provides insight into what K-8 students in the United States are expected to know and be able to do with respect to the statistical process outlined in the *GAISE Report* (Franklin et al., 2007). GLEs for each process component (formulating questions, collecting data, analyzing data, and interpreting results) were also coded as *Type I* (when students were expected to perform the process) or *Type II* (when they were expected to evaluate the process). The results indicate that Type I expectations outnumbered Type II expectations by wide margins, generally reflecting lower-levels of cognitive demand. A second key finding is that most states do not address outliers, clusters, or gaps in data until Grade 7 or 8, if at all, even as the *GAISE Report* has emphasized the need for students to recognize and understand variability.

Analysis of K–8 Probability Standards (Dingman & Tarr)

The authors of this chapter applied an existing framework (Jones & Bishop, 2005) to analyze GLEs according to four major topics in probability—sample space, theoretical probability, experimental probability, and conditional probability and independence. Overall, the authors found little consensus in the grade placement of these expectations. More than half concerned theoretical probability, reflecting the traditional preference for a classical approach to probability. However, the authors also found evidence that states are heeding recommendations for teaching probability empirically, through data collection and analysis. Perhaps the most important finding is that connections between related probability concepts are largely absent.

Major Lessons From the Second Round of Standards Analyses (Smith, Lappan, & Tarr)

The closing chapter summarizes the results around the central theme of variability. Greater attention is given to the results reported in this volume, but as they extend and complement those reported in the first (Reys, 2006a). Variability is cast in five related dimensions: grade placement & continuity, linguistic complexity, specific language, cognitive demand, and development across grades, and examples are provided to illustrate each dimension. Where appropriate, the authors identify and support more promising practices in the expression and development of expectations across grade levels. The chapter closes with three broad recommendations for the subsequent development and use of state mathematics standards.

NOTES

1. Newton completed this work during her graduate work at Michigan State University.
2. Dingman completed this work during his graduate work at the University of Missouri-Columbia.
3. See Appendix D for the 41 state documents used in the analysis of the statistics & probability expectations.

CHAPTER 2

AN ANALYSIS OF K–8 MEASUREMENT GRADE-LEVEL EXPECTATIONS

Sarah E. Kasten and Jill Newton

In the mathematics and mathematics education communities, the importance of many individual mathematical topics is often disputed. However, there is widespread agreement that it is critical for students to both understand what it means to "measure" an attribute of an object or phenomenon and become proficient in choosing appropriate tools to make or compute such measurements. The importance of measurement has been linked to both real-life applications as well as to other areas of mathematics, including opportunities for students to apply their prior knowledge (e.g., their number sense) and prepare for their future study of topics such as geometry and data analysis.

In *Principles and Standards for School Mathematics* (*PSSM*), the National Council of Teachers of Mathematics (NCTM) states that the study of measurement is important "because of the practicality and pervasiveness of measurement in so many aspects of everyday life. The study of measurement also offers an opportunity for learning and applying other mathematics" (NCTM, 2000, p. 44). On their website, Achieve, an organization created in 1996 by a group of the nation's governors and business leaders

Variability is the Rule: A Companion Analysis of K–8 State Mathematics Standards, pp. 13–40

to help states raise academic standards, improve assessments and strengthen accountability, adds,

> Geometric measurement is the basis by which we quantify the world. Through measurement, students develop respect for precision and accuracy. They also learn to spot potential and actual errors in those measurements and learn how those errors may be compounded in computations. (Achieve, 2007)

In contrast to descriptive geometry standards that concern figures and their relationships without assigning coordinates or measuring attributes of those figures that were examined in Newton's chapter (this volume), this analysis addresses geometric measurement, with specific focus on length, area, and volume. Measurement will be conceptualized in the way in which NCTM (2000) described it, "Measurement is the assignment of a numerical value to an attribute" (p. 44).

Given the importance of measurement in the K–8 curriculum, we set out to shed light on how measurement concepts are introduced and developed in the state standards documents. Our intent was not to evaluate state standards, but rather to summarize what is currently being addressed and when it is being addressed in measurement topics across 42 states. We used the "big ideas" in the research literature on the learning and teaching of measurement as another lens through which to examine the standards. These big ideas were summarized in an effort to provide information that may be of assistance to those charged with the task of writing future standards. In short, we studied what K–8 students are expected to know and be able to do with one-, two-, and three-dimensional measurement as represented in 42 state standards documents. In particular, we sought to answer the following questions:

1. What are students expected to learn with respect to measurement and when are they expected to learn it?
2. What are the differences in the treatment of one-, two- and three-dimensional measurement topics (that is, length, area, and volume) across states?
3. What is the level of agreement about the important content of measurement and the grade levels at which these ideas occur among state standards documents?
4. Do state standards address the "big ideas" of measurement suggested in the literature?

METHOD

We analyzed the complete set of 5,710 geometry and measurement grade-level learning expectations (GLEs) from 42 state documents (Appendix A). We limited our analysis to one-, two- and three-dimensional measurement (i.e., length, area, and volume) as these three measures serve as "the basis for the connection between geometry and number" (Kilpatrick, Swafford, & Findell, 2001, p. 281). We entered all geometry and measurement GLEs into a spreadsheet, searched for the presence of the following terms: "length," "perimeter," "circumference," "area," "volume," and "capacity," and selected all the GLEs with one or more search term for analysis. After we examined this set of GLEs independently, we compared our results and reached consensus, consulting a collaborating researcher as necessary. This process of analysis and comparison continued throughout each step of the process.

After consensus was achieved, we then searched the remaining GLEs for measurement content that did not contain any of our initial search terms. Examples of GLEs that were located in this second "manual" search are given below. Example 2.1 was classified as concerning two-dimensional measure; Example 2.2 was classified as addressing three-dimensional measure.

> *Example 2.1.* Cover a figure with squares and tell how many it takes. (AR, gr. 1)

> *Example 2.2.* Use tools to make predictions (e.g., using a balance scale, predicting how many cups a container will hold and then filling it to check the prediction). (NM, gr. K)

After we had identified and compiled our data (1,601 GLEs that address one-, two-, and/or three-dimensional measurement), our remaining analysis methods were largely driven by our research questions, which we will use to frame the remainder of this section.

What Are Students Expected to Learn With Respect to Measurement and When Are They Expected to Learn It?

We utilized a framework developed by Clarke, Cheeseman, McDonough, and Clarke (2003) under the auspices of the Early Numeracy Research Project (ENRP). In that framework, the authors established growth points which they defined as "primary stepping stones along the way to understanding important mathematical ideas" (p. 69). Although

ENRP's growth point descriptors were developed for many mathematical topics, we used only those developed for measurement. We chose this framework because it best fit the data that emerged from the standards documents. But even this framework was not ideal for our analysis since it was originally designed for use in the early elementary grades. However, it contained many of the topics present in the GLEs and, when modified slightly, allowed us to represent our data systematically. We present here the five levels of the modified version of the framework we used in our analysis.

> Level 1: The child shows awareness of the attribute and its descriptive language.
>
> Level 2: The child compares, orders, and matches objects by the attribute.
>
> Level 3: The child chooses and uses nonstandard units and tools for estimating and measuring.
>
> Level 4: The child chooses and uses standard units and tools for estimating and measuring, with accuracy.
>
> Level 5: The child solves a range of problems involving important concepts and skills.

To sharpen the analysis, each of the five levels was divided into finer-grained categories to capture more of the details in the GLEs (see Appendix B for this more detailed framework). Using this framework, we coded each GLE and summarized our findings. When GLEs addressed multiple measurement topics, they were included in all appropriate levels and categories.

What Are the Differences in the Treatment of One-, Two- and Three-dimensional Measurement Topics Across States?

All of the collected GLEs were sorted into one-, two-, and three-dimensional measures in order to facilitate our analysis. One-dimensional GLEs related to length, perimeter, and circumference; two-dimensional GLEs included area and surface area; and three-dimensional GLEs included references to volume and capacity. Using this method meant that many GLEs were included in more than one category since many states address one-, two-, and/or three-dimensional measurement in the same GLE. Example 2.3 illustrates a GLE that was coded for one-, two-, and three-dimensional measurement.

Example 2.3. Determine the effect on *perimeter, area* or *volume* [italics added] when one or more dimensions of two- and three-dimensional figures are changed. (NC, gr. 8)

After sorting the GLEs into one-, two-, and three-dimensional measurement, each set was analyzed individually.

What Is the Level of Agreement About the Important Content of Measurement and the Grade Levels at Which These Ideas Occur Among State Standards Documents?

We set inclusion in at least 75% of the states (that is, 32 of 42 states) as our benchmark for a reasonable level of national agreement. Using this benchmark, we summarized the topics that might be considered to represent a "*defacto* curriculum" for measurement across from K–8 in the United States (as represented by state standards). In addition to looking for consistency of placement, we looked for grade levels where a relatively high number of states addressed the topics to see if there was agreement around their placement in the standards.

Do State Standards Address the "Big Ideas" of Measurement Suggested in the Literature?

We searched the research literature and located three book chapters that proposed sets of "big ideas" in spatial measurement (Lehrer, 2003; Lehrer, Jaslow, & Curtis, 2003; and Stephan & Clements, 2003). We merged the three sets of big ideas, searched the GLEs for these big ideas, and summarized our findings.

RESULTS

Just as our research questions guided the presentation of our methods they will also be used to frame our findings.

What are Students Expected to Learn With Respect to Measurement and When Are They Expected to Learn It?

In our examination of how measurement topics are introduced and developed, we sought to determine which measurement topics are included across states and at what grades they are presented. Our findings pertaining to both aspects are presented for each level of the measurement framework. At each level, we include a brief description of the level, the relative frequency of the level compared to the total number of GLEs, the distribution of the level across K–8, and the most common categories to emerge within the level.

Level 1: The child shows awareness of the attribute and its descriptive language. Level 1 GLEs call for students to have an awareness of measurable attributes and the associated descriptive language. A major focus of NCTM's (2000) measurement standard is students' "understanding of what a measurable attribute is and becoming familiar with units and processes that are used in measuring attributes" (p. 44). Many of the GLEs assigned to Level 1 address the first two of these three foci (understanding of the measurable attribute and familiarity with its units). Other GLEs, addressing definitions and representations of measurable attributes, were also included in this level even though they may represent content more advanced than basic awareness.

Thirty-six of the 42 state standards documents contained at least one Level 1 GLE; collectively there were 192 Level 1 GLEs (approximately 12% of all measurement GLEs). Figure 2.1 summarizes the distribution of states containing these GLEs across grade levels. Figure 2.1 shows that

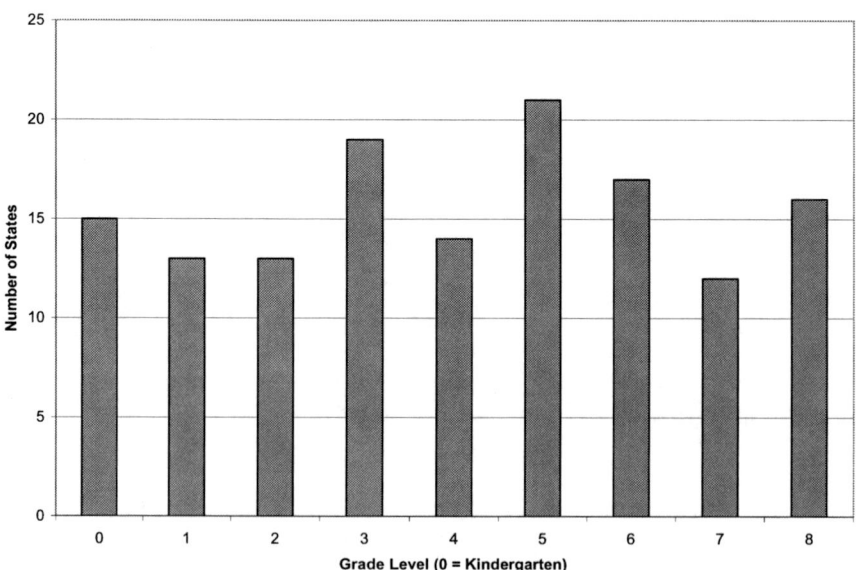

Figure 2.1.   Distribution of the number of states with Level 1 GLEs by grade.

**Table 2.1.   Level 1 Coding Categories,
Number of States, and Example GLEs**

Category	Number of States	Example
Meaning and recognition of the attribute	30	Describe the attributes of length, weight, and capacity. (MD, gr. 1)
Awareness of the units and tools associated with the attribute	27	Knows various measuring tools for measuring length, weight, or capacity. (FL, gr. K)
Representation of the attribute	20	Represent area using a rectangular array. (AZ, gr. 3)

students are expected to demonstrate awareness of attributes throughout all grades, K–8. This is not surprising given that the attributes span length, area, and volume. We found that Level 1 GLEs frequently fell into three main categories of our framework: (1) Meaning of the attribute, (2) Awareness of the units and tools associated with the attribute, and (3) Representation of the attribute. Examples from each category and the number of states with GLEs in that category are presented in Table 2.1 above, which is structured in terms of decreasing frequency, not in the order in which categories are listed in Appendix B. The meaning of the attribute category was the most common, appearing in more than 70% of the states. Awareness of the units and tools associated with the attribute GLEs were included nearly as often.

Level 2: The child compares, orders, and matches objects by the attribute. The second level of the framework concerns students' efforts to compare, order and match objects by the attributes described in Level 1. NCTM, in both the *PSSM* (2000) and *Curriculum Focal Points for Prekindergarten through Grade 8 Mathematics: A Quest for Coherence* (*CFP*) (2006), calls for students to make comparisons of objects based on their measurable attributes. At this level, 123 GLEs from 35 states were identified, representing approximately 8% of all measurement GLEs. Figure 2.2 shows the distribution of states containing these GLEs across grade levels. Figure 2.2 shows that students are most frequently expected to compare, order, and match objects in the early grades (i.e., K–2). The two most common Level 2 categories are (1) Compare/Sort objects by attributes and (2) Order objects by attributes. Examples of GLEs representing these categories and the number of states in which each are found are presented in Table 2.2. Table 2.2 reveals that the Compare/Sort objects category was the most common, appearing in all of the 35 states with Level 2 GLEs. Order objects GLEs were found in fewer states (approximately 71% of states with Level 2 GLEs).

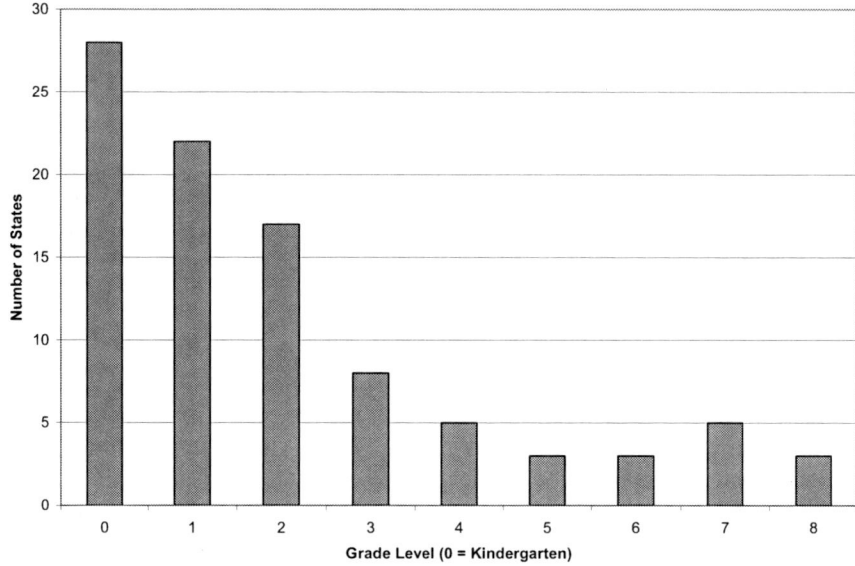

Figure 2.2.   Distribution of the number of states with Level 2 GLEs by grade.

Table 2.2.   Level 2 Coding Categories, Number of States, and Example GLEs

Category	Number of States	Example
Compare/Sort objects by attributes	35	Compare two objects or events according to one or more of the following attributes: length, height, weight, time, temperature and volume. (WV, gr. 1)
Order objects by attributes	25	Order three or more objects according to an attribute (e.g., pencil lengths, students' hand span, and thickness of books). (WA, gr. 1)

Level 3: The child chooses and uses nonstandard units and tools for estimating and measuring. Level 3 calls for students to choose and use nonstandard units and tools for estimating and measuring the attributes identified at Level 1 and compared at Level 2. Two hundred twenty-two GLEs were coded as Level 3, representing approximately 14% of all measurement GLEs, and were found in 41 of the 42 state documents. Figure 2.3 summarizes the distribution of states containing these GLEs across grade levels. As Figure 2.3 shows, students are expected to choose and use nonstandard units for estimating and measuring most often in Grades 1 through 3. Two primary categories emerged from the Level 3 GLEs: (1)

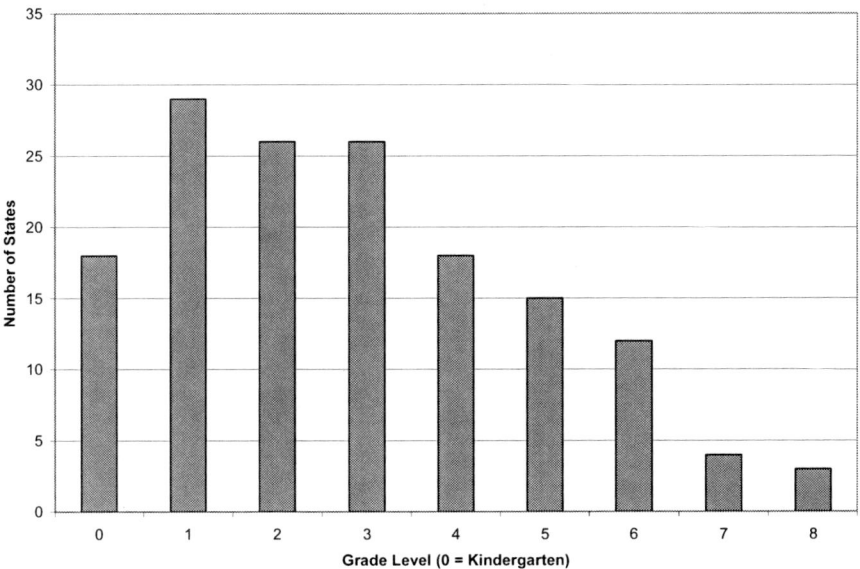

Figure 2.3.   Distribution of the number of states with Level 3 GLEs by grade.

Table 2.3. Level Coding Categories, Number of States, Example GLEs

Category	Number of States	Example
Measures with nonstandard units	36	Measures area, weight, and volume of simple rectangular prisms using an appropriate nonstandard unit. (HI, gr. 2)
Estimates with nonstandard units	23	Estimate length in standard and nonstandard units (e.g., finger lengths, pencil lengths). (OR, gr. 2)

Measures with nonstandard units, and (2) Estimates with nonstandard units. Examples from each Level 3 category and the number of states with GLEs in each category are presented in Table 2.3 above. Table 2.3 shows that measures with nonstandard units GLEs are relatively typical expectations, as 36 of the 41 states with Level 3 expectations included them. This result shows that a large majority of states expect students to measure with nonstandard units, in addition to their work with standard units and tools (see below).

Level 4: The child chooses and uses standard units and tools for estimating and measuring, with accuracy. At Level 4, students are expected to measure and estimate with standard units and tools. Thirty-nine of the 42 state

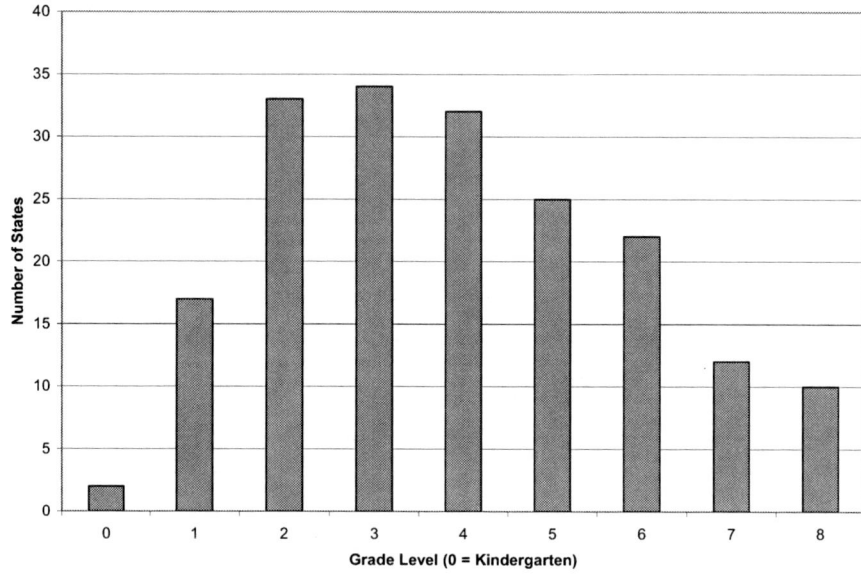

Figure 2.4.   Distribution of the number of states with Level 4 GLEs by grade.

documents contain a total of 319 Level 4 GLEs, representing approximately 20% of all measurement GLEs. The expectations not specifying standard or nonstandard tools or units will be discussed at the end of this section. Figure 2.4 above summarizes the distribution of states containing these GLEs across grade levels. Figure 2.4 shows the prominence of choosing and using standard units for estimation and measurement in Grades 2 through 4. Five primary categories emerged from the Level 4 GLEs: (1) Measures with standard units, (2) Chooses standard units, (3) Precision and accuracy, (4) Estimates with standard units, and (5) Chooses tools.[1] Table 2.4 provides examples from each of these categories along with the number of states that include such a GLE. Measures with standard units category was the most common, appearing in all 39 of the states with Level 4 GLEs. This popularity is in contrast to the category, chooses standard tools, which was found in roughly half of the states with Level 4 GLEs states. As in Level 3, estimation is somewhat less prominent than exact measurement. Additionally, in cases where states distinguish between using customary and metric units, customary units are listed slightly more frequently.

Many measurement GLEs include general statements that did not indicate the type of units or the process by which students were expected to measure and were therefore not coded in any level. Every state had a GLE

**Table 2.4. Level 4 Coding Categories,
Number of States, and Example GLEs**

Category	Number of States	Example
Measures with standard units	39	Measure length in customary units, including inches, feet, and yards. (AL, gr. 2)
Chooses standard units	31	Select and apply appropriate standard units and tools to measure length, area, volume, weight, time, temperature, and the size of angles. Example: A triangular sheet of metal is about 1 foot across. Describe the units and tools you would use to measure its weight, its angles, and the lengths of its sides. (IN, gr. 6)
Precision and accuracy	31	Estimate measures of length, volume, capacity, quantity, and weight, communicating degree of accuracy needed and when a more precise measure is required. (NV, gr. 5)
Estimates with standard units	28	Students apply estimation and measurement of length to content problems and express the results in metric units (centimeters and meters). (WY, gr. 6)
Chooses tools	21	Identify the appropriate tool used to measure length (i.e., ruler), weight (i.e., scale), time (i.e., clock, calendar) and temperature (i.e., thermometer). (ND, gr. 1)

of this type in at least one of the three dimensions, many in all three. These GLEs often included verbs like "measure," "estimate," "find," or "determine" without further description. Two examples of these GLEs come from Texas and Alabama.

Example 2.4. Measure to solve problems involving length, area, temperature, and time. (TX, gr. 3)

Example 2.5. Find the perimeter of polygons and the area of triangles and trapezoids. (AL, gr. 7)

Neither of these GLEs indicate the type of unit to be used or the process by which to measure. It is possible that their authors assumed that GLEs in earlier grades serve to identify how future expectations should be carried out. Because we did not look at the trajectory of GLEs within individual states we were not able to determine if this was so.

Level 5: The child solves a range of problems involving important concepts and skills. Finally, Level 5 GLEs ask students to solve a range of problems involving important measurement concepts and skills. At this level, a total of 799 GLEs from 42 states were coded, representing approximately 50%

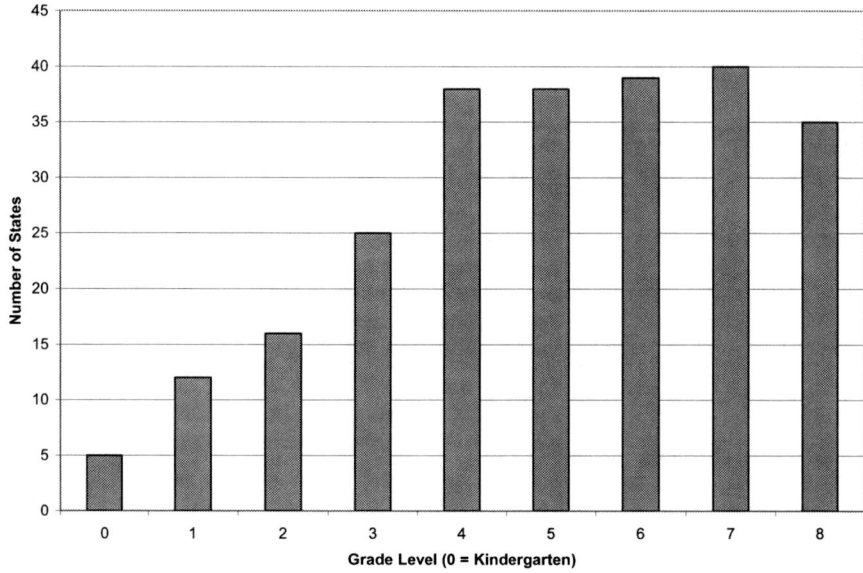

Figure 2.5.   Distribution of the number of states with Level 5 GLEs by grade.

of the total number of GLEs. Figure 2.5 summarizes the distribution of states containing these GLEs across grade levels. Figure 2.5 indicates that solving measurement problems is primarily expected in Grades 4 through 8. GLEs coded as Level 5 represented five primary categories: (1) Unit relationships, (2) Formulae, (3) Applications, (4) Relationships between one-, two- and three-dimensional measures and (5) Miscellaneous problem solving. Table 2.5 provides examples of each category along with the number of states represented in the category. Expectations in three of the categories, applications, relationships between one-dimensional, two-dimensional, and three-dimensional measures, and formulae are included in at least 80% of the state documents.

In summary, in addition to learning what measurement content is expected by states, we found that as the levels increase, the grade levels with the highest frequency of GLEs also increase, with the exception of Level 1 which is relatively evenly distributed across K–8. This can be seen in the fact that Level 2 is most prevalent in Grades K–2, Level 3 in Grades 1–3, Level 4 in Grades 2–4, and Level 5 in Grades 4–8. This pattern aligns with the intent of the developers of our framework who expressed the view that the growth points "provided a sense of the typical order in which important understandings and skills develop" (Clarke et al., 2003, p. 71).

**Table 2.5. Level 5 Coding Categories,
Number of States, and Example GLEs**

Category	Number of States	Example
Applications	41	Applies the Pythagorean Theorem to find a missing side of a right triangle, or in problem solving situations. (RI, gr. 8)
Relationships between 1-D, 2-D, and 3-D measures	36	Explore the differences and relationships between perimeter and area in both systems. (ID, gr. 5)
Formulae	35	Find the area and perimeter of a rectangle by measuring, using a grid, or using a formula, and label the answer with appropriate units. (MN, gr. 4)
Unit relationships	27	Convert basic measurements of volume, weight and distance within the same system for metric and customary units (e.g., inches to feet, hours to minutes, centimeters to meters). (OK, gr. 5)
Miscellaneous problem solving	37	Explore perimeter and area using a variety of models (e.g., geoboards, graph paper). (TN, gr. 4)

What Are the Differences in the Treatment of One-, Two- and Three-Dimensional Measures?

As we explored the type of measurement activities expected of K–8 students we noticed some differences in their frequency across one-, two- and three-dimensional measures. The findings presented in this section highlight these differences, both overall and within each level of our framework. Of the 1,601 GLEs included in this analysis, 1092 were one-dimensional (approximately 68%), 731 were two-dimensional (approximately 46%), and 629 were three-dimensional (approximately 39%).[2] Figure 2.6 shows the distribution of the number of states containing these GLEs across grade levels. We see that one-dimensional topics are the most prevalent across states until Grade 5. Two-dimensional and three-dimensional topics both increase across the grades, though the rate of increase is much shallower for three-dimensional topics. Figure 2.6 also shows that two-dimensional measurement topics occur in considerably fewer states in kindergarten and Grade 1 than one- and three-dimensional measures.

To further reveal the differences between the treatments of one-, two- and three-dimensional topics among states we will illustrate the distribution of each by state. The distribution of GLEs within states shows the grades at which the individual states are addressing these topics. This can be seen in Figures 2.7, 2.8, and 2.9 that display the grade levels at which one-, two-, and three-dimensional measures respectively appear in each

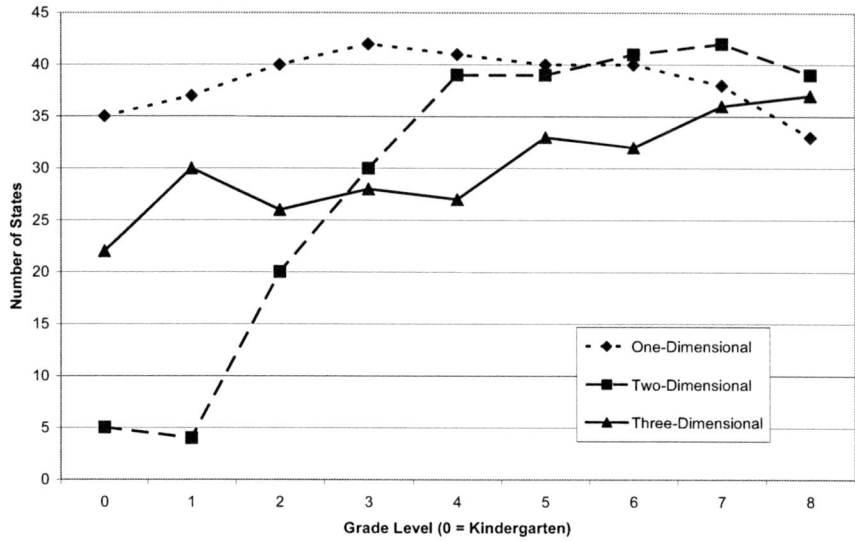

Figure 2.6.   Number of states with one-, two-, and/or three-dimensional GLEs by grade.

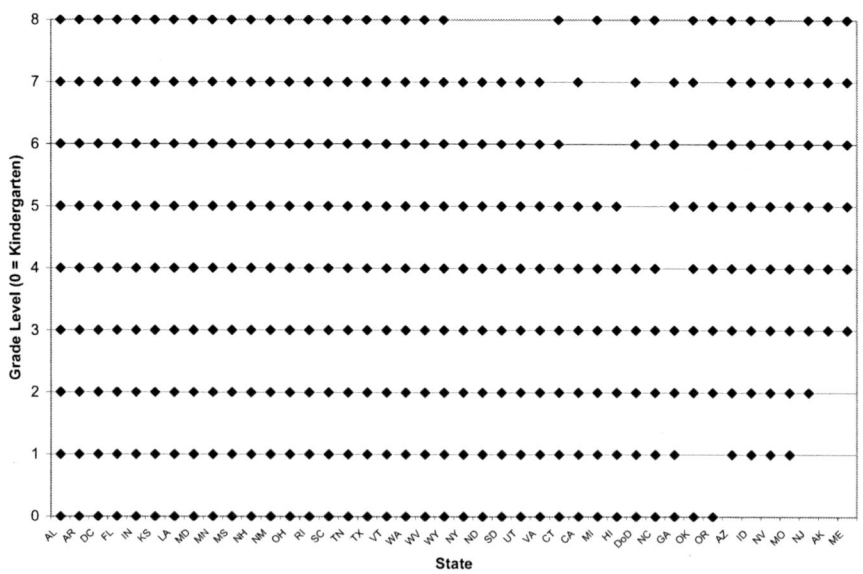

Figure 2.7.   Grade placement of GLEs addressing one-dimensional measurement by state.

state. Figure 2.7 shows that one-dimensional measurement concepts are usually introduced in kindergarten and that 39 of the 42 state documents call for the introduction by Grade 1. It also shows that 26 of the 42 states have one-dimensional measurement concepts in *every* grade of their state standards.[3] One might have expected the number of states to decrease as the grade levels increase. That they did not may indicate that states are relating one-dimensional measures to other concepts in the later grades, such as the relationship between perimeter and area. Ten states address one-dimensional measure in every grade but one, and six states in every grade but two. This indicates the emphasis on one-dimensional measures as a concept in kindergarten through Grade 8 among the 42 states.

How does this pattern change for two-dimensional measurement? The appearance of GLEs with two-dimensional content in each state is shown in Figure 2.8. Of particular interest in Figure 2.8 is the difference in the grade levels at which states begin their development of two-dimensional measurement concepts. Three states call for introducing two-dimensional measurement concepts in kindergarten, but skip Grade 1, and then continue through Grade 8, addressing the concept at eight grade levels. Nine states do not introduce the concept until Grade 4, and one state not until Grade 5. It is notable that many states do not include any GLEs that

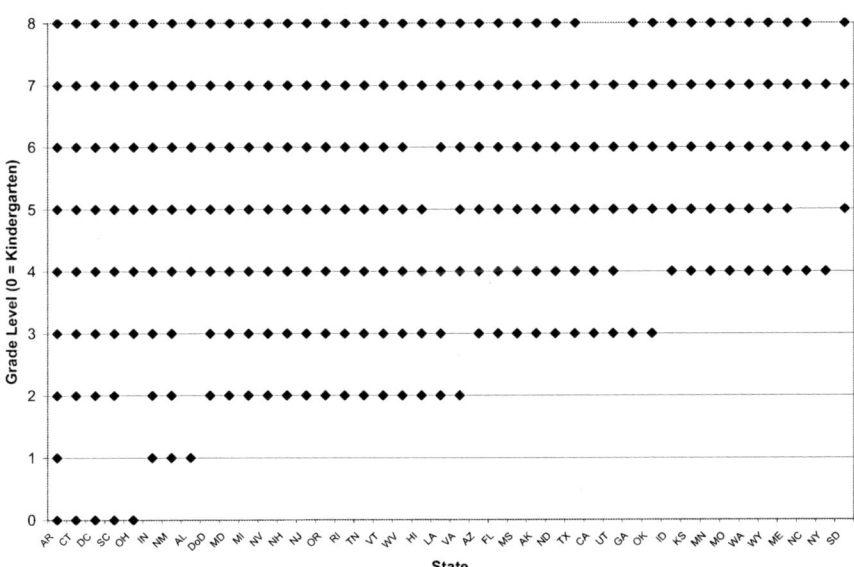

Figure 2.8.   Grade placement of GLEs addressing two-dimensional measurement by state.

address two-dimensional content in kindergarten or Grade 1. Once states begin the concept of two-dimensional measures, most continue it through Grade 7 or 8, with less than half of the states skipping one or two grade levels.

The appearance of three-dimensional measure GLEs in each state is shown in Figure 2.9. Figure 2.9 shows some consistency between states in when three-dimensional measurement is initiated, but there is little consistency between states about how to progress through the grade levels. Thirty-four of the 42 states expect that students will be introduced to three-dimensional measures by Grade 1. Five of the 42 states address the issue in all grade levels while six states address it in less than half of the grades. A comparison of Figure 2.9 with Figures 2.7 and 2.8 indicates that, unlike one- and two-dimensional measurement, three-dimensional measurement is not always, or even usually, continued in every grade through Grade 8 once introduced.

The relatively lower frequency of two-dimensional measurement expectations in the early grades was at first somewhat surprising, given the importance of area measure. Did the drop indicate lower importance assigned to the topic? Though we cannot know for sure, one possibility is that authors judged that two-dimensional measures appear less frequently

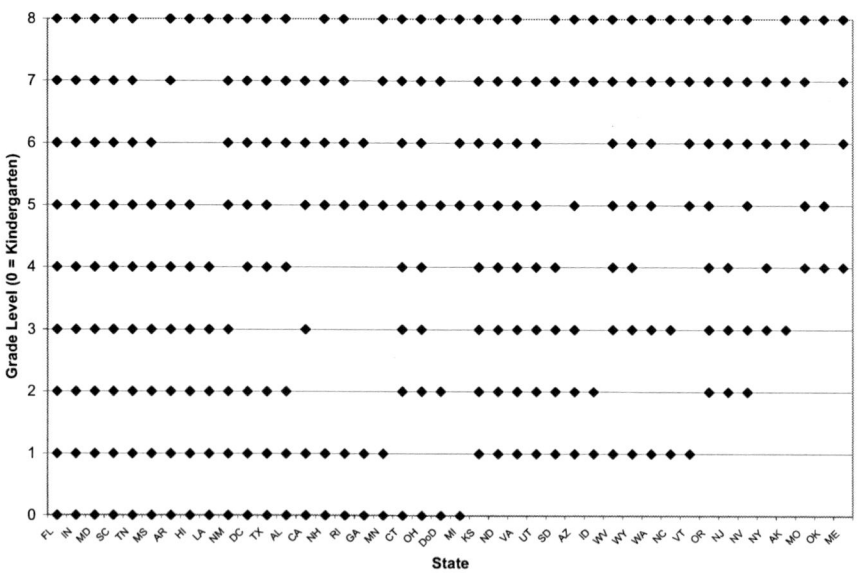

Figure 2.9.   Grade placement of GLEs addressing three-dimensional measurement by state.

in young students' everyday lives than one- and three-dimensional measures and matched the emphasis in the standards to that judgment. For example, young students are often quite familiar with length in the context of height or distance to run, or volume from filling objects with sand or water. Given such experience, they could have decided to focus attention on measures with which young students are more familiar. However, we note that the opposite argument could also be made: If students are less familiar with two-dimensional measures from their everyday experience, greater focus in the standards would be needed to generate more classroom experiences that could compensate for that lack of everyday experience.

Despite the evident differences in the appearance of one-, two- and three-dimensional measurement in their standards documents, we can safely conclude that most states do agree on addressing at least one of three measurement concepts at all grade levels. Thirty-two of the 42 documents have either one-, two-, three-dimensional measurement topics or some combination of the three at all grade levels, and the remaining ten states address them in all but one grade level. This indicates an agreement between states that at least some type of one-, two- or three-dimensional measurement activity is appropriate at all or nearly all grade levels.

To gain better insight into how these differences might play out, we now examine the distribution of one-, two- and three-dimensional GLEs across the levels of the framework. Table 2.6 highlights interesting features. The majority of states include one- and three-dimensional measure GLEs at all five levels. In addition, states containing GLEs addressing two-dimensional measures are vastly underrepresented at Levels 2 and 4, compared with the other entries in Table 2.6. Recall that Level 2 addresses the comparison, ordering, and matching of objects by attribute, and Level 4 addresses the choosing and using of standards units and tools to estimate and measure attributes. More states expect students to compare, order, measure and estimate length and volume than area. A possible explanation for this discrepancy at Level 2 may lie in the prior

**Table 2.6. Number of States With One-,
Two-, and Three-Dimensional GLEs by Level**

Level	One-Dimensional	Two-Dimensional	Three-Dimensional
1	29	29	30
2	34	12	34
3	40	36	35
4	39	27	36
5	42	41	41

experiences of students entering school, as was discussed previously. The relatively lower frequency of two-dimensional measure GLEs at Level 4 may be due to the fact that while one can directly measure length or distance with a ruler and volume or capacity with measuring cups, there are no widely available tools for measuring area directly.

What Is the Level of Agreement About the Important Content of Measurement and the Grade Levels at Which These Ideas Occur Among State Standards Documents?

Our third research question examined the level of consensus among states about what is expected of students (and when) with regard to these measurement topics. To answer this question we first identified topics that states agreed upon and then we highlighted agreement in the grade placement of these topics. We included all topics in which at least 75% of the states were represented (at least 32 of the 42 states analyzed). Using this metric, eight of the 45 identified measurement categories were included in a list of common categories. Table 2.7 presents these categories, their level in the framework, the number of states addressing the topic in each category, and a sample GLE. Noticeably absent from Table 2.7 are Level 1 categories that focus on students building an awareness of the measurable attributes of objects and their associated units of measure, measurement tools, and representations.

Table 2.8 presents the grade levels at which these topics appear in the state documents. The categories are displayed in the order in which they are found in the framework to reveal any trends that exist across levels. Frequencies of more than 15 states that address a topic at a particular level are given in boldface and enlarged to highlight these trends.

From kindergarten through Grade 3, many states expect students to compare/sort objects by attributes, measure with nonstandard units and estimate with nonstandard units. Similar clusters can be found in Grades 2 to 6 (measures using customary units and measures using metric units) and Grades 5 to 8 (applies/uses formulae and solves problems/real-world problems). While these clusters do not necessarily indicate agreement among states, one can begin to get a sense of a general trajectory of measurement topics. This trajectory begins with comparing objects by measurable attribute and measuring and estimating with nonstandard units, moves to measuring and estimating with customary and metric units, and ends with developing and using formulae and solving measurement problems, particularly those involving the Pythagorean Theorem. This trajectory supports our earlier findings regarding the progression across levels of the framework as grade levels increase.

**Table 2.7.   Most Common Measurement Coding Categories,
Level, Number of States, and Example GLEs**

Level	Category	Number of States	Example GLE
2	Compares/Sorts objects by attributes	35	Compare and order concrete objects by temperature and capacity. (SD, gr. 1)
3	Measures with nonstandard units	40	Measures length and weight to the nearest whole unit using nonstandard units. (KS, gr. 1)
3	Estimates with non-standard units	32	Develop and explain strategies for using nonstandard and standard referents to estimate measurements of length, area, weight, temperature, volume and capacity. (CT, gr. 3)
4	Measures using customary units	38	Estimate and measure the length of various line segments and objects to the nearest inch. (VA, gr. 2)
4	Measures using metric units	37	Using various types of instruments, measure: length in millimeters, meters, kilometers; weight in grams and kilograms; capacity in milliliters and liters; time to nearest minute; and temperature in Celsius and Fahrenheit. (MS, gr. 3)
5	Uses/Applies formulas	35	Use formulas routinely for finding the perimeter and area of basic two-dimensional figures and the surface area and volume of basic three-dimensional figures, including rectangles, parallelograms, trapezoids, squares, triangles, circles, prisms, and cylinders. (CA, gr. 7)
5	Solves problems/real-world problems	37	Determine perimeters of polygons and area of rectangles/squares in real-world situations. (ID, gr. 5)
5	Meanings of relationships among one-, two-, and three-dimensional measures	36	Communicate the difference between perimeter and area. (NV, gr. 5)

Do State Standards Address the "Big Ideas" Suggested in the Literature?

As we stated earlier, our framework choice for the initial analysis of the state standards was based on the mathematical content of the GLEs coded as addressing length, area, and volume measurement. In our search for such a framework, we encountered several analyses whose authors emphasized important "big ideas" in measurement. Lehrer (2003) used developmental and classroom research to suggest that children's concep-

**Table 2.8.   Number of States with GLEs in
Common Coding Categories by Level and Grade**

		Grade									
Level	Category	K	1	2	3	4	5	6	7	8	Total
2	Compares/Sorts objects by attributes	28	22	15	8	5	3	2	4	2	35
3	Measures with nonstandard units	16	27	23	24	15	13	9	0	1	40
3	Estimates with nonstandard units	9	14	14	15	11	7	7	3	2	32
4	Measures using customary units	0	13	25	24	26	19	16	5	1	38
4	Measures using metric units	0	12	17	22	20	16	12	5	2	37
5	Meanings of relationships among one-, two-, and three-dimensional measures	0	0	2	2	15	12	20	13	4	36
5	Uses/Applies formulae	0	0	0	0	11	22	28	28	21	35
5	Solves problems/real-world problems	1	3	6	9	16	19	19	26	26	37

Note: The total column in this table displays the total number of states with GLEs in each category.

tions of measure reflect a collection of emerging concepts. He put forward an informal theory of measure that suggests collective coordination among the following eight conceptual foundations: (1) unit-attribute relations, (2) iteration, (3) tiling, (4) identical units, (5) standardization, (6) proportionality, (7) additivity, and (8) origin (zero-point). He also provides the helpful and important insight that "no clear-cut 'best' sequence of instruction seems to exist in any domain of measure nor reasonable list of prescriptions or proscriptions other than the need to avoid exclusive reliance on the development of procedural competence" (Lehrer, 2003, p. 190).

Lehrer and his colleagues also published a measurement framework in NCTM's 2003 Yearbook *Learning and Teaching Measurement.* They expressed the hope "that children develop a theory of measurement rather than simply collecting measures," and add that their "approach to designing measurement instruction for children is guided by establishing a productive tension between understanding and doing" (Lehrer, Jaslow, & Curtis, 2003, p. 100). The authors then developed a set of central measurement concepts to orient a series of classroom investigations. They divided the concepts into two conceptual accomplishments: the conception of unit (including iteration, identical unit, tiling, partition, and additivity) and the conception of scale (including zero-point and precision). This framework includes many of the same big ideas represented in Lehrer's 2003 framework. However, three of his big ideas in his sole-authored publication (unit-attribute relations, standardization, and proportionality) gave way to partition and precision in the collaborative work.

In the same edited volume, Stephan and Clements (2003) expressed support for the importance of examining measurement conceptually as well as procedurally. They stated that "there are several important concepts, or big ideas, that underpin much of learning to measure" (p. 4). The concepts that they deemed most important were: (1) partitioning, (2) unit iteration, (3) transitivity, (4) conservation, (5) accumulation of distance, and (6) relation to number.

We compiled 14 "big ideas" that emerge as a composite of these three frameworks (Lehrer, 2003; Lehrer, Jaslow, & Curtis, 2003; Stephan & Clements, 2003) and used them to further analyze the measurement content of the state standards. These 14 big ideas are summarized in Table 2.9, with descriptions from the authors. We do not claim that the big ideas in these three frameworks are a comprehensive composite from the literature, nor the only possibilities for such a list of big ideas. Nonetheless, it provides a research-based framework through which to examine the state standards.

Ten of these 14 are present in one or more state's standards; the remaining 4 are not explicitly mentioned in any of them. Table 2.10 shows the frequency of mention for the first group, along with a sample GLE. As will be evident below, 4 of the 10 appear relatively frequently (in 17 or more states), where the other six are infrequently mentioned. Unit-attribute relations are well represented in the state standards. It is also notable that all 42 states include at least one GLE that partially addresses precision as described by Lehrer, Jaslow, and Curtis (2003). However, the aspect of precision that is notably absent in the GLEs is the fact that all measurements are inherently approximate. Similarly, though tiling is mentioned by 13 states, one of the key components of this skill—the generation of informal units of area measure—is not included. Most often, the students are given the units and/or objects with which to tile the object. Strom, Kemeny, Lehrer, and Forman (2001) have argued for the importance of problematizing the unit and suggest an activity in which the teacher shows their students three rectangles with the same area, but different unlabeled unit dimensions (e.g., 1 x 12, 2 x 6, 3 x 4) and asks them which would cover the most space. The children are then asked to justify their answers.

Table 2.9.   "Big Ideas" in Measurement From Three Studies

"Big Idea"	*Description*
Unit-attribute relations	Correspondence between units and the attribute being measured. (Lehrer, 2003)
Iteration	A subdivision of a length is translated to obtain a measure. (Lehrer, Jaslow, & Curtis, 2003)
Tiling	Units fill lines, planes, volumes, and angles. (Lehrer, 2003)
Identical units	Each subdivision is identical. (Lehrer, Jaslow, & Curtis, 2003)
Standardization	Conventions about units facilitate communication. (Lehrer, 2003)
Proportionality	Measurements with different-sized units imply that different quantities can represent the same measure. (Lehrer, 2003)
Additivity	Units of Euclidean space can be decomposed and recomposed. (Lehrer, 2003)
Origin (zero-point)	Any point can serve as the origin or zero point on the scale. (Lehrer, Jaslow, & Curtis, 2003)
Partitioning	The mental activity of slicing up the length of an object into the same size units. (Lehrer, Jaslow, & Curtis, 2003; Stephan & Clements, 2003)
Precision	The choice of units in relation to the object determines the relative precision of the measure; all measure is inherently approximate. (Lehrer, Jaslow, & Curtis, 2003)
Transitivity	(a) If the length of object 1 is equal to the length of object 2 and object 2 is the same length as object 3, then object 1 is the same length as object 3, (b) if the length of object 1 is greater than the length of object 2 and object 2 is longer than object 3, then object 1 is longer than object 3, and (c) if the length of object 1 is less than the length of object 2 and object 2 is shorter than object 3, then object 1 shorter than object 3. (Stephan & Clements, 2003)
Conservation	As an object is moved, its length does not change. (Stephan & Clements, 2003)
Accumulation of distance	The result of iterating a unit signifies, for students, the distance from the beginning of the first iteration to the end of the last. (Stephan & Clements, 2003); the result of iterating forms nesting relationships to each other. (Piaget, Inhelder, & Szeminska [1960], cited in Stephan & Clements, 2003)
Relation to number	Measuring is related to number in that measuring is simply a case of counting; measuring is conceptually more advanced since students must reorganize their understanding of the very objects they're counting. (discrete versus continuous units). (Stephan & Clements, 2003)

Table 2.10.   "Big ideas," Number of States, and Example GLEs

"Big Idea"	Number of States	Sample GLE
Unit-attribute relations	27	Identify appropriate units for measuring length, weight, volume, and temperature in the standard (English and metric) systems. (MS, gr. 6)
Iteration	6	Demonstrates conceptual understanding of the length/height of a two-dimensional object using nonstandard units (e.g. comparing objects to trains of small cubes, using iterations of a small unit to measure an object). (NH, gr. 1)
Tiling	13	Model (by tiling) the area of a simple geometric figure using square units (square inch, square foot, etc.). (GA, gr. 3)
Identical units	4	Knows that a uniform unit is needed to measure in real-world situations (for example, length, weight, time, capacity). (FL, gr. 1)
Standardization	5	Estimate and measure length, capacity/volume and mass with non-standard units to recognize the need for standard units. (AR, gr. 2)
Proportionality	3	Use different units to measure the length of the same object and predict whether the measure will be greater or smaller when a different unit is used. Example: If you measure your desk with a shorter pencil, will the number of pencil-lengths be more or less? Measure the desk to find out your answer. (IN, gr. 1)
Additivity	3	Determine the perimeter and area of composite plane figures by subdivision and area addition. (LA, gr. 7)
Partitioning	2	Estimate the area of a circle through partitioning and tiling and then with formula (let pi = 3.14). (Discuss square units as they apply to circles). (GA, gr. 5)
Precision	42	Determine the tool and technique to measure with an appropriate level of precision: lengths and angles. (NY, gr. 5)
Relation to number	17	Use counting techniques to explain how to find the area and perimeter of regular shapes. (DoD, gr. 3)

The procedures invented by the children led to progressive refinement of their conception of "space covered by" a form, to a point where all children were persuaded that the implausible could be true: The three forms all had the same area measure. (Strom et al., 2001, p. 736)

Four of the 14 big ideas are not explicitly mentioned: (1) origin (zero-point), (2) transitivity, (3) conservation, and (4) accumulation of distance. It is possible that the notion of transitivity as expressed in Table 2.9 is implicit in Level 2 GLEs that address comparing and ordering objects. It could be argued that comparing and ordering may include the notion that if object A is longer than object B and object B is longer than object C, then object A is longer than object C; however, this is not stated explicitly. Similarly, accumulation of distance may be included by some states as part of iteration. However, there are subtle differences between the two that may be overlooked if this is the case. Lehrer, Jacobson, Kemeny, and Strom (1999) provide an example of teacher questioning that facilitated a student investigation of the distinction between these two closely related big ideas. She asked students about the meaning of measure and pushed them to think beyond tools and units. She purposefully demonstrated an iteration of units (e.g., books) that left space between units to challenge the notion that counting and measuring are the same thing. The authors suggest that "some children think of number as a marker of the unit used (e.g., the seventh unit) but not as an indicator of the quantity of units needed to tile the distance traversed" (Lehrer et al., 1999, p. 82). It is not surprising that three of the missing big ideas (origin, conservation, and accumulation) are directly related to understanding the process of measurement since the measurement state standards seem to emphasize "doing" measurement more than "understanding" its basic principles.

Whether these big ideas should be included in the state standards or not is open for debate. Many states' standards take the form of a list of topics to be covered or skills to be mastered, and whether these big ideas, addressed using the language in the literature or other language, have a place in these documents seems dependent on the way in which the state conceptualizes the role of the standards. However, if these documents are viewed as potentially educative for classroom teachers, they certainly send a message about the importance of the conceptual understanding of measurement. In any case, the descriptions and examples in Tables 2.9 and 2.10 have been provided as a potential guide for those states interested in addressing the big ideas in measurement in future standards.

DISCUSSION

We conclude by returning briefly to the questions we set out to investigate. We will address each question in turn to summarize what we consider the most significant results from this analysis.

What Are Students Expected to Learn With Respect to Measurement and When Are They Expected to Learn It?

The compact answer to this question is difficult because of the significant breadth and depth of the topics included in this analysis (45 categories across five levels). Table 2.11 represents our effort to provide a meaningful overview. It presents an overview of each framework level, the number of states with GLEs classified at each level, the overall trends across grades with level, the most common categories within each level, and the number of states that contain GLEs classified into those categories. Table 2.11 shows, in capsule form, what we have seen above in more detail: An early focus on the awareness of measured attributes and on comparison and ordering; measuring with nonstandard units preceding measurement with standard units; and then the emphasis on formulae and problem solving.

Table 2.11.   Summary of Results: Level, Number of States, Trend, and Common Coding Categories

Level	Number of States	Trends Across Grade Levels	Common CATEGORIES (Number of States With GLEs in Category)
1	36	Fairly constant, most common in Grade 5	Meaning and recognition (30)
			Awareness of the units and tools associated with the attribute (27)
2	35	Most common in kindergarten, decreasing thereafter	Compare/Sort objects by attributes (35)
			Order objects by attributes (25)
3	41	Increases to Grade 2, decreases thereafter	Measures with nonstandard units (36)
			Estimates with nonstandard units (23)
4	39	Increases to Grade 3, decreases thereafter	Measures with standard units (39)
			Chooses standard units (31)
			Precision and accuracy (31)
			Estimates with standard units (28)
5	42	Increases from the early grades with the bulk of the work in later grades	Uses/Applies formulae (35)
			Solves problems/real-world problems (37)
			Meanings of relationships among one-, two-, and three-dimensional measures (35)

In addition, we found that in coding across the framework levels that some GLEs were not specific about whether students were expected to use standard or nonstandard units to measure and estimate. Without any greater specificity provided we wonder if classroom teachers will know how to ensure that their students have mastered such expectations.

What Are the Differences in the Treatment Of One-, Two- and Three-Dimensional Measurement Topics Across States?

Many interesting findings emerged in this analysis with regard to one-, two-, and three-dimensional measurement. One of these findings was that the state standards include more GLEs that address one-dimensional measurement (length, perimeter, and circumference) than two-dimensional (area and surface area) and three-dimensional (volume and capacity) measurement. The number of GLEs (and relative frequencies) respectively for one-, two-, and three-dimensional measurement are 1092 (68%), 731 (46%), and 629 (39%) across the 42 states. Figures 2.7, 2.8, and 2.9 showed that most states introduce one-dimensional and three-dimensional measurement in kindergarten, where two-dimensional measurement is most often not introduced until Grade 2. One-dimensional measurement topics are more prevalent than two- or three-dimensional topics in Grades K through 6. However, two-dimensional topics are emphasized more than one-dimensional topics in Grade 7, and by Grade 8, both two- and three-dimensional topics are more common than one-dimensional topics.

The analysis of the levels in our framework also produced interesting results regarding this question. At both Level 2 (comparing, ordering, and matching objects by the attribute) and 4 (choosing and using standard units and tools for estimating and measuring), two-dimensional measurement topics appeared less frequently across all categories than their one-dimensional and three-dimensional counterparts. This was also true for the Level 5 category of unit relationships. However, two-dimensional measurement topics were *much more* common than one- or three-dimensional topics in the Level 5 formulae category. These results suggest that two-dimensional measurement is dominated by computation (presumably from length measures) and less attention is given to units, tools, and unit relationships.

What Is the Level of Agreement About the Important Content of Measurement and the Grade Levels at Which These Ideas Occur Among State Standards Documents?

As found in previous analyses (Reys, 2006a), there is some agreement about the measurement topics that should be included in the K–8 state standards documents. However, the placement of topics varies significantly across states. Eight measurement topics are included in at least 75% (32 of 42 states) of the state standards documents (see Table 2.7). Forty of the 42 states expect students to measure with nonstandard units, making this the topic that occurs in the greatest number of states. Other popular topics include measuring with customary units (38 states) and measuring with metric units (37 states). Some agreement regarding when the topics should be taught can be seen in Table 2.8. Most striking is the apparent agreement among a significant number of states about the progression of students through the levels of the framework. Most states expect students first to compare and sort, then to measure and estimate with nonstandard units, then to measure with standard units, then to use formulae, solve problems involving measurement, and relate one-, two-, and three-dimensional measures.

Do State Standards Address the "Big Ideas" of Measurement Suggested in the Literature?

We collapsed three sets of big ideas found in the literature into a composite list of 14 big ideas (Table 2.9) and searched the GLEs for evidence of these ideas. Fortunately, 10 of these 14 big ideas are present in the measurement GLEs: (1) unit-attribute relations, (2) iteration, (3) tiling, (4) identical units, (5) standardization, (6) proportionality, (7) additivity, (8) partitioning, (9) precision, and (10) relation to number. Unfortunately, only two of these ideas, unit-attribute relations and precision, are present in at least half of the states analyzed, 42 and 27 states respectively. The remaining 4 of the 14 big ideas are not explicitly mentioned any of the documents: (1) origin (zero-point), (2) transitivity, (3) conservation, and (4) accumulation of distance. The absence of three big ideas that are closely related to understanding the process of measurement (origin, conservation, and accumulation of distance) leads us to question whether the state standards documents are giving sufficient attention to the development of conceptual understanding of the process of measuring.

CONCLUSION

One of our goals in completing this analysis was to provide information for those who will be charged to revise and improve their state mathematics standards. We did not set out to evaluate or to assign grades to the efforts of individual states, rather to draw attention to trends and anomalies across the 42 documents. We hope that the research-based "big ideas" we found in the literature and summarized in this chapter will serve as a useful resource in making the difficult decisions about what to include in the measurement sections of state standards. It seems that state and national standards documents will continue to shape the nature of precollege mathematics for the foreseeable future. Therefore, the mathematics education community at large will need to continue to collaborate broadly to produce standards that will ensure the richest possible experiences in measurement for students.

NOTES

1. The three collections of GLEs discussed in the text, measures with standard units, chooses standard units, and estimates with standard units, represent the combined categories of measures with customary units and measures with metric units, chooses customary units and chooses metric units, and estimates with customary units and estimates with metric units, respectively in the framework. This simplification shortens the discussion without undue loss of meaning.
2. Recall that some GLEs were coded in more than one dimension.
3. States are listed in each figure in the order in which they introduce and continue to include one-, two-, and three-dimensional measurement GLEs—that is, by grade. They are not listed in alphabetical order, and the order in which they appear differs across the figures.

CHAPTER 3

THE TREATMENT OF TRANSFORMATIONS IN K–8 GEOMETRY AND MEASUREMENT GRADE-LEVEL EXPECTATIONS

Sasha Wang and John P. Smith III

The concept of transformation has fundamentally reorganized the structure of school geometry in the last 30 years, changing the focus from studying the properties of static figures (e.g., congruence and similarity) to examining of the nature of mappings that relate figures and construct key geometric properties. This reorganization, like any fundamental change in the school mathematics, has led to changes and likely, some difficulties for teachers, mathematics supervisors and coordinators, and parents whose own geometry coursework made little to no mention of transformations. When confronted with views of geometric content structured by transformations (e.g., in mathematics textbooks), they could sensibly ask: "What's so important about transformations (since I did not learn about them), and how do they relate to the geometry that I know?" If such basic questions about the role of transformations in school geome-

Variability is the Rule: A Companion Analysis of K–8 State Mathematics Standards, pp. 41–70
Copyright © 2011 by Information Age Publishing

41

try are likely, even for some teachers, an examination of how transformations, both distance-preserving and shape-preserving, are treated in the
states' K–8 geometry and measurement content standards could be
helpful, informative, and even instructive. This chapter explores that
potential.

WHAT IS TRANSFORMATIONAL GEOMETRY?

Transformational geometry in school mathematics is the study of different classes of mappings of the plane, the properties of those mappings,
and pairs and collections of figures related by those mappings. Mumford,
Series, and Wright (2002) described, "a *transformation* [italics added] of
the plane is simply a rule that assigns to each point P a new point Q"
(p.10). More formally, transformations are 1-to-1 function mappings of
one set of points (the pre-image) onto another set of points (the image).[1]
In simple English, the mapping might be described as "the new point is 5
inches to the right of the old one," or "the new position of the figure is
obtained by rotating it 45 degrees about this point outside the figure." A
more concrete way of thinking about transformations is to see them as
procedures for physically moving the points in the plane to new locations.
Transformations may distort figures or leave their size and/or shape
intact. Properties of figures left unchanged by a given transformation are
preserved by that transformation (Mumford et al., 2002).

In the K–8 geometry curriculum, two common types of transformations are distance-preserving transformations and shape-preserving
transformations. Distance-preserving transformations (also known as
isometries or congruence transformations) preserve both distance and
shape. The four most common types are reflection, rotation, translation,
and glide reflection; most K–8 curricula introduce students to the first
three types. Shape-preserving transformations (also known as dilations or
similarity transformations) preserve shape but not size; they may increase
or decrease the size of the original figure. These two broad categories of
transformations (distance-preserving or shape-preserving) construct and
explain the traditional Euclidean properties of congruence and symmetry
(where shape and distance is preserved) and similarity (where only shape
is preserved) of geometric figures. For example, consider a figure rotated
90 degrees in a counterclockwise direction and then reflected with respect
to the *x*-axis in a coordinate plane. The positions of the pre-image and
image are different, but their size and shape remains unchanged, so the
image is congruent to the pre-image. Similarly, any pair of congruent or
similar figures in the plane can be linked as pre-image to image by an
isometry or dilation, respectively.

Before transformations were introduced in the U.S. curriculum in the late 1960s, school geometry was largely the study of Euclid's axioms, definitions, and theorems. In contrast to the traditional Euclidean geometry curriculum's presentation of points, lines and figures as fixed in the plane, transformational geometry introduced mappings and changed their characterization from static to dynamic and movable objects (Sinclair, 2008). This change connected geometry to other strands of mathematics structured by the fundamental concept of mapping or function. The change also has important implications for teaching and learning elementary mathematics. For example, some research has shown that teachers introducing transformations in elementary school through pictorial graphs can draw students' attention to transformations while providing further work with coordinate systems, counting skills, and visualization of geometric shapes (Swadener, 1987).

HISTORICAL BACKGROUND: TRANSFORMATIONS IN THE GEOMETRY CURRICULUM

In 1872 Felix Klein, a young mathematics professor at the Bavarian University in Erlangen, Germany, proposed a research program called "Comparative view of recent researchers in geometry," which later became known as the *Erlangen Program* (James, 2002). There he cast geometry as "the study of the properties of a space which are invariant under a given group of transformations" and embraced both Euclidean and non-Euclidean axiomatic systems, as well as many others (p. 219). Klein believed that in geometry one needed to study not only basic geometric objects such as triangles, circles, and points, but also the transformations that related them.

Klein's view of geometry did not influence school geometry in the United States until almost a century later. In 1969, the University of Illinois Committee School Mathematics (UICSM) published a program to help middle school students learn fractions through the study of transformations called "Stretchers and Shrinkers" (UICSM, n.d.). About the same time, the rising popularity of Escher's drawings of tessellations stimulated the move to develop more learning materials based on transformations for students at elementary and middle school. The debate over using a transformational approach to geometry reached its peak in the early 1970s. In 1971, Arthur Coxford and Zalman Usiskin published a high school geometry textbook, *Geometry, A Transformational Approach*, that developed the traditional Euclidean content through transformations (Coxford & Usiskin, 1971), and 2 years later, the National Council of

Teachers of Mathematics (NCTM) titled its Yearbook, *Geometry in the Mathematics Curriculum* (Henderson, 1973).

These volumes charted a new direction in the teaching of geometry. Curricular recommendations in the former included teaching a substantial amount of informal geometry at the K–6 level. Synthetic geometry, coordinate geometry and transformational geometry were included as "new choices" in the geometry curriculum. Spurred by these curricular recommendations, researchers examined young students' interactions with transformations, seeking answers about how early geometry or/and transformations should be taught and what sense students make of geometry at these early grades (Sinclair, 2008). This research was summarized in 1987 in *Learning and Teaching Geometry, K–12* (Lindquist, 1987), the next NCTM Yearbook devoted to geometry. Sinclair (2008) has since argued that the impact of the 1987 Yearbook reflected a growing interest in visualization, geometric thinking, computer-based exploration of geometry, and locating geometrical connections to other mathematical domains. The development and proliferation of dynamic computer software was another important factor in supporting the study of transformations in geometry classrooms because the effects of transformations on figures were easily and immediately seen.

In 1989, NCTM's *Curriculum and Evaluation Standards for School Mathematics* articulated standards for geometry at each of three grade bands (K–4, 5–8, 9–12). The Grade 5–8 standards explicitly or implicitly refer to transformations in multiple passages, including "explore transformations of geometric figures" (p. 112), "tessellations with regular polygon" (p. 115) and "reflections in water" (p. 115). Likewise, the subsequent *Principles and Standards for School Mathematics (PSSM)* included transformations in both geometry and measurement standards from kindergarten to Grade 8 (NCTM, 2000). The Geometry standard cited transformations as an important component of school geometry from pre-kindergarten through Grade 12. For example, in the middle grades (5–8), *PSSM* asserts that, "students should learn to understand what it means for a transformation to preserve distance, as translations, rotations, and reflections do" (p. 43).

Because transformations are a relatively recent addition to the school geometry curriculum, they may be a novel concept for many K–12 teachers, especially those teaching in elementary and middle schools, whose collegiate mathematics coursework may not have included this concept in any substantial way. Also, the curriculum materials that experienced teachers used earlier in their careers may not have included significant, if any work, with transformations. For these reasons, transformations are likely one of the concepts in the states' geometry and measurement standards for which U.S. teachers have the most questions and the least knowledge of and experience teaching.

With these issues in mind, this chapter addresses three interrelated questions: Where, for how long, and for what mathematical purpose have transformations been included in the state standards? We will approach these questions in two main steps. First, we will examine the states and grade levels where the concept of transformation appears in grade-level learning expectations (GLEs) (to address "where?") with specific attention to the continuity of development from their first mention (to address "for how long?"). Then we turn to the issue of purpose and explore how, how often, and how well transformations have been linked to three central and more traditional topics in the K–8 geometry and measurement curriculum, congruence, similarity, and symmetry.

METHOD

All 42 states dealt with the concept of transformation somewhere in the their standards document. Most ($n = 34$) placed their GLEs that concerned transformations in their Geometry strands. Two of those states (Alabama and Georgia) also placed transformation GLEs in their Measurement strands. Because similarity transformations (dilations) change the size of figures, the inclusion of some transformation GLEs in Measurement strands is quite sensible. Example 3.1 illustrates one such GLE from Alabama.

*Example 3.1.*Using dilations on the coordinate plane to determine measures of similar figures. (AL, gr. 8)

The remaining eight states placed their transformation GLEs in a combined Geometry & Measurement strand. Overall, these frequencies show that most standards authors saw transformations as primarily geometric content.

Of the total geometry and measurement GLEs in all 42 state documents ($N = 5710$), a relatively small proportion, $n = 335$ (6%), were coded as "transformation GLEs," based on the presence of one or more terms directly related to transformations. These terms were: "motion," "rigid motion," "mapping," "rotation," "turn," "reflection," "flip," "dilation," "translation," "slide," "enlargement," "shrinking," "stretching," "magnifying," "reduction," "contraction," and "transformation" itself. Note that this list includes the accepted mathematical terminology for different types of transformations (e.g., reflection, dilation, rotation, mapping) and a corresponding set of informal terms tailored for younger students (e.g., turn, flip, slide, shrinking, stretching)—an issue that we will examine below. The more commonly used terms were "rotation," "turn," "reflection," "flip," "dilation," "translation," "slide," and "transformation." There was no mention of glide reflection (a reflection composed with a translation) in any state document.

Frequently, transformation GLEs included more than one of these terms. Example 3.2 illustrates GLEs that included multiple search terms and mixed formal and informal terms.

> *Example 3.2.* Recognizing the results of changing the position (*transformation*) [italics added] of objects or shapes by *sliding* (*translation*) [italics added], *turning* (*rotation*) [italics added], or *flipping* (*reflection*) [italics added]. (AL, gr. 2)

Grade-level expectations were also coded as "congruence GLEs" if they included at least one of the following terms: "congruence," "congruent," "congruency," "match exactly," and "same shape and size." Three typical examples are given below. As Example 3.3 indicates, our coding of GLEs did not create disjoint sets. Numerous GLEs were coded as both "transformation GLEs" and "congruence GLEs", and the same was true for similarity and symmetry (Examples 3.4 and 3.5).

> *Example 3.3.* Describe congruent figures as having the *same size and shape* [italics added]. (MD, gr. 2)

> *Example 3.4.* Understand that congruent shapes *match exactly* [italics added]. (VA, gr. 3)

> *Example 3.5.* Examine the *congruence* [italics added] similarity, and line or rotational symmetry of objects using transformations. (AR, gr. 7)

Our search terms for similarity were: "similar/similarity," "proportion/ proportionality," "same shape and different size," "scale factor," "scale drawing," "reduce/reduction," "enlarge/enlargement," "magnify/magnifying," "shrink/shrinking," "stretch/stretching," and "dilation." Similarity GLEs most often appeared in the states' Measurement strand (for states that distinguished geometry from measurement), principally due to mention of "scale factor" and "scale drawing." Some typical GLEs are given in Examples 3.6, 3.7, and 3.8 below. Note the frequency with which congruence terms co-appear with similarity terms.

> *Example 3.6.* Identify and determine whether two-dimensional shapes are congruent (same shape and size) or *similar* (*same shape different size*) [italics added] by copying or using superposition (lay one thing on top of another). (OH, gr. 2)

Example 3.7. Identify, define, and describe similar and congruent polygons with respect to angle measures, length of sides, and *proportionality* [italics added] of sides. (NC, gr. 7)

Example 3.8. Use *scale drawings* [italics added] involving indirect measurement (determining the *scale factor* [italics added] and applying it to find missing dimension). (AR, gr. 8)

Finally, our search terms for symmetry were: "symmetry/symmetries," "symmetric/symmetrical," "line(s) of symmetry," "rotational symmetry," and "reflection/reflective symmetry." Though all contain the same root term, the full list illustrates the ways in which that root term was expressed. Examples 3.9 and 3.10 illustrate some of the range of expression among the symmetry GLEs.

Example 3.9. Build and identify shapes that have one or more lines of *reflective symmetry* [italics added] or that can be divided into two congruent parts. (CT, gr. 2)

Example 3.10. Determine the type of *symmetry (point or line)* [italics added] found in a reflection or a rotation. (SC, gr. 7)

LOCATION AND CONTINUITY:
WHERE AND FOR HOW LONG DID TRANSFORMATIONS APPEAR?

Though every state included at least one transformation GLE in their Geometry, Measurement, or Geometry & Measurement standards, there was great variation in focus across states. Two (California and Maine) mentioned transformations only once; by contrast, Washington did so 27 times from Grades K–8. Given this extreme value, the median ($n = 6.5$) is a more meaningful measure of central tendency for the frequency of transformations GLEs. The range, mean, median and mode of the distribution of transformation GLEs are given in Table 3.1.

Transformation GLEs, like those in other content areas, varied in length. Some states include only a single sentence; some states include four or five sentences that could have been listed as different GLEs. So the simple frequencies of GLEs are not a reliable indicator of the importance assigned to this concept by the authors.

To better understand when states expect students to study and learn transformations, we present the distribution of GLEs across grades in Figure 3.1. The darker bars show the number of states with at least one transformation GLE at each grade (e.g., 37 states included at least one transformation GLE in Grade 4). The lighter bars show the total number

Table 3.1.   Descriptive Statistics for Transformation GLEs

States Mentioning Transformations	42
Overall Total of Transformation GLEs	335
Range	1–27
Mean Frequency	7.98
Median Frequency	6.5
Modal Frequency	5

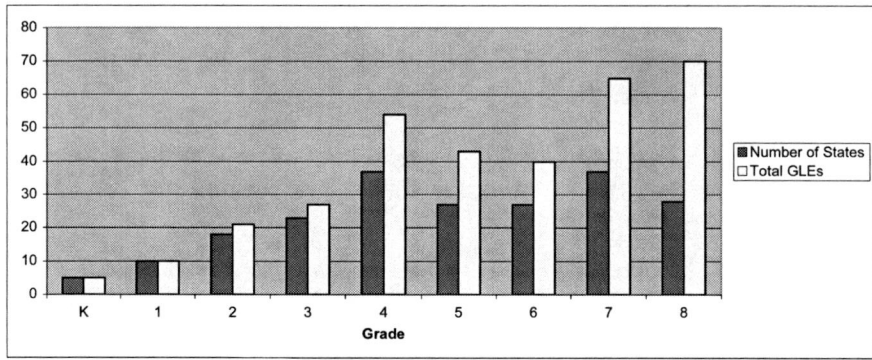

Figure 3.1.   Frequency of states and transformation GLEs by grade.

of transformation GLEs across the states at each grade (e.g., there were 54 transformation GLEs in Grade 4).

Figure 3.1 shows that attention to transformations generally increased by grade, with the most focused attention occurring between Grades 4 and 8. Though the number of states with transformation GLEs was not constant across grades, there was, on average, more mention of this construct as the grade level increased. From kindergarten to Grade 3, states included about one GLE per state at each grade. But between Grades 3 and 6, the average increased to about 1.5 GLEs per state per grade, and by Grades 7 and 8 the average was about 2.5 GLEs per state.

The complete distribution of transformation GLEs across states and grades is shown in Figure 3.2. In each state column, the triangles indicate the grade level in which transformation first appeared in that state's standards, and the squares represent the subsequent grade levels where the concept was mentioned. The states have been arranged from earliest introduction and most continuous mention on the far left to latest introduction on the far right. For example, Arkansas was one of three states that introduced transformations in kindergarten and included at least one GLE in each subsequent grade. By contrast, Wyoming's first transfor-

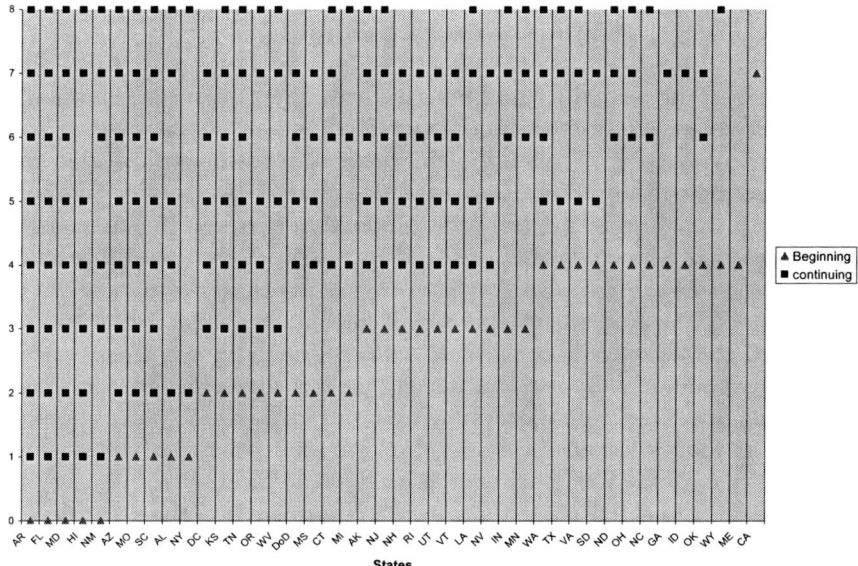

Figure 3.2.   Distribution of transformation GLEs by state and grade.

mation GLE appeared in Grade 4 and the concept did not appear again until in Grade 8.

Figure 3.2 highlights the variation across states in when students are first expected to demonstrate knowledge of transformations. Significant numbers of states first introduced the concept in each grade from kindergarten to Grade 4. Thirty-four states, once they introduced transformations, continued the topic in subsequent grades with no gaps greater than one grade, and 23 of those 34 skipped only one grade once the concept was first mentioned. In contrast, six states introduced the topics and then dropped it (i.e., for each, there was at least one gap of two grades or more). For example, Indiana and Minnesota first mentioned transformations in Grade 3, skipped the topic in Grades 4 and 5, and returned to it in middle school (Grades 6–8). As noted earlier, the remaining two states, Maine and California, gave little attention to transformations, with only one GLE, K–8.

But where these analyses are informative, they provide only a surface view of how states portray the role of transformations in geometry and measurement, leaving many important questions unanswered. In the following section, we examine how and when transformations GLEs have been used to articulate learning expectations for three traditional geometric topics—congruence, similarity, and symmetry.

HOW WERE TRANSFORMATIONS RELATED TO CONGRUENCE, SIMILARITY AND SYMMETRY?

As described above, the mathematical concept of transformation is intimately related to the traditional geometric topics of congruence, similarity, and symmetry. In brief, the character of transformations that map pre-image figures on their images determine their shared geometric properties. But despite the intimate connection between the character of mappings and what they map, we did not assume that transformations would always co-appear with congruence, similarity, and symmetry in the states' geometry and measurement expectations. So as an initial step, we examined the distributions of GLEs across grades to see when each of these four concepts was introduced. Figure 3.3 shows the frequencies of transformation GLEs, congruence GLEs, similarity GLEs, and symmetry GLEs by grade level, and Figure 3.4 shows the frequencies of states with at least one of each GLE of each type at each grade level.

Figures 3.3 and 3.4 show quite similar patterns for the treatment of these four broad topics. Both the number of GLEs and the number of

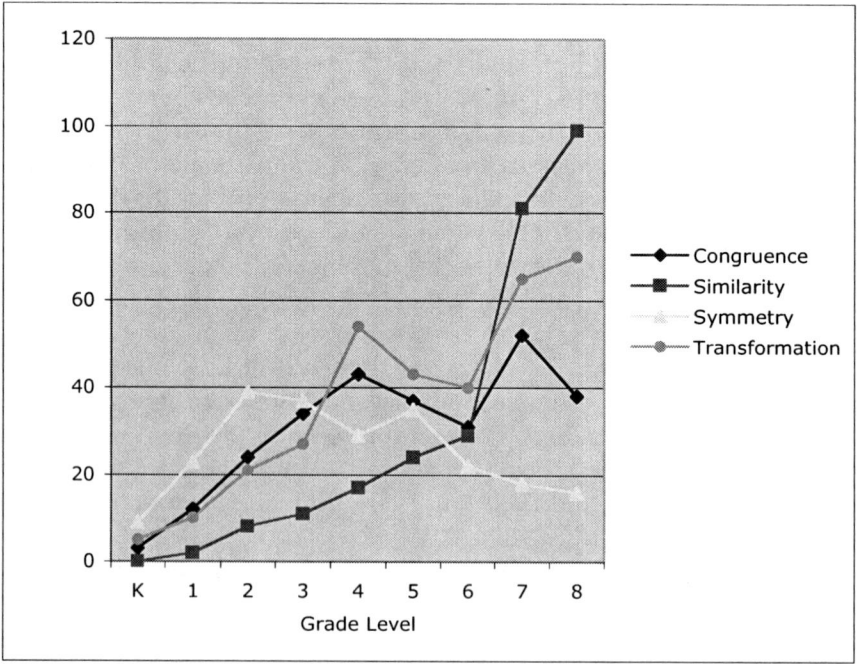

Figure 3.3.   Frequency of congruence GLEs, similarity GLEs, symmetry GLEs, and transformation GLEs by grade.

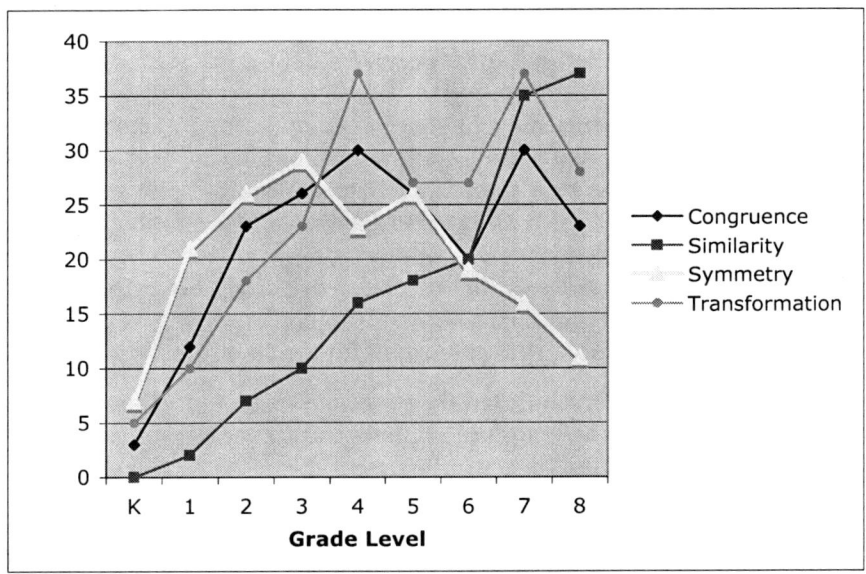

Figure 3.4. Frequency of states with at least one congruence, similarity, symmetry, and transformation GLEs by grade.

states increased steadily from kindergarten to Grade 4 (where nearly all states included at least one transformation GLE), declined in Grades 5 and 6 and then increased again at Grade 7. In Grade 8, fewer states addressed transformations in their documents, but those that did dealt with the concept more intensively, as indicated by the rise in the number of GLEs. The shape of the graphs for congruence and symmetry are nearly identical. Attention to congruence increased steadily until Grade 4, dropped until Grade 6, rose again in Grade 7 and dropped again in Grade 8. On average, the typical state included between one and 1.5 congruence GLE per grade. Attention to symmetry rose until Grade 3 and then declined relatively uniformly, except for the steeper drop at Grade 4. The typical state also included between one and 1.5 symmetry GLE at each grade. By contrast, the treatment of similarity was delayed; both the number of GLEs and the number of states increased gradually to Grade 6. However, in Grades 7 and 8 the topic was treated by most states and typically with more than one GLE at each grade. Finally, as shown in part in Figures 3.1 and 3.2, the frequency of transformation GLEs increased by state and total frequency to Grade 4, declined in Grades 5 and 6, and rose again in Grade 7. At Grade 8, fewer states addressed the topic, but those that did gave it more attention. The average number of transformation GLEs at Grade 8 was 2.5.

Explicit Relations Between Concepts

Of all 335 transformation GLEs, only 76 (23%) in 31 state documents explicitly included a transformation term with a congruence, similarity, or symmetry term. The remaining 11 states developed the topic of transformations entirely separately from congruence, similarity, and symmetry. However, the 76 GLEs that mentioned transformation with one of the other three topics included both cases where the transformation term simply co-appeared with a congruence, similarity, or symmetry term and cases where transformations were explicitly related to one of those three topics. For example, one of the Indiana's Grade 7 GLEs (Example 3.11) explicitly indicated that isometries create congruent figures by preserving distance.

Example 3.11. Understand that transformations such as slides, turns, and flips preserve the length of segments, and that figures resulting from slides, turns, and flips are congruent to the original figures. (IN, gr. 7)

In contrast, in one of Florida's Grade 3 GLEs (Example 3.12), the term "reflection" appeared in a list with "symmetry" and "congruency," suggesting that the three mathematical concepts were of the same type.

Example 3.12. Knows symmetry, congruency, and reflections in geometric figures using concrete materials (for example, pattern blocks, geo-boards, mirrors). (FL, gr. 3)

Where the Indiana GLE related one type of transformation to the properties of the figures involved in that type of mapping, the Florida GLEs did not clarify that reflections are mappings that establish the symmetry and congruence of mapped figures.

Given the importance of clarity about these connections to communicate clearly with the readers of the standards about potentially "new" mathematics, we separated GLEs that related transformation to one of the other three topics from those where a transformation term simply co-appeared with a term for one of the other three topics. Table 3.2 presents these frequencies by grade level.

The entries in Table 3.2 represent good news. In general, co-appearance without any expression of relationship was infrequent. Subsequent sections will present more detail on how states related transformations to congruence, similarity, and symmetry.

The Development of Transformations Across Grades

Thus far, we have examined when and how often states have included transformations in their geometry and measurement expectations, when

Table 3.2.   Frequencies of Transformations GLEs That Co-Appear or are Related to Congruence, Similarity

| | Number of GLEs | | | | | |
| | Congruence | | Similarity | | Symmetry | |
Grade	Co-Appear	Related	Co-Appear	Relate	Co-Appear	Relate
2	0	1	0	0	0	0
3	1	7	0	0	1	2
4	1	13	0	2	1	2
5	1	8	0	2	1	2
6	0	7	0	1	0	2
7	0	12	0	5	0	8
8	1	6	1	9	0	6
Total GLEs	4	54	1	19	3	22
Total States	2	23	1	14	1	15

Note: The number of entries exceeds the total number of GLEs ($n = 76$) because some GLEs contained two or more terms, for example, a congruence term and a symmetry term.

the closely related concepts of congruence, similarity, and symmetry were introduced and developed, and whether linkages between transformations and these three concepts have been simply mentioned together or more closely connected. But the aggregate nature of this data makes it difficult to see, in detail, how states have developed the notion of transformation across grade levels and how they have related these mappings to the properties of the images they generate.

In this section, we address that limitation by examining two states' treatment of transformations. In each the complete list of their transformation GLEs is given. These two are among the majority of states ($n = 29$) that have given serious attention to the development of transformations in their standards. We have selected them to illustrate development across grades and to show the challenges and choices involved in so doing. The remaining states ($n = 13$) dealt with transformations more peripherally and therefore are less interesting cases of development.

Case 1: Arkansas

The first case (Arkansas) illustrates three important features common to other states that have given serious attention to transformations: (1) the concept is introduced via intuitive and informal terminology, (2) it is developed across grade levels, and (3) explicit connections are drawn to congruence, similarity, and symmetry. Arkansas's ten transformation GLEs in their Geometry strand are shown in Table 3.3.

**Table 3.3. Arkansas' Transformation GLEs From
Their Geometry Standards**

Grade	Grade-Level Expectation
K	Explore slides, flips and turns.
1	Manipulate two-dimensional figures through slides, flips and turns.
3	Describe the motion (transformation) of a two-dimensional figure as a flip (reflection), slide (translation) or turn (rotation).
4	Determine the result of a transformation of a two-dimensional figure as a slide (translation), flip (reflection) or turn (rotation) and justify the answer.
5	Predict and describe the results of translation (slide), reflection (flip), rotation (turn), showing that the transformed shape remains unchanged.
6	Describe positions and orientations of shapes under transformation (translation, reflection and rotation) recognizing the size and shape do not change.
7	Examine the congruence, similarity, and line or rotational symmetry of objects using transformations.
7	Perform translations and reflections of two-dimensional figures using a variety of methods (paper folding, tracing, graph paper).
8	Determine a transformation's line of symmetry and compare the properties of the figure and its transformation.
8	Draw the results of translations and reflections about the x- and y-axis and rotations of objects about the origin.

Their development of transformations began with the exploration of "slides, flips, and turns" in kindergarten, added the figures to be transformed in Grade 1, and introduced the formal terminology for isometries in Grade 3 but with linkages to the informal terms. By Grade 5, the formal terms have taken precedence, though the linkage to the informal remains. Linkages were then drawn to congruence, similarity, and symmetry in Grades 7 and 8. However, these GLEs did not clearly distinguish between dilations (similarity transformations) and isometries (congruence transformations), left similarity undefined and the meaning of congruence implicit, and mistakenly made lines of symmetry properties of transformation rather than the figures themselves (in the first Grade 8 GLE).

Case 2: Louisiana

In contrast, the second case represents another group of states that weakly connected congruence, similarity, and symmetry to transformations, but still have developed the concept in a careful and thoughtful way. Louisiana included seven transformation GLEs in their Geometry strand (see Table 3.4).

**Table 3.4. Louisiana's Transformation GLEs From
Their Geometry Standards**

Grade	Grade-Level Expectation
3	Recognize and execute specified flips, turns, and slides of geometric figures using manipulatives and correct terminology (including clockwise and counterclockwise).
4	Make and test predictions regarding transformations (i.e., slides, flips, and turns) of plane geometric shapes.
4	Identify, manipulate, and predict the results of rotations of 90, 180, 270, and 360 degrees on a given figure.
5	Identify and use appropriate terminology for transformations (e.g., translation as slide, reflection as flip, and rotation as turn).
7	Draw the results of reflections and translations of geometric shapes on a coordinate grid.
8	Predict, draw, and discuss the resulting changes in lengths, orientation, angle measures, and coordinates when figures are translated, reflected across horizontal or vertical lines, and rotated on a grid.
8	Predict, draw, and discuss the resulting changes in lengths, orientation, and angle measures that occur in figures under a similarity transformation (dilation).

Like Arkansas but three grades later, Louisiana introduced transformations via the informal terminology of flips, turns, and slides and then a grade later focused attention on the figures being mapped. Also like Arkansas, Louisiana introduced the formal terminology in a later grade and explicitly attached the formal to the informal. Grade 7 and 8 expectations focused on reflections and translations applied on coordinate grids and to examining the effects of those isometries and of dilations on the mapped figures. But where the term "similarity" was mentioned and explicitly related to dilations, the corresponding relationship between isometries (reflections, rotations, and translations) and congruence was left entirely to the reader. Similarly, symmetry and its relation to reflection were never mentioned.

One important contrast between the two states is in the cognitive processes they ask students to undertake and the verbs they used to do so. Where Arkansas generally used a single verb to request one cognitive activity of students in each GLE (e.g., "explore," "manipulate," "describe," etc.) and varied these verbs/activities substantially over the grades, Louisiana frequently included a sequence of verbs in their GLEs (e.g., "predict, draw, and discuss") and focused a great deal of attention on the cognitive process of predicting the results of applying transformations.

CONGRUENCE

As we recounted above, the introduction of transformations into the school geometry curriculum reconceptualized the traditional treatment of congruent figures (plane figures with same size and shape). Where before congruent figures were treated as unrelated (if identical) figures, they were now seen as related via a particular kind of transformation (isometries) that preserved distance and shape. Three types of isometries in the K–8 curriculum map pre-image figures onto their images: reflections, translations, and rotations.

All 42 states mentioned congruence at least once in their standards documents. Thirty-one states developed the topic only in their Geometry strands, two states in both Geometry and Measurement strands, and nine states in combined Geometry & Measurement strands. But only 5% ($n = 274$) of all geometry and measurement GLEs involved this construct. As was the case with transformation, the range was large; three states mentioned the concept only once (Maine, Minnesota, and Missouri) where Florida mentioned it 15 times. The mean frequency was 6.52 per state and the median was 6. Of the 274 congruence GLEs, relatively few ($n = 60$, 22%) explicitly related congruence to transformations.

Some GLEs were written with the apparent intent of defining congruence, strictly or loosely as "figures as having the same size and shape," "sides and angles have equal measures," "map one figure onto another," or "shapes match exactly." Four expectations, Examples 3.13 through 3.16, illustrate the diversity of focus among these "definitional" GLEs.

> *Example 3.13*. Recognize that two objects having the same shape but oriented differently in space are congruent. (DoD, gr. K)
>
> *Example 3.14*. Compare two-dimensional shapes to determine if they exactly match (congruency). (SC, gr. 3)
>
> *Example 3.15*. Understand that for polygons, congruence means corresponding sides and angles have equal measures. (MI, gr. 6)
>
> *Example 3.16*. Use a translation, a reflection, or a rotation to map one figure onto another congruent figure. (NJ, gr. 5)

Other nondefinitional GLEs focused on the congruence of angles, related angle congruence to the properties that generated them (e.g., parallel lines cut by a transversal), and/or to similar or congruent figures, as the following examples from the Grades 7 and 8 illustrate (Examples 3.17 to 3.20)

Example 3.17. Identify, define, and describe similar and congruent polygons with respect to angle measures, length of sides, and proportionality of sides. (NC, gr. 7)

Example 3.18. Develop the properties of similar figures (ratio of sides and congruent angles). (AR, gr. 7)

Example 3.19. Identifying angle bisectors, perpendicular bisectors, congruent angles, and congruent figures. (AL, gr. 8)

Example 3.20. Identify the properties of angles created by a transversal intersecting two parallel lines (e.g., corresponding angles are congruent). (AZ, gr. 8)

Congruence Across the Grades

As was the case for transformations, the grade level at which congruence was first introduced ranged widely across the states—from kindergarten and Grade 5. The distribution of all 274 congruence GLEs across states and grades is shown in Figure 3.5. As before, the triangles indicate the grade in which congruence first appeared, and the squares indicate the subsequent grades where the topic was treated.

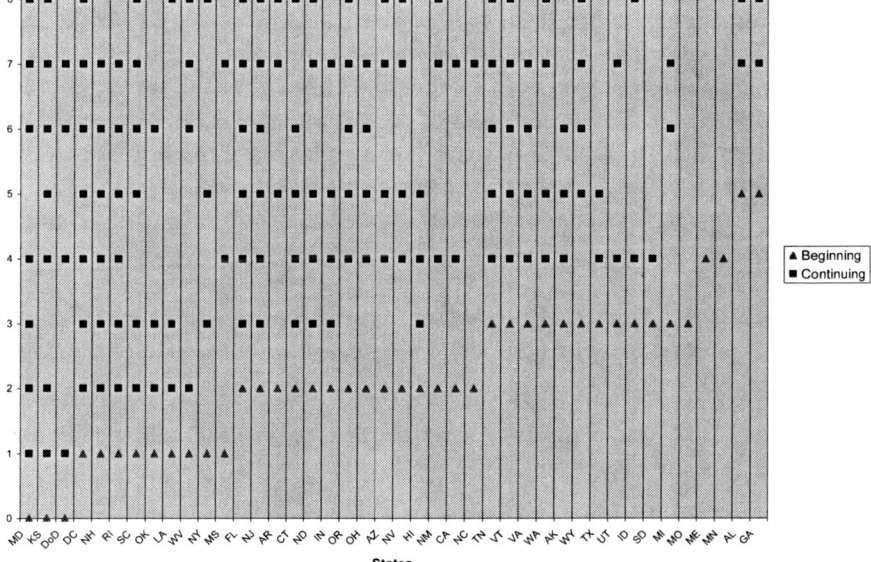

Figure 3.5.   Distribution of congruence GLEs by state and grade.

The vast majority of states ($n = 38$) introduced congruence by Grade 3, and a simple majority ($n =26$) had by Grade 2. As they did for transformations, some states introduced the topic and developed it relatively continuously, whereas other states dropped the topic entirely or skipped multiple grade levels after they introduced it. Once introduced, a thin majority ($n = 23$ states, 55%) developed the topic relatively continuously in subsequent grades—no gaps were greater than one grade. Eighteen of those 23 skipped only one grade after they introduced the concept. Most of the remaining states ($n = 16$; 38%) had significant discontinuities in their treatment of congruence (i.e., there was at least one gap of two grades or more). For example, West Virginia introduced the topic in Grade 1, developed it in Grade 2, but then skipped it entirely in Grades 3, 4 and 5, before returning to it in middle school (Grades 6–8). As noted earlier, the remaining three states, Maine, Missouri, and Minnesota, mentioned the topic only once.

Relations Between Transformations and Congruence

About one in five congruence GLEs ($n = 60$; 22%) linked that properties of geometric figures to isometries—a sensible number given the need to introduce the congruence of figures, possibly in informal terms (see below), and also to apply the concept to parts of figures, e.g., angles and sides of polygons. But these "linking" GLEs were not distributed evenly across the states; only slightly more than half of the states ($n = 26$, 62%) included them. Of those 26, 10 states included only one GLE that linked transformations to congruence, 7 others included 2, and 2 states included the maximum of 5. Three examples of such "linking" GLEs are given below in Examples 3.21 to 3.23. The first two examples leave the necessity of the relationship implicit, casting isometries as tools for determining or verifying if two figures are congruent, where the third makes that necessity explicit.

> *Example 3.21.* Apply techniques such as reflections (flips), rotations (turns), and translations (slides) for determining if two shapes are congruent. (DC, gr. 3)
>
> *Example 3.22.* Use translations, reflections, and rotations to verify that two shapes are congruent. (TX, gr. 4)
>
> *Example 3.23.* Understand that transformations such as slides, turns, and flips preserve the length of segments, and that figures resulting from slides, turns, and flips are congruent to the original figures. (IN, gr. 7)

Formal and Informal Terms for Congruence Transformations

Early in our analyses, we noticed that states used different terms to describe transformations, particularly isometries. In the primary grades (kindergarten to Grade 2) transformations were often identified by terms like "flip," "turn," and "slide" in the place of the standard mathematical terms ("reflection," "rotation," and "translation"). As the grade level increased, most authors replaced their informal terms to the standard ones—sometimes, as we have seen, linking the informal to the formal explicitly. Because the notion of introducing a mathematical concept via more accessible, descriptive terms and then shifting to later to standard terms could be important for teaching and learning, we examined this pattern more closely, beginning with reflection/flip.

Figure 3.6 shows the frequencies with which states used the terms "flip" and "reflection" across the grades.

From kindergarten to Grade 3, the informal term ("flip") was used more frequently; by Grade 4, the formal term ("reflection") appeared almost as often; and thereafter the formal term has dominated, to the point that "flip" nearly disappeared by Grade 8.

We also found the same pattern held for the other isometries (slide/translation, turn/rotation), as shown in Table 3.5, whose entries count all 42 states at least once.

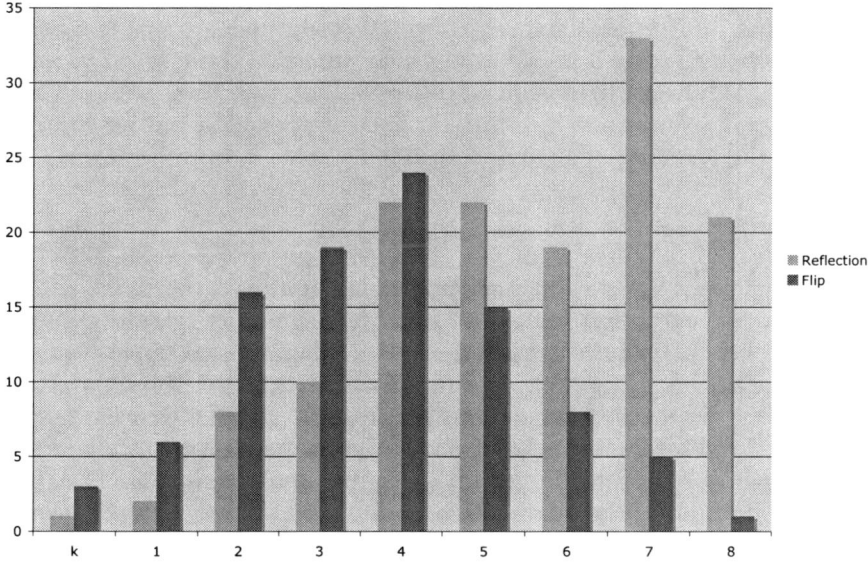

Figure 3.6. Frequency of states using "flip" and "reflection" by grade.

**Table 3.5.   Frequency of States Using Formal and
Informal Terms for Isometries by Grade**

			Number of States			
Grade	Flip	Reflection	Turn	Rotation	Slide	Translation
K	3	1	4	1	5	1
1	6	2	8	1	10	3
2	16	8	14	6	14	5
3	19	10	19	9	20	8
4	24	22	21	21	24	22
5	15	22	14	20	14	19
6	8	19	8	21	7	18
7	5	33	4	28	5	33
8	1	21	1	20	1	21
Total	36	40	35	40	35	39

Note: Some states used both informal and formal terms and are double counted.

The results shown in Table 3.5 above closely parallel the results for flip/
reflection: Informal terms for rotation and translation predominated in
the primary grades, Grade 4 usage was roughly equal, and the formal
terms increasingly dominated in the upper grades (5 to 8). So for congruence transformations at least, most states introduce this concept with
informal terms before shifting to the official mathematical terminology.
In tracking and reporting this pattern for congruence transformations,
we are not suggesting that the use of these informal terms is sufficient to
introduce children the specific transformations that they name. These
terms may be educationally useful, but they are not sufficient for students
to grasp the meaning of any type of isometry, even in intuitive terms.

SIMILARITY

In an analogous way to congruence, similar figures in the plane can be
seen as pre-images and images of dilations (similarity transformations)
that preserve their shape but not their size. Dilations increase or decrease
the size of the image figure according a fixed scale factor (the ratio of corresponding distances in image and pre-image). Those with scale factors
between 0 and 1 generate smaller image figures (reductions); scale factors
larger than one produce larger image figures (enlargements). The location of the center of the dilation determines the location of the image relative to its pre-image. Dilations with negative scale factors invert the
image on the opposite side of the center. Two dilations with the same center O, one with a positive scale factor greater than 1 (generating image

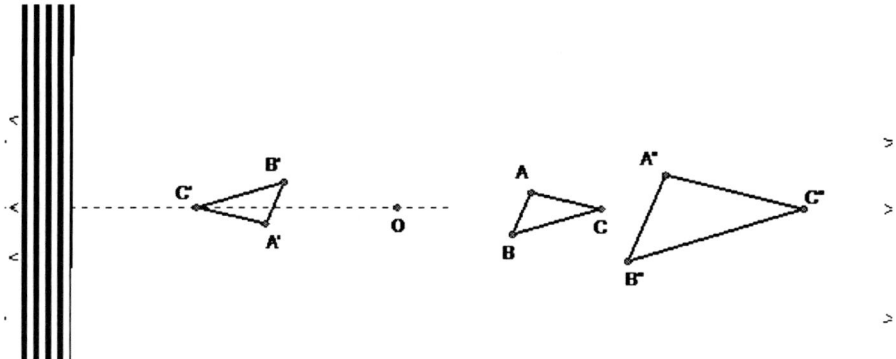

Figure 3.7. Two example dilations.

A"B"C") and one with a negative scale factor (generating image A'B'C'), are shown in Figure 3.7 above.

Overall, the standards documents contained nearly the same number of similarity GLEs ($n = 271$) as congruence GLEs. Their mean frequency across the 42 states was 6.45, and the median was 6. The range was again quite large: Two states (Maine and Mississippi) included one similarity GLE; one state (Kansas) included 19. As with congruence, all 42 states mentioned the concept of similarity at least once in their standards documents. Fourteen states addressed the topic only in their Geometry strands, 20 states included expectations in both their Geometry and Measurement strands, and eight states in their combined Geometry & Measurement strands. Similarity was treated as a measurement topic more often than other concepts discussed in this chapter, largely because of its connection to issues of proportionality and scale and changes of scale, primarily in Grades 7 and 8.

Figure 3.8 displays the distribution of similarity GLEs across states and grades. As before, the triangles represent the grade level when similarity was first introduced and the squares represent the subsequent grades where the topic was developed.

The general shape of the distribution in Figure 3.8 closely parallels that of Figure 3.5 (congruence), though shifted upward in the grade range, showing that similarity was generally introduced after congruence. No state introduced similarity before Grade 1, but most included at least one similarity GLE by middle school ($n = 36$, Grade 7; $n = 38$, Grade 8). In between, the timing of introduction was relatively evenly distributed across grades. As was the case with congruence, similarity was not always developed continuously. Two early introducers (the Department of Defense and Mississippi) dropped the topic entirely or for an extended

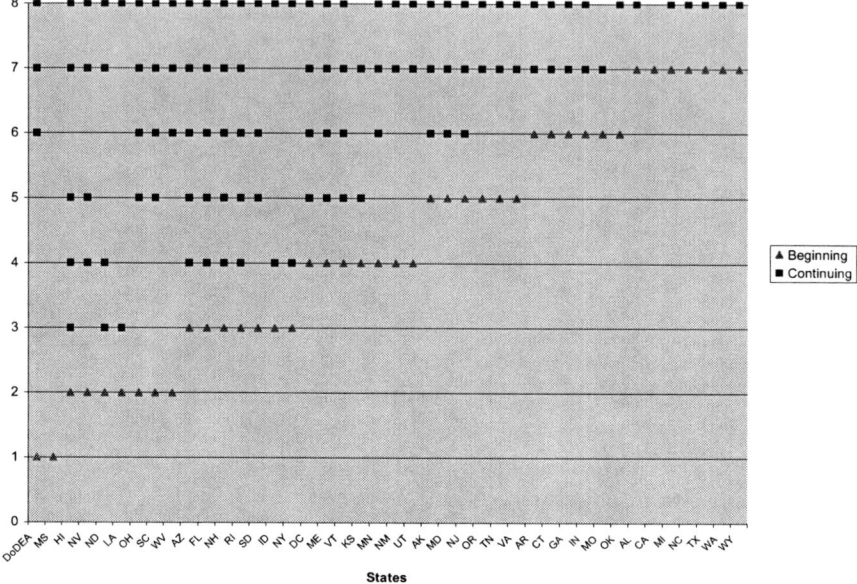

Figure 3.8.   Distribution of similarity GLEs by state and grade.

period. However, half of the states ($n = 18$) introduced similarity in the early grades and continued the topic, with no gaps were greater than one grade.

In terms of content, the most frequent expression of similarity was in terms of "scale drawing" ($n = 24$ states) or "scale factor[s]" ($n = 27$ states), as illustrated in Examples 3.24 and 3.25.

> *Example 3.24.* Applies concepts of similarity using constant of proportionality/scale factor to make larger and smaller scale drawings. (VT, gr. 6)

> *Example 3.25.* Solve problems involving scale factors using ratio and proportion. (TN, gr. 8)

Fifteen states, including New York, linked similarity to proportional reasoning using the lengths of corresponding sides of similar figures (Example 3.26).

> *Example 3.26.* Calculate the length of corresponding sides of similar triangles, using proportional reasoning. (NY, gr. 6)

Fifteen states also targeted the change in area or perimeter of similar figures when the linear dimensions are changed respectively, as did Texas (Example 3.27).

> *Example 3.27.* Describe the resulting effects on perimeter and area when dimensions of a shape are changed proportionally (TX, gr. 8)

Relations Between Transformations and Similarity

Among the 271 similarity GLEs, only 53 (about 20%) explicitly referred to transformations, generally either via the general term "transformation" or the more specific term "dilation." Note that none of the four examples above, 3.26 through 3.29, include a transformation term. These results closely parallel the results for congruence (n = 60 of 274 total GLEs, 22%). Most of these "linking" similarity GLEs in the upper elementary grades related similar figures to the action of dilations, as Example 3.28 does below. In the middle grades (Grades 6 to 8), the focus expanded to include effects of dilations on properties of similar figures, typically their perimeter and/or area (Example 3.29).

> *Example 3.28.* Compare two-dimensional shapes to determine if they are similar by transformations of magnifying or shrinking. (SC, gr. 5)
>
> *Example 3.29.* Describe the relationship between the scale factor and the area of the image using a dilation (stretching/ shrinking). (MO, gr. 8)

Informal and Formal Terms for Similarity Transformations

Recall that most states introduced congruence transformations in the early grades (before Grade 4) via informal terms such as "flip," "slide" and "turn" before shifting to the more accepted terms for isometries in the later grades. Given the availability of corresponding informal terms for similarity transformations ("contracting/contraction," "enlarging, enlargement," "reducing/reduction," "shrink/shrinking," "stretch/stretching," and "magnify/magnifying"), we expected that the same pattern might hold for dilations as well. That was not the case. In the 53 GLEs from 27 states that mentioned similarity transformations, either in formal or informal terms, the formal term "dilation" dominated. The frequencies of formal and informal terms for similarity transformations across grades are shown in Table 3.6.

**Table 3.6.   Frequency of
States Using Formal and
Informal Terms for
Similarity Transformations by Grade**

	Number of States	
Grade	Formal	Informal
K	0	0
1	0	0
2	0	1
3	0	0
4	0	0
5	0	2
6	1	1
7	8	2
8	18	6

In contrast to congruence, similarity transformations (not similarity, more broadly) did not commonly appear in geometry and measurement GLEs until Grade 7. When they did, the formal term "dilation" was used much more commonly than the various informal terms. This difference makes sense if the age of the student was the primary consideration in the authors' choice informal/formal terms. The introduction of congruence transformations in the primary grades for younger children may have motivated the use of informal terms. Since similarity transformations were not typically introduced until Grade 7, students at that age were likely judged capable of learning the formal mathematical term.

SYMMETRY

K–8 school mathematics curricula typically focus on the symmetry produced by reflections and rotations. Most commonly, figures are symmetric about lines of reflection that bisect them. Because of its commonality, figures that possess this form of symmetry are referred to as "symmetric" in some texts, or more precisely as having "reflection symmetry," "line symmetry," or "bilateral symmetry" in others. Other figures, for example, parallelograms, possess rotational symmetry about a point in their interior for some given angle of rotation and orientation (clockwise or counterclockwise). Both of these forms of symmetry are illustrated in the figure shown in Figure 3.9 below.

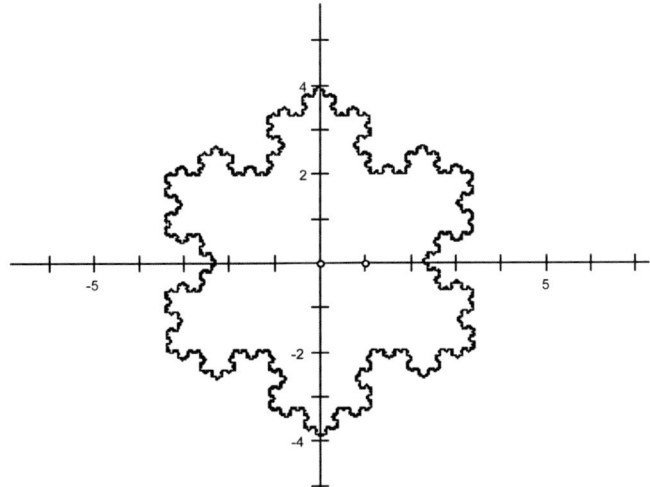

Figure 3.9.   An example plane figure with reflection and rotational symmetry.

This snowflake has reflection symmetry with respect to the *x*-axis and the *y*-axis and also rotational symmetry about the origin (the center of the rotation) for angle of 60 degrees, clockwise or counterclockwise. But symmetry, like congruence and similarity, can be introduced as a property of certain figures and transformations that operate on them or quite independently, as simply the visual property of figures.

A smaller number of GLEs ($n = 228$) concerned symmetry than was the case for congruence and similarity. All 42 states mentioned symmetry at least once in their geometry and measurement GLEs. Expectations that mentioned symmetry either appeared in states' Geometry strands ($n = 34$ states) or in combined Geometry & Measurement strands ($n = 8$). No state considered symmetry in a separate Measurement strand. The mean frequency of mention across states was 5.43 GLEs; the median was 5; and the range was again larger—one (Hawaii) to 14 (California and South Dakota). Figure 3.10 presents the distribution of symmetry GLEs across states and grades.

Figure 3.10 shows that most states introduced symmetry in the primary grades. Eight included a symmetry GLE in kindergarten, and a large majority ($n = 32$) included at least one GLE by Grade 2. Florida considered the topic at every grade; 19 states included symmetry GLEs in at least five grades. So overall, symmetry was widely considered across the states and introduced and developed in the primary grades.

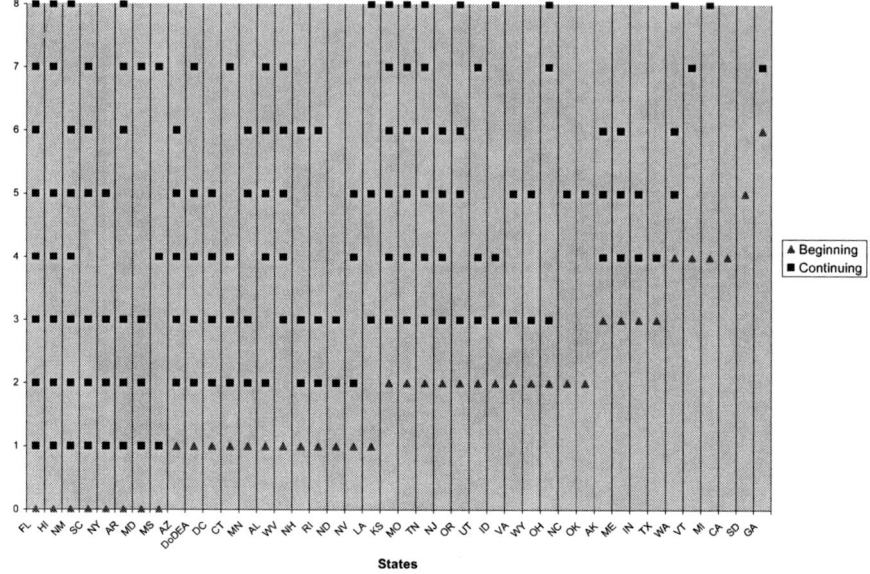

Figure 3.10.   Distribution of symmetry GLEs by state and grade.

Reflection Symmetry of Two-Dimensional Figures

About half of all symmetry GLEs (n = 127) referred to reflection symmetry, and more than one-third of those (n = 43) appeared between kindergarten and Grade 2. Thirty-nine states used the term "line[s] of symmetry" to refer to figures with reflection symmetry, where three, Idaho, Oklahoma, and Vermont, used the general term ("symmetry"). Of those 39 states, ten also used the term "reflection symmetry." Primary grade GLEs typically focused on drawing the lines of symmetry for given figures (as in Example 3.30) or selecting figures that possessed reflection symmetry (as in Example 3.31).

Example 3.30. Identifies plane figures that are reflection symmetrical. (HI, gr. 2)

Example 3.31. Draw one or more lines of symmetry in a polygon. (AR, gr. 3)

But at the later grades, reflection symmetry was more commonly explicitly connected to transformations, as discussed below.

Rotational Symmetry of Two-Dimensional Figures

Slightly more than 20% of all symmetry GLEs ($n = 31$) addressed rotational symmetry. Most states did not introduce this idea until the upper elementary grades. Of the 49 expectations in 27 states, more than half ($n = 23$) appeared in Grades 5 and 6, and typically addressed the rotational symmetry of polygons, as illustrated in Example 3.32 below.

Example 3.32. Identify polygons and designs with rotational symmetry. (MO, gr. 5)

Symmetry of Three-Dimensional Figures

A relatively small number of GLEs ($n = 12$ in 8 states) also considered the symmetry of three-dimensional figures. However, there was no consistency in when such GLEs appeared; the small set spanned kindergarten to Grade 8. Note that Example 3.33 addresses both reflection and rotational symmetry.

Example 3.33. Identifies and justifies reflectional symmetry (plane) and rotational symmetry (line, axis) in three-dimensional object. (HI, gr. 5)

Relations Between Transformations and Symmetry

Of the 228 symmetry GLEs, relatively few ($n = 27$ in 18 states; 11%) explicitly related transformations (reflections and/or rotations) to symmetry. Of those 18 states, 11 did so at Grades 7 and 8, more frequently for reflection symmetry ($n = 24$ GLEs) than rotational symmetry ($n = 15$ GLEs). As we have seen above for congruence and similarity, the role of transformations in determining symmetry was not always precisely stated. Examples 3.34 and 3.35 illustrate how transformations were linked to symmetry, either generally or more specifically, in the small number of cases where those linkages were explicitly drawn.

Example 3.34. Identify and describe transformations that result in rotational and reflectional symmetry. (MD, gr. 7)

Example 3.35. Investigates congruency, similarity, and symmetry of geometric figures using transformations. (KS, gr. 8)

Seven states extended this linkage to include congruence, sometimes in ways that clarified their relationship, at least partially, and sometimes in ways that left that relationship obscure. Line symmetry is linked to congruence in Example 3.36, but the nature of the linkage remains unclear. In contrast, Example 3.37 explicitly draws attention the role that line reflection plays in each.

> *Example 3.36.* Demonstrates conceptual understanding of congruency by composing and decomposing two-dimensional objects using models or explanations (e.g., using triangular pattern blocks to construct a figure congruent to the hexagonal pattern block); and uses line symmetry to demonstrate congruent parts within a shape. (NH, gr. 2)

> *Example 3.37.* Relate symmetry and congruence to reflections about a line. (TN, gr. 7)

DISCUSSION

Like other chapters, in this volume and the previous one (Reys, 2006a), we found striking variety in the role that transformations played in the states' geometry and measurement standards, as a topic in themselves and in their capacity to explain and develop the traditional Euclidean topics of congruence, similarity, and symmetry. We found this variation in: (a) the large range in the distribution of transformation GLEs across states, (b) the timing of their introduction by grade, (c) the degree of continuity/ discontinuity in development across grades, and crucially (d) how relationships between transformations and congruence, similarity, and symmetry were described. We also found similar variations in each of the three content areas (congruence, similarity, and symmetry) when GLEs addressing those topics were analyzed separately. As yet there appears to be no national consensus about the importance, role, and timing of the teaching and learning of transformations in the K–8 geometry and measurement curriculum. The minimal consensus that does exist is limited to the view that transformations merit some attention, somewhere in the K–8 standards, in some form, and with or without connection to the properties of plane figures.

As measured by the aggregate number of GLEs, states give greater attention to the traditional Euclidean topics of congruence, similarity, and symmetry ($n = 274 + 271 + 228 = 773$, respectively) than to transformations ($n = 335$). Moreover, the overlap between these two sets of GLEs was not that large; only 140 ($60 + 53 + 27$) of the 335 transformation GLEs made some explicit reference to congruence, similarity or symmetry, respectively. These totals elaborate the claim made just above: The concept of transformation has only partially penetrated the traditional Euclidean core of school geometry and measurement. Expectations to learn about transformations have often appeared in the state standards without explicit connections to those three central properties, and conversely, congruence, similarity, and symmetry have been introduced and developed without clear and explicit connection to transformations.

We believe this disconnect is quite unfortunate for teachers and merits the attention of standards writers to address. Well-written standards, like well-written textbooks, can become resources for teachers' on-going learning of mathematics. Expectations that concern transformations but do not clarify how they are related to, indeed how they construct, the Euclidean properties of plane figures represent missed opportunities to support teacher learning. As we stated earlier, these missed opportunities may be more costly for transformations than other topics in the K–8 curriculum. Where all well-written GLEs have the potential to teach readers about the nature and interconnection of topics in the school mathematics curriculum, that potential is needed much more for transformations, because it may be a new and relatively underdeveloped aspect of many elementary and middle school teachers' mathematical knowledge. We hope that standards authors will attend to this issue as they work to refine their state documents.

More positively, standards authors have clearly given attention to the role of terminology can play in giving young children access to advanced concepts, like transformations. We consider the general practice of introducing transformations via descriptive informal terms before shifting to the standard mathematical terms in latter grades quite sensible. (Informal terms for similarity transformations appear unnecessary when the concept is introduced in middle school.) The general point made above, however, needs underscoring: Mention of such intuitive terms is no substitute for the teaching children about congruence transformations.

Finally, we note that similarity could be presented in state standards as a site for learning other important mathematical ideas such as rational numbers and spatial reasoning. Dilations that enlarge or reduce figures by non-integral scale factors are a useful and sensible context for developing fractions and rational numbers, and their multiplication and division. No transformation GLEs, however, explicitly connected dilations to fractions or rational numbers. In this case, the disjunction between geometry & measurement and number & operation is unfortunate, for teachers and students.

NOTE

1. The terms, "pre-image" and "image," are used to refer both to individual points and sets of points that are mapped by transformations.

CHAPTER 4

AN EXAMINATION OF K–8 GEOMETRY STATE STANDARDS THROUGH THE LENS OF THE VAN HIELE LEVELS OF GEOMETRIC THINKING

Jill Newton

When should students be introduced to the properties of three-dimensional figures or the concept of similarity? How (i.e., at what rate and in what direction) does geometric thinking develop? Do current K–8 mathematics curricula provide a coherent view of that development? Are K–8 students expected to reason geometrically? Does the level of this reasoning increase across the curriculum? Does the middle school geometry curriculum prepare students for high school geometry courses? These questions have been asked before and student interviews and assessments and textbook analyses have been used to investigate them (e.g., Fuys, Geddes, & Tischler, 1988; Senk, 1989). However, given the "growth in authority and specificity" of state-level curriculum standards on the mathematics taught

Variability is the Rule: A Companion Analysis of K–8 State Mathematics Standards, pp. 71–94

in classrooms (Reys, 2006b), it was appropriate to examine these questions again, this time through an investigation of the state standards documents.

In this chapter, I examine the states' K–8 geometry standards using the lens of the van Hiele levels of geometric thinking. This theory was introduced by a Dutch husband and wife team of mathematics educators, Pierre Marie van Hiele and Dina van Hiele-Geldof, in their doctoral theses in 1957.[1] They continued to develop the theory together (van Hiele & van Hiele-Geldof, 1958) until Dina's untimely death in 1959. Since then, Pierre has continued their joint project independently (e.g., van Hiele, 1986, 1999). The van Hiele theory of geometric thinking was selected for use in this analysis of the K–8 geometry state standards for several reasons: (a) it is content-specific (i.e., it was developed for use in geometry); (b) it has strong research support from both qualitative (e.g., Burger & Shaughnessy, 1986; Monaghan, 2000) and quantitative (e.g., Clements, Swaminathan, Hannibal, & Sarama, 1999; Senk, 1989) studies; and (c) it has "elegance, comprehensiveness, and wide applicability" (Usiskin, 1982, p. 6). Over the period of the last 2 decades, other authors have acknowledged the importance of the theory. Van de Walle (2000) referred to it as "the most influential factor in the American geometry curriculum" (p. 309). Drawing on his study of the use of the theory in the Soviet national curriculum, Hoffer (1983) adds that "the van Hiele model provides us with a peephole through which we can use our mathematical eye to view children's interaction with mathematics" (p. 215).

The theory was first introduced in the United States by Russian mathematician Izaak Wirszup (1974, 1976) following its incorporation into the Soviet geometry curriculum. During the period of 1980–83, the National Science Foundation funded three major investigations of the van Hieles' theory in the United States directed by William Burger at Oregon State University, Dorothy Geddes at Brooklyn College, and Zalman Usiskin at the University of Chicago. Burger's research set out to determine the usefulness of van Hiele's model for describing children's geometric thinking in elementary, middle, and high school. Geddes focused her investigation on geometric thinking in sixth- and ninth-grade students. Usiskin's project utilized the levels for assessing the geometric reasoning of students enrolled in high school geometry courses. Since these three studies, further research using the work of the van Hieles has continued in the United States (e.g., Clements et al., 1999; Mason, 1989; Mistretta, 2000; Senk, 1989), Spain (e.g., Gutierrez, 1996; Gutierrez, Jaime, & Fortuny, 1991; Llorens Fuster & Pérez Carreras, 1997), South Africa (Govender, & de Villiers, 2002; Nixon, 2005), England (Monaghan, 2000), and Australia (e.g., Pegg, 1997), as well as in international collaborations (e.g., Gutierrez, Pegg, & Lawrie, 2004; Whitman et al., 1997). This body of work has both continued the application of van Hiele's work in two-dimensional and three-dimensional geometry and extended its use into other mathematical topics (e.g., local approximation, abstract algebra).

In 1999, Clements and his colleagues encouraged the theory's use in guiding curriculum development, stating that "helping children move through these [van Hiele] levels may be taken as a critical educational goal" (Clements et al., 1999, p. 193). The following year in *Principles and Standards in School Mathematics*, the National Council of Teachers of Mathematics (NCTM) cited the van Hieles and others who studied their theory to develop the importance of "building understanding in geometry across the grades, from informal to more formal thinking" (NCTM, 2000, p. 40). More recently, Clements (2003) added that "the [van Hiele] theory also provides a reminder that students think about geometry in quite different ways and serves as a framework that helps us understand students' varied notions" (p. 154).

This chapter, unlike the two preceding it, does not present a complete summary of the content of state' geometry standards. Rather, I examine the development of geometric thinking in those documents using the van Hiele theory. The chapter begins with an introduction to the van Hiele levels of geometric thinking; follows with a review of relevant research, a description of the methods used in the analysis, a summary of the findings from the K–8 state standards documents; and concludes with a discussion of the implications for the teaching and learning of geometry.

THE VAN HIELE LEVELS OF GEOMETRIC THINKING

Pierre Marie van Hiele and Dina van Hiele-Geldof began their careers in education as high school mathematics teachers. They were surprised by the difficulty of teaching geometric ideas to their students and began working on a theory to explain the phenomena they observed in their classrooms. One of their initial observations was that they spoke about geometry in a different way than their students. For example, when they described a square as a type of rectangle, students were confused because they saw squares and rectangles as quite different. This led the van Hieles to consider the existence of various levels of geometric reasoning and the possibility that individuals thinking at different levels may have difficulty communicating with one another. The van Hiele theory of geometric thinking arose from further investigation of this hypothesis. The couple contributed to the model in different ways: "P[ierre] van Hiele (1957) formulated the scheme and psychological principles. D[ina] van Hiele-Geldof (1957) focused on the didactics experiment to raise students' thought levels" (Hoffer, 1983, p. 207).

The van Hiele levels were originally numbered zero through four. Many researchers, particularly in the United States, have adopted an alternate numbering system that begins the numbering at one, reserving the zero level for students who are unable to recognize and name basic geometric figures. For example, Level 0 students may classify ovals as circles and shapes with three curved sides as triangles. We used the more recent numbering system (i.e., Levels 1 through 5) in this analysis in order to easily compare results with other studies conducted in the United States.[2] As characterized by Mayberry (1983, p. 59), but with my emphasis added, the van Hiele levels are:

> *Level 1*. At this level, figures are *recognized by appearance alone*. A figure is perceived as a whole, recognizable by its visible form, but properties of a figure are not perceived. At this level, students should recognize and name figures and distinguish a given figure from others that look somewhat the same.

> *Level 2*. Here, *properties are perceived*, but they are isolated and unrelated. Since each property is seen separately, no relationship between properties is noticed and relationships between different figures are not perceived. A student at this level should recognize and name properties of geometric figures.

> *Level 3*. At this level, definitions are meaningful, with *relationships being perceived* between properties and between figures. Logical implications and class inclusions are understood. The role and significance of deduction, however is not understood.

> *Level 4*. At this level, *deduction is meaningful*. The student can construct proofs, understand the role of axioms and definitions, and know the meaning of necessary and sufficient conditions. A student at this level should be able to supply reasons for steps in a proof.

> *Level 5*. The student at this level understands the *formal aspects of deduction*. Symbols without referents can be manipulated according to the laws of formal logic. A student at this level should understand the role and necessity of indirect proof and proof by contrapositive.

At least two studies of the theory have proposed single word descriptive labels for the levels. I have adopted the descriptors suggested by Burger and Shaughnessy (1986) for use in this report: *Visualization, Analysis, Informal Deduction, Formal Deduction*, and *Rigor*, for Levels 1 through 5, respectively.

Crowley (1987) provided examples of level-specific responses, except for Level 5, that might be given by a typical student who is asked why a given shape is a rectangle (p. 15).

Level 1   "It looks like one."
            "Because it looks like a door."
Level 2   "Four sides, closed, two long sides, two shorter sides, opposite sides parallel, four right angles"
Level 3   "It is a parallelogram with right angles."
Level 4   "This can be proved if I know this figure is a parallelogram and that one angle is a right angle."

A student operating at Level 1 answers based on a visual model, identifying the rectangle by its overall appearance. At Level 2, a student is aware that the rectangle has properties; however, redundancies (i.e., properties that can be derived from other properties) are not noticed. A student working at Level 3 attempts to provide a minimum number of properties (i.e., a definition), and finally, at Level 4, a student seeks to prove the fact deductively.

Van Hiele also emphasized several important properties of the levels.[3] First, the levels are discrete and sequential. *Discrete* indicates that the levels are qualitatively different from one another. *Sequential* refers to the fact that students pass through the levels in the same order, albeit at varying rates, and that it is not possible to skip levels. Second, what is intrinsic at one level becomes extrinsic (i.e., objectified) at the next level. For example, students operating at Level 1 are able to name geometric figures only by their appearance as a "whole;" the properties of the figure remain intrinsic. However, at Level 2, these properties become extrinsic and in fact, are the new objects of study. Third, each level has its own language and symbols. Van Hiele believed that "in general, the teacher and the student speak a very different language" (van Hiele, 1988, p. 245). Therefore, teachers and students often have difficulty communicating with one another about geometric concepts. This linguistic challenge can also be extended to communication difficulties between students when they are functioning at different levels of geometric thinking. The example provided earlier of students' responses to the question about rectangles illustrates how geometric language can vary among levels. Fourth, instructional methods have a greater influence than either age or grade on a student's progress through the van Hiele levels because teachers' instructional activities can either foster or impede movement through the levels.

Dina van Hiele-Geldof developed a model of five phases of teaching that were intended to move students through the levels of geometric thinking (Fuys et al., 1988, p. 7). These five phases were defined as follows:

Phase 1   *Information*: The student gets acquainted with the working domain (e.g., examines examples and nonexamples).

Phase 2   *Guided orientation*: The student works on tasks involving different relations of the network that is to be formed (e.g., folding, measuring, looking for symmetry).

Phase 3   *Explicitation*: The student becomes conscious of the relations, tries to express them in words and learns technical language which accompanies the subject matter (e.g., expresses ideas about properties of figures).

Phase 4   *Free orientation*: The student learns, by doing more complex tasks, to find his/her own way in the network of relations (e.g., knowing properties of one kind of shapes, investigates these properties for a new shape, such as kites).

Phase 5   *Integration*: The student summarizes all that he/she has learned about the subject, then reflects on his/her actions and obtains an overview of the newly formed network of relations now available (e.g., properties of a figure are summarized).

The van Hieles adamantly encouraged children's investigations in geometry. In fact, van Hiele (1999) began with the statement, "For children, geometry begins with play" (p. 310). This emphasis on hands-on exploration is illustrated in Phases 2 (*Guided orientation*) and 5 (*Free orientation*) described above. Dina estimated that it took approximately 20 lessons to move from Level 1 to Level 2 and 50 lessons to move from Level 2 to Level 3, suggesting that the rate of development through levels was not constant. Though the phases of teaching will not be further elaborated in this chapter, an analysis of the standards through the lens of the teaching phases would be an important contribution. Such an analysis would be difficult since not all states address pedagogy in their standards. However, it would be interesting to examine whether the standards encourage the types of investigations advocated for by the van Hieles.

Van Hiele cautioned that it is possible to misjudge a student's level of geometric thinking without careful analysis because students often memorize or learn patterns in order to accomplish tasks without understanding the underlying concepts. For example, students are sometimes taught to recognize alternate interior angles by finding the "Z" that is formed when two lines are intersected by a transversal (see Figure 4.1). This technique simplifies the mathematics and allows the students to avoid the "crisis of thinking" that van Hiele claimed is essential for true understanding; students can derive the answer without recognizing the relationships between the angles in Figure 4.1 (e.g., supplementary angles, angles at a point, alternate interior angles). Van Hiele warned that these types of

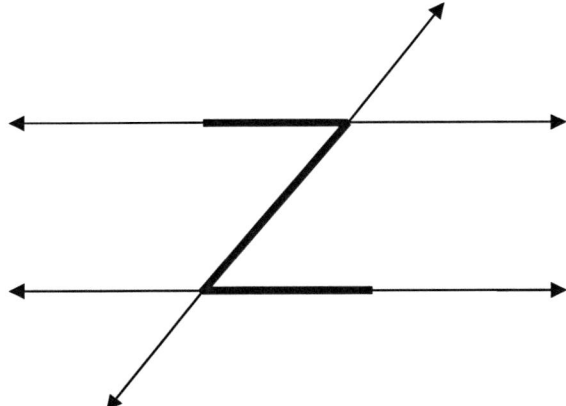

Figure 4.1.   Alternate interior angles formed when two lines are intersected by a transversal.

"tricks" may actually prevent students from moving to the subsequent level of reasoning (van Hiele, 1986).

A REVIEW OF RESEARCH APPLYING THE VAN HIELE LEVELS

Many researchers have found van Hiele's levels useful in describing students' geometric thinking (e.g., Hoffer, 1983; Senk, 1989; Wirszup, 1976) and have confirmed their hierarchical nature (e.g., Burger & Shaughnessy, 1986; Gutierrez & Jaime, 1988; Usiskin, 1982). Several studies have also identified linguistic differences between levels (e.g., Fuys et al.,1988; Mayberry, 1983), that a student's level is not necessarily related to their age or grade (e.g., Burger & Shaughnessy, 1986; Usiskin, 1982), and that instructional methods can facilitate students' progress through the levels (e.g., Mistretta, 2000; Wirszup, 1976). For example, Mayberry's research (1983) lent support to two specific implications of van Hiele's theory. First, a student cannot function adequately at a level without having had experiences that enable intuitive thinking at each preceding level. Second, if the language of instruction is at a higher level than students' thought processes are, they will not understand the instruction.

Although research has produced a great deal of support for van Hiele's theory, researchers have also questioned and modified certain of its aspects. For example, many studies have indicated that students may not be working at the same level on all concepts (e.g., Burger & Shaughnessy, 1986; Gutierrez & Jaime, 1988; Mason, 1989). In a study of the van Hiele levels of gifted middle school students, Mason (1989) found that individuals performed at a higher van Hiele level on content with which they had greater familiarity. For example, 1.6% of the subjects were below Level 2 on the square strand compared to 26.5% below Level 2 on the right triangle strand. Additionally, many studies have questioned whether the van Hiele levels are discrete and have provided evidence for a more dynamic and continuous model (e.g., Fuys et al., 1988; Gutierrez et al., 1991; Usiskin, 1982). For example, the research by Gutierrez et al. (1991) illustrated "the possibility that a student can develop two consecutive levels of reasoning at the same time, although what usually happens is that the acquisition of the lower level is more complete than the acquisition of the upper level" (p. 250).

Several studies have also supported an extension of the five original levels to include a "pre-recognition" level as mentioned earlier (Clements et al., 1999; Fuys et al., 1988; Mayberry, 1983; Senk, 1989; Usiskin, 1982). In fact, this pre-recognition level, where students are unable to consistently identify basic geometric shapes, has been found to occur, not only among young children (e.g., Clements et al., 1999), but also among sixth and ninth graders (Fuys et al., 1988), high school students (Senk, 1989; Usiskin, 1982) and pre-service teachers (Mayberry, 1983). Some of these identification problems have been attributed to the use of specific visual prototypes to represent various shapes. Figure 4.2 provides two such examples. The first shape presented in Figure 4.2 is the most common prototype for a square whereas the second shape, a square with a different orientation, is often referred to as a diamond particularly in the early grades. Once established, it can be difficult to convince some students that, in fact, both of these figures are squares.

The overall results for the van Hiele levels of U.S. students are discouraging. Fuys et al.'s (1988) study of the geometric reasoning of sixth- and

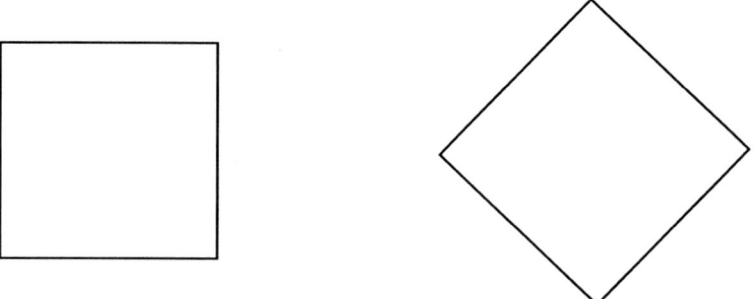

Figure 4.2.   Prototype of a square and a diamond.

ninth-grade students found that: (a) 19% of sixth graders performed consistently at Level 1 (*Visualization*), (b) 31% performed sometimes at Level 1 and sometimes at Level 2 (*Analysis*), and (c) the remaining 50% performed sometimes at Level 2 and sometimes at Level 3 (*Informal Deduction*). The corresponding percentages for ninth graders were 12, 44, and 44, respectively. Research conducted by Mistretta (2000) with eighth-grade students produced similar results: 22% of the students were consistently functioning at Level 1, 30% at Level 2, and 13% at Level 3. The remaining 35% were not functioning consistently at any one given level.

Research on secondary students documented that nearly 40% of U.S. students finish high school functioning below van Hiele Level 2 (*Analysis*) (Usiskin, 1982). Senk's (1989) study of high school students found that 27% were functioning at Level 0 (*Pre-recognition*), 51% at Level 1, 15% at Level 2, and 7% at Level 3. In addition, she provided evidence that students entering high school geometry courses with higher van Hiele levels were more likely to be successful at proof writing by the end of the school year. Of those studied, only 9% of the students who entered geometry functioning at van Hiele Level 0 succeeded in writing proofs by the end of the year. Thirty percent of the students entering geometry at Level 1 had success in proof writing and 56% of the students entering at Level 2 succeeded at proof writing by the end of the year. All students entering at Level 3 were successful at proof writing by the end of the school year. Though these data provide an initial picture of the students' status and assess their progress, Hoffer (1983) warned that "we should avoid labeling people by the levels. The value of the van Hiele model resides not so much in a stratification of student thought as in a prescription for instruction" (p. 224).

Wirszup (1976) argued that many students leave middle school operating at Level 1 (*Visualization*) and that the typical high school geometry classes are taught at Level 4 (*Formal Deduction*). Usiskin (1982) confirmed the "spirit" of this claim and expanded concern for the large number of students entering high school not yet operating at Level 1. He stated that "many if not most students in the U.S. enter geometry at van Hiele levels that are too low to insure success" (p. 84). Hoffer (1983) added that "the geometry experiences that are offered there [in junior high school grades] seem inadequate to prepare students for the thought levels that are demanded in the high school geometry course" (p. 211). Clements and Battista (1992) suggested that "in fact, because many students have not developed Level 3 [*Informal Deduction*] thought processes, they may not benefit from additional work in formal geometry because their knowledge and the information presented in the textbook will be organized differently" (p. 430). My decision to examine the K–8 geometry state standards documents using the van Hiele theory was reinforced by these concerns regarding both the lack of adequate geometry experiences in the K–12 curriculum and the possible gap between the K–8 geometry curriculum and the curricular expectations of high school geometry courses. I wanted to examine current curriculum documents to see if there had been changes in the K–8 geometry curriculum since these studies were conducted in the 1980s and 1990s and whether the aforementioned gap had persisted.

METHODS

The primary question guiding my analysis was:

> How consistent is the progression of K–8 Geometry state standards with the van Hiele levels of geometric thinking?

More specifically, I asked whether there is evidence of a gradual progression toward higher levels of geometric thinking across the K–8 standards and whether these standards appear adequate to prepare students for formal deduction in high school?

In this analysis, we included only the grade-level learning expectations (GLEs) that addressed aspects of descriptive geometry. We defined *descriptive geometry* as geometry concerned with figures and their relationships, not with coordinates or exact quantities. We did not analyze GLEs that addressed measurement or the use of known quantities to calculate unknown quantities related to geometry (see Kasten & Newton, this volume, for such an analysis).

In the analysis described here, two researchers identified the descriptive geometry GLEs independently and discussed any discrepancies until consensus was reached, eliciting additional information or opinions in several cases. Table 4.1 provides examples of GLEs that were included in the analysis as well as examples of GLEs that were not. The descriptive geometry GLEs in the left column of Table 4.1 concern figures and their relationships while those in the right column pertain to measurement with emphasis on coordinates or exact quantities. The decision to focus on descriptive geometry was based on two important considerations: (a) the van Hiele theory has most often been applied to this content, and (b) it provided us with a distinct and manageable subset of GLEs for comparison purposes across states.

Once selected, the GLEs were classified into van Hiele levels using the descriptors provided earlier, examples given by the van Hieles in their writings, and examples provided in other previously mentioned research studies (e.g., Burger & Shaughnessy, 1986; Fuys et al., 1988). Again, we

Table 4.1. Examples of GLEs Included and Excluded From the Analysis

GLEs Included	GLEs Excluded
Use the attributes and properties of plane figures to model, identify, compare, or describe plane figures (circles, rectangles, squares, and triangles). (AK, gr. 3)	Estimate or determine area or perimeter of rectangular or square shapes on grids. (AK, gr. 3)
Describe and compare angles in a variety of objects. (WA, gr. 5)	Measure angles in assorted polygons and determine the total number of degrees in the polygon. (WA, gr. 5)
Identify the right angle, hypotenuse, and legs of a right triangle. (NY, gr. 7)	Use the Pythagorean Theorem to determine the unknown length of a side of a right triangle. (NY, gr. 7)

independently sorted the GLEs, this time into van Hiele levels, and compared the results, soliciting additional input as necessary to reach consensus. This process brought light to several important concerns. First, whereas the van Hiele's levels have been most often used to assess individual student thinking, we were attempting to classify standards that were written for all students in a particular grade level. This dilemma was expressed well by van Hiele (1986): "[T]he levels are situated not in the subject matter but in the thinking of man" (p. 41). Gutierrez et al. (1991), however, suggested that tasks elicit the thinking and therefore interact with the students. We argue that tasks and standards that describe desired reasoning more generally matter in determining the levels to which students are exposed and therefore have access. Second, we categorized the GLEs based solely on their content without consideration for the grade level in which they appeared. For example, the two GLEs given below (Examples 4.1 and 4.2) were assigned the same van Hiele level (i.e., Level 2, *Analysis*) even though their grade placement (Grades 1 and 7) might suggest that they targeted different points in development.

Example 4.1. Classify two and three-dimensional figures according to characteristics (e.g., square, rectangle, circle, cube, prism, sphere, cone, and cylinder). (MS, gr. 1)

Example 4.2. Classify 2- and 3-dimensional shapes based on their properties. (MO, gr. 7)

It may be that the use of "characteristics" in the Mississippi GLE and "properties" in the Missouri GLE distinguish these GLEs, but it is not possible to determine the nature of this distinction without further information from the authors. Third, many states wrote supporting documents with their standards, but these documents were not considered in this analysis since the nature of these documents varies greatly. Only the standards document itself was analyzed which limited, to some extent, knowledge of the intent of the authors. Finally, some of the standards documents were written to specify curriculum content while others were produced for the primary purpose of providing assessment standards. While this distinction is important, their content relative to the van Hiele levels can be productive for both purposes.

The GLEs classified into Level 1 expect students only to perceive geometric figures as whole objects. The Level 2 GLEs suggest an analysis of geometric figures in terms of their component parts or properties. Finally, Level 3 GLEs take several forms (this will be discussed later in the chapter); however, definitions, informal deduction, and the ordering of classes of figures are characteristic of this level. Table 4.2 provides examples of GLEs that were coded into van Hiele Levels 1 through 3. Four GLEs included some type of formal deduction (i.e., Level 4); however, none of

Table 4.2.   Sample GLEs Representing van Hiele Levels 1–3

Level	Grade-Level Expectation	Explanation
1	Identify circles, triangles, rectangles, and squares. (UT, gr. K)	These GLEs expect students to recognize the figures by their overall visual appearance (e.g., finding shapes in their surroundings).
	Recognizes and finds two- and three-dimensional shapes in familiar surroundings (e.g., at home, in the classroom). (HI, gr. K)	
	Cut geometric shapes apart and identify the new shapes made. (TX, gr. 2)	
2	Sorts plane figures and solids (circles, squares, rectangles sorts, triangles, ellipses, cubes, rectangular prisms, cylinders, cones, spheres) by a given attribute. (KS, gr. 1)	These GLEs focus on an analysis of the properties of the figures (e.g., sorting by a given attribute, identifying relationships).
	Recognize the angles formed and the relationship between the angles when two lines intersect and when parallel lines are cut by a transversal. (OH, gr. 8)	
	Identify relationships among points, lines, and planes (e.g., intersecting, parallel, perpendicular). (DC, gr. 5)	
3	Develop definitions for classes of two- and three-dimensional shapes. (SC, gr. 5)	These GLEs require students to utilize various forms of informal deduction (e.g., developing definitions, understanding proofs).
	Understand at least one proof of the Pythagorean Theorem. (MI, gr. 8)	
	Understand that a quadrilateral can belong to one or more subsets of the set of quadrilaterals. (VA, gr. 7)	

these GLEs explicitly expected students to construct formal proofs. Therefore, these GLEs were coded as Level 3. Level 5 (*Rigor*) GLEs were not found in the K–8 state standards documents. After placing each GLE into a van Hiele level, the coded GLEs were aggregated across states and grade levels in an effort to determine the relationship between the state standards and van Hiele's levels of geometric thinking.

Finally, I conducted a brief analysis of the 18 states that had provided expectations for a high school geometry course at the time of our K–8 analysis.[4] My purpose was to test the claim stated in the literature (e.g., Mayberry 1983; Wirszup, 1976; Usiskin, 1982) that high school geometry courses include expectations for formal deduction (Level 4) since these studies were completed more than a decade ago. I looked first for any explicit mention of formal deduction or proof in the geometry course expectations and then searched the documents again for more details regarding the nature of the expected formal deduction. The results of this analysis are stated briefly below, but also in more detail in Appendix C.

RESULTS

This section is framed by a series of questions that systematically address the primary research question: How consistent is the progression of K–8 Geometry state standards with the van Hiele levels of geometric thinking?

1. How prevalent are descriptive geometry GLEs in the standards documents?[5]

2. How are the descriptive geometry GLEs distributed across the grade levels?

3. How many GLEs were categorized into each of the van Hiele levels?

4. How are GLEs at each van Hiele level distributed across grade levels?

5. When are standards that are associated with van Hiele Levels 2 and 3 first introduced in the states?

6. Do different van Hiele levels occur in the same grade level in the same state?

7. What forms of Level 3 (*Informal Deduction*) are present in the standards?

8. Do the standards documents provide examples in which a progression through the van Hiele levels is evident within a topic?

9. Do current high school geometry courses as represented by state standards contain Level 4 (*Formal Deduction*) content?

Each question will be taken in turn and the chapter will conclude with a discussion of the implications of the results.

How Prevalent Are Descriptive Geometry GLEs in the Standards Documents?

Of the 5,710 GLEs contained in the K–8 Geometry and Measurement strands of 42 states, 1,667 GLEs (approximately 29%) were labeled as descriptive geometry and included in this analysis. The total number of descriptive geometry GLEs across K–8 in individual states ranges from nine to 129, indicating a lack of consensus across the states. The grain size of these GLEs varies markedly among states. For example, the following GLEs (Examples 4.3 and 4.4) occur in Michigan and Maryland in Grade 3, respectively:

> *Example 4.3.* Identify, describe, compare and classify two-dimensional shapes, e.g., parallelogram, trapezoid, circle, rectangle, square and rhombus, based on their component parts (angle, sides, vertices, line segment) and the number of sides and vertices. (MI, gr. 3)

> *Example 4.4.* Identify right angles. (MD, gr. 3)

The Michigan GLE contains more individual objectives than the GLE from Maryland's document. In spite of this difference, the range ($n = 9$ to 129) still seems striking if the hope is to provide reasonably similar knowledge of geometry to all students. In fact, the two states at the extremes of the range contain a combination of the types of GLEs included above. The mean number of descriptive geometry GLEs is approximately 40 per state and the median is 32.5. To provide a more comprehensive picture, we calculated the proportion of descriptive geometry GLEs as a percentage of the total number of geometry and measurement GLEs in each state. The range was from 12% to 45%, with a mean and median of approximately 31%. It is interesting to note that the equivalent measure (i.e., mean) in the NCTM's *Principles and Standards for School Mathematics* is approximately 53% (NCTM, 2000) indicating that NCTM places more relative emphasis on descriptive geometry than the states included in this analysis.

How Are the Descriptive Geometry GLEs Distributed Across the Grade Levels?

Figure 4.3 presents the distribution of descriptive geometry GLEs across grade levels. Figure 4.3 reveals a relatively symmetric pattern with the increase from kindergarten through Grade 2 mirroring the decrease

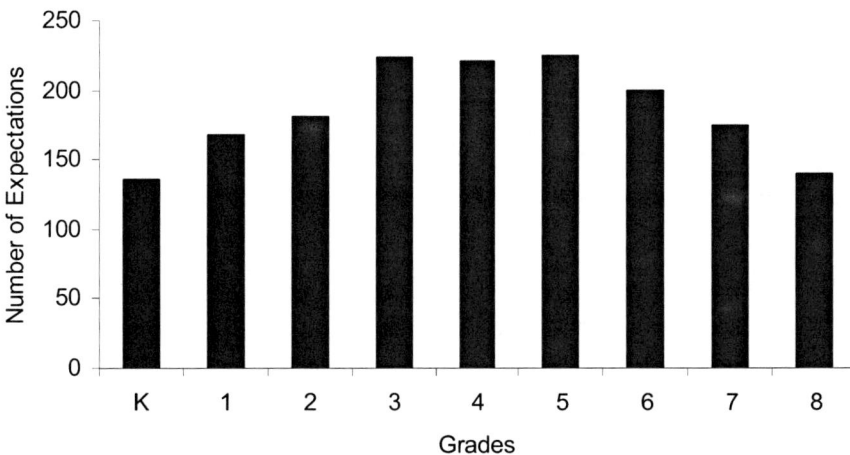

Figure 4.3.   Distribution of the descriptive geometry GLEs by grade.

from Grades 6 through 8. The smallest and greatest frequencies occur in kindergarten ($n = 136$ GLEs) and Grade 5 ($n = 224$ GLEs), respectively. The symmetry of this distribution may indirectly reflect the strong emphasis on whole number computation topics in kindergarten through Grade 2 (Reys, Dingman, Olson, Sutter, Teuscher, & Chval, 2006) and on algebra topics in Grades 6 through 8 (Newton, Larnell, & Lappan, 2006). These emphases may reduce the number of GLEs addressing geometry topics in these grades.

How Many GLEs Were Categorized Into Each of the van Hiele Levels?

All 42 states include Levels 1 and 2 GLEs. These two levels collectively represent the vast majority of descriptive geometry GLEs: $n = 785$ (47%) and $n = 818$ (49%), respectively. Level 3 GLEs occur much less frequently: $n = 64$ (4%) in 24 state documents with no Level 3 GLEs in the other 18 states. As mentioned earlier, Levels 4 and 5 are not represented in the K–8 state standards in descriptive geometry. The average number of Level 1, Level 2, and Level 3 GLEs per state are approximately 18.5, 19.5, and 1.5, respectively.

Recall that Dina van Hiele suggested that it takes approximately 20 lessons to move from Level 1 to Level 2 and 50 lessons to move from Level 2 to Level 3. If we presume a rough equivalence of lessons to GLEs, her estimate suggests that the ratio of Level 2 to Level 1 GLEs should be approximately 2.5:1, rather than the ratio of approximately 1:1 currently represented in the state standards. The impact of the relatively low number of appearances of Level 3 GLEs will be discussed later in the chapter.

How Are the van Hiele Levels Distributed Across Grade Levels?

Figure 4.4 summarizes the distribution of van Hiele Level 1, 2, and 3 GLEs across grade levels. Although the total number of Level 1 and Level 2 GLEs is similar, their placement across Grades K–8 is quite different. Figure 4.4 indicates the prevalence of Level 1 GLEs in kindergarten through Grade 3, with a steady decrease thereafter. In contrast, Level 2 GLEs slowly increase over the early grades, but are primarily found in Grades 4 through 8, with a gradual decrease after Grade 5. Level 3 GLEs appear in Grades 3 through 8 with greatest emphasis in Grades 7 and 8. This distribution is consistent with van Hiele's basic claim about the sequential nature of the levels: An emphasis on Level 1 (*Visualization*) in the lower grades, followed by GLEs representing Level 2 (*Analysis*) in upper elementary and middle school, and finally, Level 3 (*Informal Deduction*) GLEs occur primarily in middle school. The most striking information presented in Figure 4.4 is the small number of GLEs at Level 3.

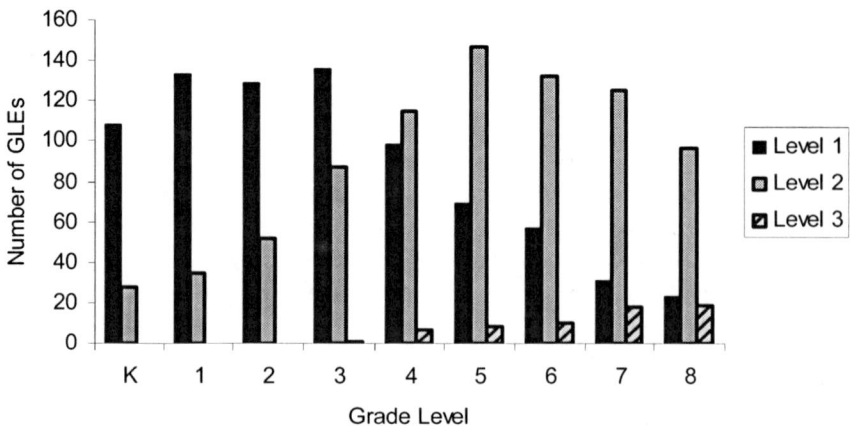

Figure 4.4.   Distribution of GLEs at three van Hiele levels by grade.

The number of Level 1 (*Visualization*) GLEs in an individual state ranges from 2 to 46; Level 2 (*Analysis*) from 6 to 73; and Level 3 (*Informal Deduction*) from 0 to 10. Thus the overall wide range among states for descriptive geometry GLEs discussed earlier holds, particularly for those categorized at Levels 1 and 2. Some states include substantially more Level 1 than Level 2 GLEs (e.g., 42 Level 1 and 24 Level 2 GLEs), while the reverse is true in other states (e.g., 24 Level 1 and 41 Level 2 GLEs).

The main message in these frequencies is the lack of consensus across states regarding the emphasis needed to develop the particular levels of geometric thinking. Additionally, the relatively small number of Level 3 GLEs across the states (more than 40% of the states have no Level 3 GLEs) seems to support the concern mentioned previously that the K–8 geometry curriculum may not be preparing students for success in high school geometry courses, as numerous authors have argued (Clements & Battista, 1992; Hoffer, 1983; Mayberry, 1983; Senk, 1989; Usiskin, 1982; Wirszup, 1976).

When Are Standards Associated With van Hiele Levels 2 and 3 First Introduced in the States?

Table 4.3 shows the number of states that introduce their first Level 2 and Level 3 GLEs at each grade level. For example, in Grade 4, one state

Table 4.3. Number of States With the First Appearance of Levels 2 and 3 GLEs by Grade

Grade	Number of States	
	Level 2	*Level 3*
K	19	–
1	10	–
2	5	–
3	7	1
4	1	4
5	–	5
6	–	4
7	–	6
8	–	4
Total	42	24

introduces its first Level 2 GLE and four states introduce their first Level 3 GLE. It is interesting to note the wide range of grades at which the first introduction of Levels 2 and 3 GLEs occur. Twenty-nine states introduce Level 2 GLEs in kindergarten or Grade 1, while the remaining states (*n* = 13) do so in Grades 2, 3 or 4. In almost all cases, the early Level 2 GLEs address the classification of two- and three-dimensional shapes using descriptive attributes (e.g., Identify, sort and classify objects by attribute and identify objects that do not belong in a particular group. [MI, gr. K]). Given that 29 states introduce Level 2 in kindergarten or Grade 1, it is surprising how few Level 3 GLEs are included in the K–8 curriculum. The range of grade levels over which Level 3 is first introduced is even larger than for Level 2, as early as Grade 3 and as late as Grade 8, but relatively consistently in Grades 4 to 8.

Do Different van Hiele Levels Occur in the Same Grade Level in the Same State?

States frequently include GLEs coded at more than one van Hiele level in the same grade. For example, Table 4.4 shows three GLEs from Alabama, Grade 8, that were coded at three different van Hiele levels. In this case, students are expected to identify a set of geometric figures (Level 1); construct, and therefore know the properties of, a slightly different set of geometric figures (Level 2); and develop mathematical arguments about the relationships between classes of a third set of geometric figures (Level 3). This is consistent with van Hiele research cited earlier that indicates that it is possible, in fact probable, that students can be simultaneously operating on different van Hiele levels across different geometric content. For example, Fuys et al. (1988) found that students working at Level 3 on familiar content often reverted back to Level 1 when confronted with new content. However, the students were able to quickly reach Level 3 for the new content when provided with instruction consistent with the van Hieles' model.

Table 4.4.   Sample GLEs at the Same Grade Level That Differ by van Hiele Level and Content

Van Hiele Level	Grade-Level Expectation
1	Identifying angle bisectors, perpendicular bisectors, congruent angles, and congruent figures.
2	Constructing congruent and similar polygons, congruent angles, congruent segments, and parallel and perpendicular lines.
3	Developing mathematical arguments about the relationships among types of quadrilaterals and triangles.

Table 4.5. Types of van Hiele Level 3 GLEs

Type of Level 3	Number of States	Sample Grade-Level Expectation
Hierarchical nature of classes of figures	6	Classify quadrilaterals according to their sides and angles (e.g., determine whether all squares are rectangles). (OK, gr. 7)
Relationships between properties of figures	14	Make, with and without appropriate technology, and test conjectures about characteristics and properties between two-dimensional figures and three-dimensional objects. (AR, gr. 8)
Defining properties	8	Precisely describe, classify, and understand relationships among types of one-, two-, and three- dimensional objects using their defining properties. (ID, gr. 7)
Proof	4	Agrees/disagrees with a given argument about geometric ideas/relationships and gives supporting evidence or counterexamples (e.g., polygons, similarity, proof). (HI, gr. 8)

Note: Several states include more than one type of Level 3 GLEs in their standards.

What Types of Level 3 (Informal Deduction) GLEs Are Present in the Standards?

Four types of Level 3 GLEs were identified in the K–8 state standards documents, including those that addressed: (a) the hierarchical nature of classes of figures (e.g., quadrilaterals), (b) the relationships between the properties of figures, (c) the definitions of classes of figures, and (d) experiences with proof. Recall that these experiences with proof were coded as Level 3 because students are not explicitly expected to construct formal proofs. Table 4.5 above presents these types of Level 3 GLEs with the number of states where they appear and an example GLE. These types are suggested repeatedly in various studies of the van Hiele levels (e.g., Crowley, 1987; Fuys et al., 1988; Van de Walle, 2000). Therefore, it is encouraging that 24 states include such types in their state standards documents. On the other hand, it is also surprising that 18 states do not include any Level 3 GLEs in their descriptive geometry GLEs.

Do the Standards Documents Contain Examples in Which the van Hiele Levels Are Evident Within the Development of a Topic?

Given these general analyses, it was sensible to ask: What might a trajectory through the van Hiele levels look like? Several states provide examples of such trajectories. Table 4.6 provides a sample development

Table 4.6. A Selection of Descriptive Geometry GLEs From Virginia by Grade and van Hiele Level

Grade	Grade-Level Expectation	Level
K	Compare and group plane geometric figures (circle, triangle, square, and rectangle) according to their shapes.	1
1	Develop strategies to sort and/or group plane geometric figures and refine the vocabulary used to explain their strategies.	1
3	Understand more precise ways to describe shapes by focusing on properties and the specialized vocabulary associated with these shapes and properties.	2
4	Identify and describe the properties of squares, rectangles, triangles, parallelograms, rhombi, and circles.	2
6	Understand that plane figures are identified and described by their similarities, differences, and defining properties.	3
7	Understand that a quadrilateral can belong to one or more subsets of the set of quadrilaterals.	3

sequence from Virginia's state standards that contains GLEs addressing circles and polygons in kindergarten through Grade 7 in ways that indicate the need for increasingly higher levels of geometric reasoning. The first two GLEs in Table 4.6 ask students to recognize and sort figures (Level 1). In Grades 3 and 4, students are expected to identify and describe the properties of the figures (Level 2). Finally, definitions and the class structure of quadrilaterals (Level 3) are introduced in Grades 6 and 7. This progression and the emphasis on language explicit in the GLEs are consistent with van Hiele's levels of geometric thinking. According to van Hiele, a similar sequence of expectations is necessary for each new set of figures that are introduced to students (e.g., circles, polygons, angles, parallel lines). We did not find states that contain developmental sequences such as the one included here for a variety of geometric figures.

Do Current High School Geometry Standards Contain Level 4 (Formal Deduction) Content?

Standards for a high school geometry course were available from 18 states at the time of this analysis. Of these 18 states, 14 explicitly require formal deduction (Level 4) in their expectations. Examples 4.5, 4.6, and 4.7 are typical expectations from these documents.

Example 4.5. Write geometric proofs, including proofs by contradiction. (CA)

Example 4.6. Prove and apply theorems involving segments divided proportionally. (IN)

Example 4.7. Prove lines parallel or perpendicular using slope or angle relationships. (UT)

The most common proofs required by states involved congruence, similarity, and the Pythagorean Theorem. Thirteen of the 18 states explicitly mention the expectation that students demonstrate familiarity with some or all of the components of an axiomatic system, including undefined terms, axioms/postulates, definitions, and theorems. Interestingly, two states expect students to compare and contrast Euclidean and non-Euclidean geometries. Such comparisons may be considered reasoning representative of van Hiele Level 5. Overall, this analysis indicated what we expected, that states with high school geometry standards expect students to think at Level 4, if not higher, in their geometry courses. Further discussion of the results of the high school standards analysis is provided in Appendix C.

DISCUSSION

I return now to my primary question: How consistent is the progression of K–8 geometry grade-level learning expectations with the van Hiele theory of geometric thinking? The distribution of the GLEs across the grades in the 42 states analyzed is consistent with the general thrust of the van Hiele theory, particularly the claim that levels of geometric thinking are sequential. Level 1 GLEs are more abundant in kindergarten through Grade 3, whereas Level 2 GLEs are more frequently included in the upper elementary grades, and Level 3 GLEs are found primarily in middle school. In spite of this overall trend across states, individual states vary markedly. In addition, GLEs coded at more than one van Hiele level are frequently present in the same grade level. This mixing of levels may reflect the variation in geometric development among students at any grade level and the fact that students can function at different van Hiele levels in different geometric content.

This analysis of the descriptive geometry GLEs indicated that approximately 47% of the GLEs are Level 1, 49% are Level 2, and 4% are Level 3. Since the van Hiele theory has not connected levels to age or grade, and in fact to the contrary, has suggested that these factors do not play a significant role in determining an individual's level, it is difficult to make any definitive statements about the appropriate proportions of each van Hiele level in states' K–8 curriculum standards. However, based on studies cited earlier, there is a clear basis for concern regarding the fact that a mere 4% of the K–8 descriptive geometry GLEs represent van Hiele Level 3, and further, that the GLEs making up this 4% are present in only 24 of the 42 state documents.[6] The results from this analysis are strikingly similar to findings from the Fuys et al.'s (1988) analysis of the geometric content of three popular K–8 textbook series. That study revealed that no more than 1–2 % of the lessons contained content or expectations that required geometric thinking at van Hiele Level 3 and that all of the lessons at this level appeared in Grades 7 and 8. The remaining 98–99% represented van Hiele Levels 0, 1, and 2. Fuys and colleagues (1988) expressed further concerns that "students do not need to think above level 1 for almost all of their geometry experience through Grade 8 because even though some lessons include what appears to be level 2 content, most often they are reduced to memorizing" (p. 169).

The absence of Level 3 GLEs in more than 40% of the states and the near absence in the remaining 60% represents the most compelling result of this analysis, particularly since formal deduction is generally expected in high school geometry courses. The current K–8 geometry curriculum, as represented in these 42 state standards documents, shows little prospect of bridging the gap between K–8 geometry expectations and high school geometry courses. Since the van Hiele theory was first introduced in the United States in the late 1970s, researchers have expressed concern about the lack of Level 3 geometric thinking (*Informal Deduction*) prior to high school (Clements & Battista, 1992; Fuys et al., 1988; Hoffer, 1983; Mayberry, 1983; Mistretta, 2000; Senk, 1989; Usiskin, 1982; Wirszup, 1976). This absence has meant that students enter high school unprepared for the formal deduction required in many geometry courses. Our analysis confirms the legitimacy of that concern. Clements and Battista (1992) point out that "most researchers agree that achieving Level 2 and 3 thinking is an important goal of pre-secondary geometry instruction" (p. 433). Clements (2003) reiterates similar sentiments: "The finding that most U.S. students are not developing through the [van Hiele] levels at all, but that such development is possible given better curriculum and teaching, cannot be ignored" (p. 154). So, why are we no further ahead on this front? What can those interested in K–8 geometry teaching and learning take away from this analysis?

First, expectations and experiences in K–8 geometry must address content at van Hiele Level 3 (*Informal Deduction*) if we intend to prepare students for success in future geometry courses. The van Hiele theory provides us with useful guidelines for creating curricular materials to facilitate the development of geometric thinking which moves students through the levels. Dina van Hiele-Geldof laid the groundwork with a series of five teaching phases and supporting activities to develop students' geometric reasoning. Since her initial work, many others have created additional curricular materials for specific topics that reflect the van Hiele levels (e.g., Crowley, 1987; Fuys et al., 1988; Groth, 2005; Hartweg, 2005; Malloy, 1999; Sharp & Hoiberg, 2001; Van de Walle, 2000). For example, Van de Walle (2000) provides 40 pages of activities for developing geometric thinking using the van Hiele model. At Level 3, he recommends several areas for consideration: (a) definitions and properties, (b) informal proofs, and (c) other topics, including the Pythagorean Theorem, area and volume formulas and the platonic solids. He emphasizes that these topics should be "explored or extended in a way that challenges students to reason in a deductive manner" (p. 344).

Second, we need more dialogue and collaboration among mathematics educators with knowledge of the van Hiele theory, teachers, and curriculum writers including authors of textbooks and standards. The evidence provided from this analysis indicates that in spite of research conducted over the past 30 years that support the use of this model, few changes have been made in the K–8 geometry curriculum that reflect knowledge gained from this research. Do we want to continue to send geometrically deprived students out of U.S. schools? If not, changes will need to be made.

Finally and most importantly we need to bridge the gap between K–8 and high school geometry curricula and the van Hiele theory of geometric thinking provides the tools to do just that. Mathematics education researchers need to continue to refine instructional and assessment models for the levels; state standards writers need to use van Hiele's levels in creating consistent, supportive geometry learning trajectories when revising standards documents; curriculum developers need to develop textbooks that better reflect the necessary geometric reasoning skills in coherent trajectories; and teachers need to be supported in recognizing and facilitating students' progression through the levels. Only this type of systemic approach will provide K–8 students with geometrically rich learning experiences and adequate preparation for future geometry courses.

NOTES

1.   The van Hieles' theory has been given many different titles, and the words "theory" and "model" seem to be used interchangeably in the literature related to their work, as do the words "thinking" and "reasoning." I use "van Hiele's theory of geometric thinking," the phrase Pierre used in his 1999 publication (van Hiele, 1999), or more simply "the theory" in this chapter.

2. The first person plural pronoun ("we") will be used in all references to the data analyses reported in this chapter since they were conducted by two researchers. The second researcher was my colleague, Sarah Kasten, whose assistance was invaluable.

3. The use of the singular "van Hiele" (in contrast to "van Hieles" as a reference to both Pierre and Dina) in many places in the paper is due to the fact that Pierre's major contribution to the model was the levels of geometric thinking, whereas Dina's contribution was the teaching phases which were not the focus of this analysis.

4. A list of the states included in this analysis is included in Appendix C.

5. I use present tense verbs when describing what is in the state standards documents, recognizing that some of these documents are still in use and others are not.

6. My conclusions are based solely on the analysis of state standards documents. I do not have any data to suggest how these standards are being implemented in classrooms. Teachers may enact an expectation coded at van Hiele Level 2 using activities or discussions that would place it at a different van Hiele level.

CHAPTER 5

VERBS AND COGNITIVE DEMAND IN K–8 GEOMETRY AND MEASUREMENT GRADE-LEVEL EXPECTATIONS

Gregory V. Larnell and John P. Smith III

The purpose of standards is to describe what students should know and be able to do. Standards establish performance expectations for students. This means that when developers of standards choose a verb for an indicator or objective, they are sending a message about teaching, learning and assessment. Verb choice is of paramount importance. (Achieve, 2005, p. 9)

In the words of the National Research Council (1989, p. 58–59), for students to understand what they learn "they must enact for themselves verbs that permeate the mathematics curriculum: 'examine,' 'represent,' 'transform,' 'solve,' 'apply,' 'prove,' and 'communicate.' " (Price, 1997, p. 191)

The focus of this chapter differs from others in this volume (Dingman & Tarr; Kasten, & Newton; Newton, Horvath, & Dietiker; and Wang & Smith) and from chapters in the previous volume (Reys, 2006a). As in Newton's chapter (this volume), the focus is less on the mathematics content of state curriculum standards in mathematics and more on how

Variability is the Rule: A Companion Analysis of K–8 State Mathematics Standards, pp. 95–117

grade-level learning expectations (GLEs) describe the character of mental work that students must carry out to fulfill them. In particular, we report an analysis of how well one important component of GLEs, their primary verbs, performs as an index of cognitive demand, using the content areas of geometry and measurement as our test-bed.

As the opening quote from Achieve indicates, some see a strong connection between the verbs that structure learning or performance expectations, their mathematics content, and the teaching necessary to support students' learning of that content. From this perspective, different verbs carry different messages about the cognitive character, difficulty, and depth of grade-level expectations. For example, a verb like "analyze" expresses a more challenging expectation than "recognize" because the mental processes involved in any sort of analysis are more complex and/or extensive than those involved in simple recognition. But it is not obvious that such a tight linkage between verb choice and cognitive demand exists. If the Achieve position is questionable and verbs alone do not determine what students are expected to know and do, then it is sensible to ask, "What does?" In the current climate of accountability, teachers have a right and a need to know, whether they are involved in composing GLEs or interpreting their meaning as they try to help their students meet them.

In exploring this issue, we address the question: How well do distinctions among the meanings of primary verbs appearing in geometry and measurement GLEs define the cognitive demand on K–8 students in this content area? We appeal to one longstanding analysis of how verbs relate to cognitive demand: Bloom's Taxonomy of educational objectives (Bloom, 1956).[1] That framework supports the analysis of all specific verbs in the geometry and measurement GLEs that are associated with different levels of cognitive activity. Our analysis will show that verbs alone are often imprecise measures of cognitive demand and that, while precise measures are difficult to construct via any means, combining the mathematical predicates of GLE verbs with the verbs themselves is a more promising indicator of cognitive demand.

This sort of analysis could be revealing if it were carried out in *any* major content area of mathematics. But selecting geometry and measurement allowed a parallel analysis of two frequently joined content strands that are arguably quite different in the cognitive activity they require. Geometry, in K–12 U.S. schools, typically involves the *descriptive* study of properties and relations of one-, two-, and three-dimensional objects (e.g., points, lines, prisms, prismoids) and relationships among them (e.g., parallelism, congruence, similarity). This definition suggests certain verbs and associated cognitive actions, such as "describe," "identify," and "construct" (Examples 5.1–5.3 below). Here and throughout the chapter, we indicate the mathematical strand—Geometry, Measurement, or

Geometry & Measurement—as well as the state and grade where the example GLE appeared.

> *Example 5.1.* Students classify and *describe* [italics added] one- and two-dimensional geometric objects, including:
>
> • lines, rays, segments, and angles;
> • parallel and perpendicular relationships; and
> • regular polygon types. (WI, Geometry, gr. 7)
>
> *Example 5.2.* Use the attributes and properties of plane figures to model, *identify* [italics added], compare, or *describe* [italics added] plane figures (circles, rectangles, squares, and triangles). (AK, Geometry, gr. 3)
>
> *Example 5.3. Construct* [italics added] two-dimensional patterns for three-dimensional models (e.g., cylinders, prisms, cones). (NM, Geometry, gr. 8)

Measurement, though inextricably tied to geometric contexts, is characterized by the *quantification* of spatial attributes of objects (e.g., length and area) and the enumeration of those quantities (e.g., the rectangle's length is 6 centimeters). This characterization suggests a quite different set of actions, such as "measure," "estimate," "compare," and "solve," as illustrated in Examples 5.4–5.6 below.

> *Example 5.4. Measure* [italics added] the length of objects by repeating a nonstandard unit or a standard unit. Example: *Measure* [italics added] the length of your desk in pencil-lengths. (IN, Measurement, gr. 1)
>
> *Example 5.5. Solve* [italics added] and justify solutions to real-life problems involving the measurement of time, length, and temperature including using a ruler to measure length to the nearest inch and whole centimeter. (ME, Measurement, gr. 3)
>
> *Example 5.6. Compare* [italics added] and *estimate* [italics added] measurements between the U.S. and metric systems in terms of common reference points (e.g., l vs. qt., m vs. yd.). (LA, Measurement, gr. 5)

Studying the frequency of verbs used in geometry grade-level expectations in contrast to those used in measurement will indicate whether GLEs in these two content areas require different intellectual skills, as a complement to the central question of whether verbs alone provide a good index of cognitive demand.

In the sections that follow, we present, analyze, and discuss examples of verb choice in geometry and measurement GLEs from 42 state standards documents listed in Appendix A. Our analysis attempts to balance breadth (first) and then depth, in a more detailed analysis of three specific, commonly-used verbs—*recognize, compare*, and *explain*. First, we apply Bloom's taxonomy to the entire collection of primary verbs to show that, for most verbs, Bloom's framework supports no clear and simple relation between verbs and cognitive demand. In other words, most verbs do not map one-to-one onto specific levels in the taxonomy of cognitive processes. By "primary," we mean the verb (or verbs) that indicates the main and necessary mental work with which students are expected to engage. They are central to the meaning of expectations. Often, several verbs are listed, all of which could be considered primary (see Example 5.2 above and Example 5.7 below). In both examples, the selection of one verb as more important or focal than the others would be arbitrary.

> *Example 5.7. Identify, compare* or *describe* [italics added] attributes and properties of circles (radius, and diameter). (AK, Geometry, gr. 6)

Stringing primary verbs together complicates both our analysis and readers' interpretation of the GLEs by varying the cognitive complexity of expectations—an issue that we will return to below.

The second part of the analysis is, by necessity, illustrative rather than exhaustive. The sheer number of GLEs and primary verbs prohibit an exhaustive analysis for all verbs, so we have been forced to make choices. Our more detailed analysis of *recognize, compare*, and *explain* will show the same general result we report in the initial analysis: There is no clear and simple mapping between verb choice and the cognitive demand of the GLEs where those verbs appear. Moreover, we report similar results for two verbs that appear more frequently in geometry GLEs (*recognize* and *explain*) and for the one (*compare*) that was more common in measurement GLEs. Overall, our analysis suggests that a more appropriate scheme for analyzing the cognitive demand of GLEs is to pair the verb with the specific mathematical concept(s) that is the verb's predicate. In Example 5.7 above, the mathematical predicate of the three verbs is "the attributes and properties of circles."

To underscore what has been stated earlier in this volume, we do not understand or present our analysis as either a critique or defense of the standards we have analyzed. Instead, we hope this work will support mathematics educators' and standards writers' efforts to examine, interpret, and when possible revise their standards with attention to what students should know and be able to do. Writing educationally useful grade-level expectations is hard work. So we hope our analysis will support that work by challenging one overly simplistic model of cognitive demand and suggesting a more sophisticated model to replace it.

APPLYING BLOOM'S TAXONOMY TO THE ANALYSIS OF PRIMARY VERBS

Researchers and teachers have often used verbs to describe and analyze the cognitive activity called for in written statements and to develop questions and assessments in classrooms (e.g., Kastberg, 2003; Vidakovic, Bevis, & Alexander, 2003). The cognitive domain of Bloom's Taxonomy (Bloom, 1956) is an especially common and enduring framework for assessing "cognitive levels" in various educational contexts.[2] The taxonomy features six hierarchically-ordered levels: Knowledge, Comprehension, Application, Analysis, Synthesis, and Evaluation (see Table 5.1) This analysis has been used to assess the cognitive demand of texts and assess-

Table 5.1. Bloom's Taxonomy of Educational Objectives (Cognitive Domain)

Category/Level	Representative Verbs
Knowledge: Make observations and recall data or information.	Defines, describes, identifies, knows, labels, lists, matches, names, outlines, recalls, recognizes, reproduces, selects, states.
Comprehension: Understand information, making interpretations and making predictions from that understanding.	Comprehends, converts, defends, distinguishes, estimates, explains, extends, generalizes, gives examples, infers, interprets, paraphrases, predicts, rewrites, summarizes, translates.
Application: Use a concept or information in a new situation or to solve specific problems.	Applies, changes, computes, constructs, demonstrates, discovers, manipulates, modifies, operates, predicts, prepares, produces, relates, shows, solves, uses.
Analysis: Recognizes meanings and patterns in information or data.	Analyzes, breaks down, compares, contrasts, diagrams, deconstructs, differentiates, discriminates, distinguishes, identifies, illustrates, infers, outlines, recognizes, relates, selects, separates.
Synthesis: Creates new meaning by combining, recomposing, or generalizing given information.	Categorizes, combines, compiles, composes, creates, devises, designs, explains, generalizes, generates, modifies, organizes, plans, rearranges, reconstructs, relates, reorganizes, revises, rewrites, summarizes, tells, writes.
Evaluation: Assess or make conclusions about the value of information or theories. Verify evidence.	Appraises, compares, concludes, contrasts, criticizes, critiques, defends, describes, discriminates, evaluates, explains, interprets, justifies, relates, summarizes, supports.

Adapted from Bloom (1984) and Clark (1999).

ments, and Bloom's levels have also appeared in mathematics textbooks and state standards documents to facilitate instruction (e.g., South Dakota Department of Education, 2004). Our analysis assigns primary verbs to particular levels in the Taxonomy based on their definition and associated examples.

Since its publication, many versions of Bloom's Taxonomy have appeared. Table 5.1 presents just one of many examples of the model described in Bloom's (1984) *Taxonomy of Educational Objectives* in which verbs have been assigned to each level.

As Table 5.1 shows, some verbs, e.g., *identifies, describes, defends,* and *compares,* appear in two or more levels of the Taxonomy. The verb, *relates,* is listed four times, spanning Application to Evaluation. Frequently, verbs appear in quite different levels in the table. For example, *describes* appears both as a low-level Knowledge verb and as high-level Evaluation verb. This complexity has also been noted by other authors. The verb, *identify,* has often been categorized as indicating a low-level skill (Burger & Shaughnessy, 1986). But according to a number of interpretations of Bloom's Taxonomy (e.g., Clark, 1999), *identify* can also be interpreted as an act of analysis (e.g., identifying distinctions and relationships). Without a one-to-one mapping of verbs to levels, the Taxonomy becomes much less helpful in making clear and explicit statements describing the knowledge and skills students are expected to acquire in geometry and measurement, or any other content area of school mathematics.

Thus far, all we have shown is that not all verbs typically associated with Bloom Taxonomy correspond one-to-one with its different levels. In other words, it looks doubtful that verbs alone will serve as reliable indicators of cognitive demand of GLEs. But what verbs do we find in the geometry and measurement GLEs ($N = 5,710$), and where do they fall in the Taxonomy? In our analysis, we compiled and searched with verbs from two sources. First, we chose the most common verbs in the GLEs at each grade level using search and filter functions in Microsoft Excel. Second, we added three verbs from Table 5.1 (*categorize, compose,* and *critique*) that did not frequently appear in the geometry and measurement GLEs, but (a) seemed applicable to geometry and measurement and (b) represented the higher levels of the Taxonomy (Synthesis and Evaluation).

In Table 5.2, we present the verbs that appeared in only one level of the Taxonomy and their frequency of appearance. Table 5.2 shows the frequency with which the GLEs used a primary verb associated with a single Taxonomy level and which specific verbs were most commonly used. This tabulation includes states that distinguished geometry from measurement in their state documents and those that combined them in a single geometry & measurement strand.

Table 5.2.   Verbs Associated With One Level of Bloom's Taxonomy

Taxonomy Level	Verb	Frequency
Knowledge	Define	30
	Know	146
	State	29
	Subtotal	205
Comprehension	Distinguish	42
	Estimate	369
	Extend	26
	Translate	16
	Subtotal	453
Application	Apply	213
	Compute	36
	Construct	82
	Demonstrate	200
	Show	52
	Solve	386
	Subtotal	969
Analysis	Analyze	45
	Distinguish	42
	Select	208
	Subtotal	295
Synthesis	Categorize	1
	Combine	34
	Compose	8
	Create	144
	Write	62
	Subtotal	249
Evaluation	Critique	1
	Evaluate	12
	Justify	41
	Verify	19
	Subtotal	73
	Total	2,244

Overall, Table 5.2 shows that Comprehension and Application verbs far outnumber those associated with other levels and that higher-level verbs appeared less frequently, especially verbs associated with Evaluation. For example, *solve* and *estimate* were commonly used, where *create*, *justify*, and *verify*—verbs associated with higher levels in the Taxonomy—were far less frequent. These results show a clear focus on lower levels of cognitive demand in this large collection of GLEs. Second, the frequency of verbs within and between levels was not uniform. Only seven verbs—*knows*, *estimates*, *applies*, *demonstrates*, *solves*, *selects*, and *creates*—accounted for almost three-quarters (74%) of all entries in Table 5.2. There were no instances of *deconstructs*, *summarizes*, *concludes*, and *proves*, reflecting the subject-specificity of mathematical actions and the K–8 grade level.[3] These results suggest that a relatively small number of verbs, mostly associated with the lower half of Bloom's Taxonomy, play a dominant role in grade-level expectations in this content area.

The contents of Table 5.2 represent the best-case scenario for linking verb use to cognitive demand, listing verbs that associated with only *one* level in Bloom's Taxonomy. But Table 5.1 listed numerous verbs, such as *describes*, *relates*, and *compares* that appear in *two or more* Taxonomy levels. Table 5.3 shows the frequency of appearance of those verbs in the GLEs. As before, this tabulation includes states that distinguished geometry from measurement in their state documents and those that combined them.

If we divide the six levels of Bloom's Taxonomy into two parts, grouping Knowledge, Comprehension, and Application as relatively lower levels of cognitive activity and Analysis, Synthesis, and Evaluation as relatively higher levels, the contents of Table 5.3 reveal some interesting patterns. One verb, *predict*, corresponds only to lower-level demands;

Table 5.3.   Verbs Associated With Two or More Levels of Bloom's Taxonomy

Verb	Taxonomy Level	Frequency
Compare	Analysis, Evaluation	462
Describe	Knowledge, Evaluation	747
Explain	Synthesis, Evaluation	168
Generalize	Comprehension, Synthesis	3
Identify	Knowledge, Analysis	966
Recognize	Knowledge, Analysis	261
Interpret	Comprehension, Evaluation	46
Predict	Comprehension, Application	78
Relate	Analysis, Synthesis, Evaluation	74
Total		2,805

three verbs, *compare*, *explain*, and *relate*, correspond only to higher-levels. *Describe*, *generalize*, *identify*, *recognize*, and *interpret* correspond to both a lower-level and a higher-level activity, and within that group, *identify*, *describe*, and *recognize*, were three of the four most frequently used verbs. So as Table 5.1 suggested and Table 5.3 confirms, states' current grade-level expectations in geometry and measurement frequently use verbs that, according to Bloom's Taxonomy, can either correspond to relatively low levels of cognitive demand or relatively high levels.

Given these general results, we now present a more detailed analysis of specific examples of three particular verbs—*recognize*, *compare*, and *explain*. We aim to show how the cognitive demand of geometry and measurement GLEs changes as the mathematical content shifts, with primary verbs held constant. We selected these three verbs for different reasons. We chose *recognize* because it combined lower and higher levels of cognitive demand and appeared with a frequency that was both large enough to merit our attention, yet still modest enough to permit a thorough analysis. The frequency of *identify*, a possible alternative, was much larger ($n = 966$), and our preliminary analysis of *recognize* or *identify* indicated that these verbs were often used as near synonyms (see Examples 5.8 and 5.9 below). Therefore we did not feel we were losing much in choosing the less frequent verb (*recognize*).

> *Example 5.8. Identify* [italics addded] geometric shapes and structures in the environment and specify their location. Example: Find as many rectangles as you can in your classroom. Record the rectangles that you found by making drawings or using a camera. (IN, Geometry, gr. 1)
>
> *Example 5.9. Recognize* [italics addded] geometric shapes in the student's environment (stop sign, number cube, ball). (MO, Geometry, gr. K)

We chose *compare* for similar reasons: It combined lower and higher levels of demand and appeared frequently—in numbers greater than *recognize* but less than *identify*. In contrast to *recognize*, however, it was commonly used in measurement GLEs. Finally, we selected *explain* to round out this trio because it combined the two highest levels of demand, Synthesis and Evaluation. Given the dominance of relatively low-level demands in our emerging results, it seemed prudent to examine the use of a verb associated with higher levels of demand.

RECOGNIZE: VARIATION IN DEMAND FOR A GEOMETRIC VERB

As indicated in Table 5.2, *recognize* was used frequently across states and grades ($n = 201$ instances). So we first sorted these instances by grade and by specific content area (geometry or measurement), setting aside the GLEs that appeared in GLEs in state documents that combined geometry and measurement into a single content area ($n = 79$). Figure 5.1 presents these results.

As shown, more geometry than measurement GLEs asked students to recognize at each grade level. In light of our initial questions, this suggests that *recognize* was more a "geometry verb" than a "measurement verb." Furthermore, students were expected to recognize geometry content more often in the early grades (K–3) than in subsequent grades (4–7). Interestingly, this pattern did not continue in Grade 8, where the frequency of *recognize* in measurement GLEs returned to primary grade levels.

This information about distribution across grades and broad content area, however, tells us very little about *what* students are expected to recognize, particularly from one grade level to the next. In other words, what is the object that should be recognized? In geometry GLEs in the primary years, we found that students are generally expected to recognize the two-dimensional objects that would later serve as components or representations of three-dimensional objects (see Examples 5.10–5.12 below).

Example 5.10. Students *recognize* [italics added], name, compare, and sort geometric shapes (circle, square, triangle and rectangle). (WY, Geometry, gr. K)

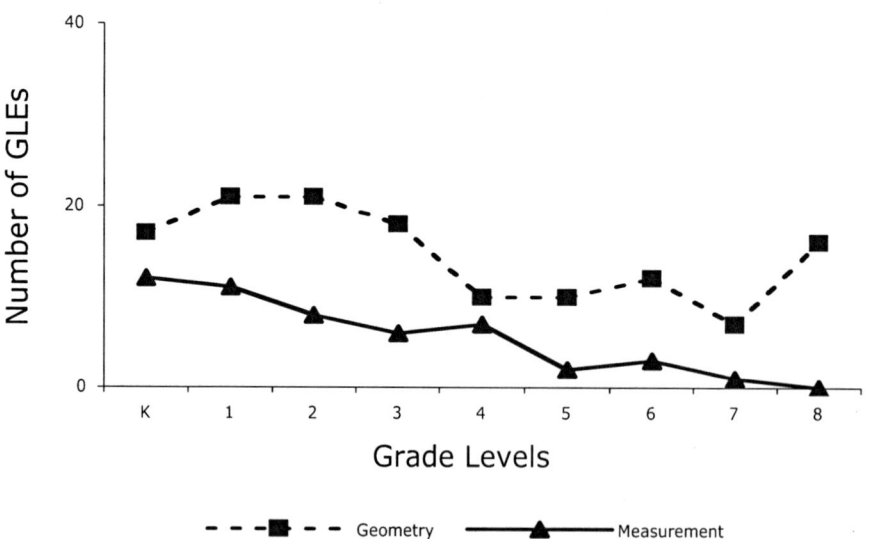

Figure 5.1.   Frequency of *recognize* in geometry and measurement GLEs by grade and content area.

Example 5.11. Recognize [italics added] and create shapes that have symmetry. (MS, Geometry, gr. 2)

Example 5.12. Recognizes [italics added] and compares properties of plane figures and solids using concrete objects, constructions, drawings, and appropriate technology. (KS, Geometry, gr. 6)

In the early grades (e.g., Examples 5.10 and 5.11), recognition was cast as a visual process, matching the low-level (Knowledge) use of the verb. In measurement, students were often expected to recognize general and specific aspects of time, money, and the calendar (as in Examples 5.13 and 5.14). Note that Example 5.13 is another instance of visual recognition.

Example 5.13. Recognize [italics added] the following coins: penny, nickel, dime and quarter. (MN, Measurement, gr. K)

Example 5.14. Recognize [italics added] that there are 24 hours in a day. (AR, Measurement, gr. 2)

Whereas the last five examples (5.10–5.14) clearly illustrate the Knowledge level use of *recognize* as an immediate and direct visual recognition, these examples also point to an important pattern that we found more widely in our analysis, that of verb concatenation. In these examples, students were asked not only to *recognize*, but to *name, compare,* and *sort* (Example 5.10), to *compare* (Example 5.11), or to *create* (Example 5.12). Concatenation significantly reshapes the task of analyzing verb use in relation to cognitive demand, because different verbs in the same GLE may indicate different levels of cognitive activity. In the examples above, *recognize* generally indicates an initial lower-level cognitive process that could support, in the eyes of the standards' authors, more complex higher-level processes. So if *recognition* leads to *comparison*, that step lifts the level of cognitive demand from Knowledge to Analysis. If *recognition* leads further to *creation*, demand is elevated still further to Evaluation. But in the process, concatenation makes it less clear to teachers what students are expected to do. For instance, in Example 5.12, the recognition of the geometric properties of plane figures and solids is clear enough, but what does it mean to compare their properties? At a minimum, verb concatenation distributes teachers' attention over different cognitive processes.

Within the set of *recognize* GLEs, we found evidence that the mathematical object of recognition changes, sometimes in the same grade, and with it the expected level of cognitive activity. For example, consider the following two Grade 1 GLEs that ask students to recognize geometric figures (Examples 5.15 and 5.16).

Example 5.15. Recognizes [italics added] cubes, rectangular prisms, cylinders, cones, and spheres (solids and three-dimensional figures). (KS, Geometry, gr. 1)

Example 5.16. Recognizes [italics added] and investigates attributes of circles, squares, rectangles, triangles, and ellipses (plane figures) using concrete objects, drawings, and appropriate technology. (KS, Geometry, gr. 1)

In Example 5.15, students are expected to recognize three-dimensional *figures*, whereas in 5.16, they are expected to recognize (as well as investigate) the *attributes* or *properties* of two-dimensional figures. It does not seem sensible to consider that these two acts of recognition create the same level of cognitive demand, especially for first graders. In addition, in Example 5.16 precisely which attributes of the listed figures should be recognized and investigated is left to the reader's interpretation. But the analysis of cognitive processes in geometry proposed by van Hiele clearly distinguishes reasoning about figures and reasoning about the properties of figures as different and hierarchically-ordered (Newton, this volume). Students must first recognize the object before they isolate and analyze the attributes of those objects.

We found similar uses of *recognize* in geometry GLEs in the later grades (3–8). As expected, students in these grades were asked to recognize more complex mathematical relationships that build on object and property recognition. In Examples 5.17 and 5.18, students are expected not only to recognize objects and their attributes, but to also recognize the *patterns* and *relationships* between specific attributes or properties.

Example 5.17. Recognizes [italics added] patterns and relationships between the coordinates and properties of figures. (HI, Geometry, gr. 7)

Example 5.18. Recognize [italics added] that rectangles with the same perimeter do not necessarily have the same area and vice versa. (NJ, Geometry & Measurement, gr. 5)

In Example 5.18, students are expected to recognize the relationships between area and perimeter after recognizing that some geometrical objects (squares, in this case) have the same perimeter. These examples of recognition of relatively complex patterns and relationships clearly qualify as examples of Analysis as characterized in Table 5.1. Moreover, where Example 5.18 targets a single relationship, Example 5.17 carries a very wide scope, apparently including an almost infinite number of patterns and relationships for students to recognize. We will see other instances of this problem of vagueness in the mathematical predicates of verbs in later sections of this chapter.

These are not the only complex acts of recognition that Grade 3–8 students are expected to learn (and that teachers are expected to teach). As Example 5.19 illustrates, students are expected not only to recognize certain attributes of figures, but *strategies* for measuring unknown lengths as well. And as Example 5.20 shows, they are also expected to recognize *when to apply* such strategies.

> *Example 5.19. Recognizes* [italics added] how ratios and proportions can be used to measure inaccessible objects, e.g., using shadows to measure the height of a flagpole. (KS, Geometry, gr. 8)

> *Example 5.20. Recognizes* [italics added] when to use properties of right triangles to solve problems. (HI, Geometry, gr. 8)

In both cases, recognition involves judgments of when and how to apply mathematical concepts and procedures to solve problems. As judged by the contents of Table 5.1, these examples of *recognize* most closely match the Application level of Bloom's Taxonomy—an association not suggested in either Table 5.1 or Table 5.3. This mismatch does not undermine, in any serious way, our prior analysis of overall verb use in relation to the Taxonomy. What it does suggest is that verb use, absent other information, can tell us little about cognitive demand. In these latter examples, *recognize* is far from the visual process suggested in the examples discussed early this section. *Apply* would be a more accurate verb to express what Examples 5.19 and 5.20 expect students to do.

These examples (5.10–5.20) show the multiple ways in which students are expected to think and act in response to the verb *recognize* and the differential cognitive demands of these acts. Across grade levels, they are expected to (a) *recognize* by identifying, labeling, or naming simple geometric objects; (b) *recognize* the attributes or properties of such objects; (c) *recognize* the relationships between objects and/or their attributes; or (d) *recognize* strategies and decide when and how they should be applied. Within these broad types, students must also *recognize* increasingly sophisticated mathematical ideas as objects of recognition (e.g., ratios and cross-sections of three-dimensional objects). The permutations of the different types of recognition and the objects to be recognized create a much more complex picture of cognitive demand than is suggested by the simple correspondences in Bloom's Taxonomy. But as our analysis has suggested, the fault does not entirely rest with Bloom. In at least some cases, standards authors have used *recognize* when other verbs would seem more appropriate choices.

COMPARE: VARIATION AND VAGUENESS IN
DEMAND IN A MEASUREMENT VERB

Our second verb, *compare*, which is listed in both the Knowledge and Analysis levels of Bloom's Taxonomy in Table 5.1, appeared more frequently than *recognize* ($n = 462$ instances, compared to 201 for the latter). Figure 5.2 shows the use of *compare* as a primary verb across grades and content area.[4]

The verb *compare* appeared more frequently in measurement GLEs in states with distinct Measurement strands. Figure 5.2 also shows that *compare* was used most often in the primary years (Grades K–2). As noted above, the prevalence of topics like money, temperature and time in the primary grades—now as objects of *comparison*, not *recognition*—accounts for these high relative frequencies. So *compare* can be considered predominately a "measurement" verb. But in what ways are students expected to *compare*, and how do these uses relate to measurement?

In the primary grades, students are expected to compare a wide variety of attributes of objects, sometimes apparently by visual inspection (Example 5.22 below) and sometimes after measurement or counting (Examples 5.21 and 5.25). The common attributes are money, time, temperature, length, and weight.

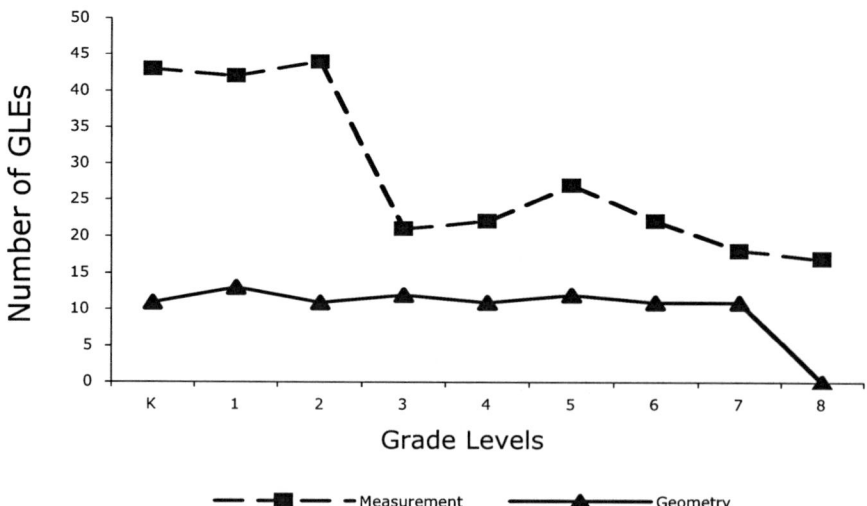

Figure 5.2.   Frequency of *compare* in geometry and measurement GLEs by grade level and content area.

Example 5.21. Compare [italics addeded] situations or objects according to temperature such as hotter or colder. (TX, Measurement, gr. K)

Example 5.22. Compare [italics addeded] attributes of two objects using appropriate vocabulary (color, weight, height, width, length, texture). (NC, Measurement, gr. K)

Example 5.23. Identify units of time (day, week, month, year) and *compare* [italics addeded] calendar elements; e.g., weeks are longer than days. (OH, Measurement, gr. K)

Example 5.24. Knows and *compares* [italics addeded] amounts of money in coins, to one dollar or more. (FL, Measurement, gr. 2)

Example 5.25. Measure and *compare* [italics addeded] the length of common objects using metric and U.S. customary units to the nearest centimeter or inch. (DC, Measurement, gr. 2)

Example 5.26. Compare [italics addeded] U.S. and metric measurements using approximate reference points without using conversions (e.g., a meter is longer than a yard). (LA, Measurement, gr. 3)

With the possible exception of Example 5.25, all these examples suggest that comparison involves judgments of more or less (that is, qualitative comparisons) without specifying the magnitudes of the differences. But in some cases, the meaning of *compare* is left to the reader to determine. Where comparisons of money, time and temperature (Examples 5.21, 5.23, and 5.24) call for judgments of more or less on a single scale, Example 5.22 calls for same/different judgments and on many different attributes. Likewise, Example 5.26 calls for the use of "reference points" in comparing measurements across systems but fails to clarify that those reference points are and how they are to be used in making those comparisons.

We raised the general issue of verb concatenation in our analysis of *recognize*. Here we identify another general problem that was common in, but not limited to GLEs where *compare* was a primary verb. This is the problem of vagueness—the lack of specificity about the act (or acts) of comparison that students are supposed to carry out. We found that compare GLEs frequently did not clearly articulate *how* and/or *on what dimension* students are expected to compare two or more objects.

Consider the following four examples.

Example 5.27. Identify and *compare* [italics addeded] three-dimensional shapes. (DC, Geometry, gr. K)

Example 5.28. Compares [italics addeded] geometric solids. (HI, Geometry, gr. 1)

Example 5.29. Compare [italics addeded] and analyze attributes and other features (e.g., number of sides, faces, corners, right angles, diagonals, and symmetry) of two- and three-dimensional geometric shapes. (DC, Geometry, gr. 4)

Example 5.30. Identifies, *compares* [italics addeded], analyzes, and clearly explains the classification of two- and three-dimensional shapes, using appropriate descriptive vocabulary to define the class. (HI, Geometry, gr. 4)

In contrast to the prior set (Examples 5.21–5.26) where comparison was presented as a visual or numerical process and in some cases clarified the target dimension of comparison, Examples 5.27 through 5.30 do not clearly identify the dimensions and/or extent of the expected comparisons. Does Example 5.27 expect kindergarteners to compare three-dimensional shapes by type (i.e., judge objects as the same shape or different) or size? Must spheres be distinguished from prisms (only), or are finer distinctions among prisms expected? Examples 5.29 and 5.30 raise a slightly different problem: What is the complete set of dimensions (5.29) and shapes (5.30) along which Grade 4 students are expected to *compare*? This lack of clarity in specifying target comparisons translates into a large burden for teachers and supervisors to interpret the expected range of comparison called for in those GLEs. Given the demands on our teachers, it seems unreasonable to expect them to make the same (and sensible) interpretations of vaguely stated expectations.

More generally, these examples support our main claim: The mere presence of the same primary verb, *compare*, does not designate the same or even similar level of cognitive demand. The main feature that distinguished low-demand from high-demand instances of *compare* in these examples (5.21–5.30) was the complexity of the mathematical predicate. In the second collection (Examples 5.27–5.30), comparison requires a visual-cognitive framework for seeing and analyzing the *properties* of three-dimensional objects, a broad capacity that cannot be expected of primary age children (Clements, 1999).

EXPLAIN: HIGH-LEVEL VERBS CAN EXPRESS LOW-LEVEL EXPECTATIONS

In contrast to *recognize* and *compare*, *explain* did not appear as frequently in the state documents ($n = 168$ total instances compared to 462 and 201, respectively). But it represented the higher levels of the Bloom's Taxonomy (Synthesis and Evaluation) in greater numbers than any other verb in our set. For example, *justify* and *evaluate* appeared considerably less frequently (n = 41 and 12 instances, respectively). Our analysis of *explain* allowed us to explore the demands of an apparently high-demand verb when it was coupled with geometric and measurement content. Figure 5.3 presents the distribution of appearances of *explain* over grade levels and specific content area.[5]

As Figure 5.3 shows, *explain* was used more often in measurement GLEs with a marked increase in Grades 3 and 5, where its appearance in geometry GLEs was more constant across the grades. Though this display provides little insight into specific content and demand of the GLEs where the verb appeared, it does show that *explain* was more commonly associated with measurement than geometry (especially in Grades 3 through 5). But what were students asked to *explain*?

The GLEs employed the verb *explain* in various ways and with a variety of objects. In our analysis, we identified five different types of objects of explanation: (1) a strategy, procedure, or theorem, (2) a relationship, property, or concept, (3) an answer or result, (4) a problem or the nature of a problem, and (5) some general, unspecified reasoning. Without claiming that these categories are ordered in cognitive complexity, we do claim (and show through the examples given below) that within and across categories, *explain* GLEs called for both cognitively demanding reasoning *and* relatively low-level reasoning, depending on the apparent meaning of the verb and its mathematical predicate. Though *explain* is

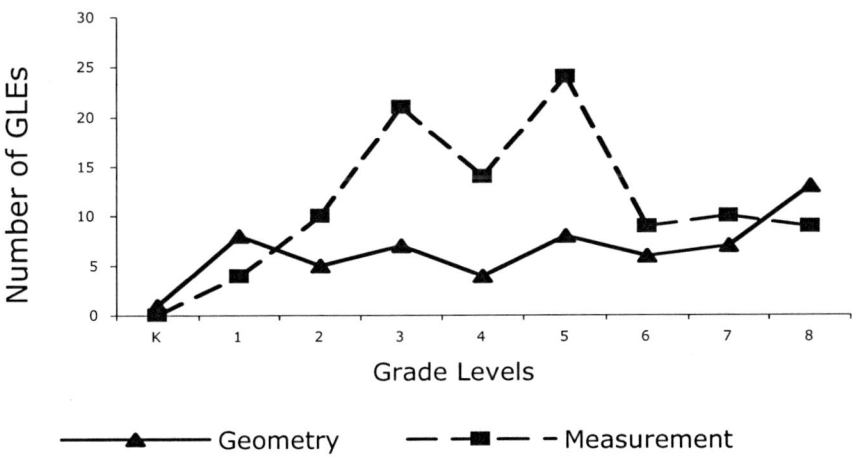

Figure 5.3.   Frequency of explain in geometry and measurement GLEs by grade level and content area.

commonly considered a relatively high-level verb in Bloom's Taxonomy, this analysis suggests that states may be using it to identify low-level cognitive processes.

Explain a Strategy, Procedure, or Theorem: Explain or State?

In many cases, geometry and measurement GLEs asked students to explain a strategy, procedure, or theorem for solving some class of problems, and most of those instances involved measurement topics (see Examples 5.31–5.33).

> *Example 5.31.* Use counting techniques to *explain* [italics addeded] how to find the area and perimeter of regular shapes. (DoD, Measurement, gr. 3)
>
> *Example 5.32.* Apply and *explain* [italics addeded] appropriate estimation strategies using standard units of measure. (TN, Measurement, gr. 5)
>
> *Example 5.33. Explain* [italics addeded] and use the Pythagorean theorem. (NM, Geometry, gr. 7)

In each of these examples, the call to *explain* was combined with an application—of a procedure (counting units of length and area in Example 5.31), a set of strategies (estimating quantities with standard units in Example 5.32), or a theorem (stating the Pythagorean relationship in Example 5.33). Though we cannot know the authors' intentions when they composed these GLEs, in each case *explain* could be interpreted simply as a call to *tell* or *state* the targeted mathematics. Indeed, what could it mean to *explain* the Pythagorean Theorem? In our view, *state* would be a sensible expectation for Grade 7 students. And in Example 5.31, do the authors intend students to state the procedures for finding perimeter and area or explain *why* those procedures work—two quite different tasks? Explaining why a strategy, procedure, or theorem works/is true sets a relatively high cognitive demand, because the explanation must appeal to more fundamental mathematical principles (e.g., to the relationship between the measures of angles and opposite sides in all triangles in the case of the Pythagorean Theorem). *Explain* in that sense is consistent with Bloom's placement of this verb at the Synthesis and/or Evaluation level of the Taxonomy. In contrast, *stating* a strategy, procedure, or theorem may also be demanding, especially as the complexity of the content rises, but this meaning of *explain* is more consistent with Bloom's Knowledge and Comprehension levels.

Explain a Relationship, Property, or Concept: Clarity in the Predicate is Not Sufficient

We have argued throughout this chapter that assessing the cognitive demand of grade-level expectations is not a straightforward task. Further, we have shown that the primary verbs used in GLEs are often not, by themselves, sufficient indicators of cognitive demand. We have argued that combining the verb with the relevant mathematical content appears to be a more promising index of cognitive demand, as we have demonstrated for *recognize, compare,* and several examples of *explain.* But to underline again the complexity of the task, we show that simple clarity in the object of explanation (the mathematical concept[s] that must be explained) is not sufficient for clarity in the GLE. Coherence in the verb-predicate pairing is required.

Alongside GLEs that ask students to explain a strategy, procedure or theorem are those that call for explaining relationships, properties, or concepts in geometry and/or measurement. Often, the connection between the verb and the mathematical predicate indicates relatively sophisticated mathematical thinking, but the indeterminate language of the GLE make the estimation of cognitive demand difficult. For instance, in Example 5.34, students are expected to (among other things) explain geometric properties and relations among a variety of geometric figures.

> *Example 5.34.* Observes, *explains* [italics addeded], and makes conjectures regarding geometric properties and relationships (among angles, triangles, squares, rectangles, parallelograms). (FL, Geometry, gr. 6)

Taken by themselves, the "properties and relationships" among the listed two-dimensional shapes seem a reasonably well-formed mathematical topic. Teachers could list a set of statements that describe the regions in terms of their angles and in relation to each other, for example, "all squares are rectangles but the reverse is not true." However, what does it mean to *explain* this hypothetical list of properties and relationships? Is this another case of using *explain* when *state* would be a more accurate term? Or, alternatively, do the authors of this GLE intend that students should possess and express the complete hierarchy of quadrilaterals, with specific attention to their interior angles? In this case, even if we look past the concatenation of verbs, the verb *explain,* when matched to a relatively broad mathematical topic, fails to support a clear and straightforward interpretation.

Consider a second example. In Example 5.35 (below), the verb *explain* is matched to the relationship between perimeter/circumference and area.

Example 5.35. Model and *explain* [italics added] the relationship between perimeter and area (how scale change in a linear dimension affects perimeter and area) and between circumference and area of a circle. (LA, Geometry, gr. 7)

Here students must first recognize and understand the relationship (with possible analysis and application, to borrow from Bloom's framework) before explaining it, suggesting a hierarchical increase in the complexity in mathematical thinking (higher cognitive demand). But more fundamentally this GLE could be clearer with respect to its mathematical goal. Which of the many relationships between perimeters and areas of polygons or between the circumferences and areas of circles are students expected to model and *explain*? While this particular grade-level expectation specifies parenthetically that students should *explain* linear scale change, is that the only relationship they are expected to explain? Are students, for example, also expected to *explain* that while perimeter and area often co-vary, it is also possible to increase the perimeter as much as desired and will holding constant or even reducing the area?

The central lesson of this analysis is that expectations with the primary verb *explain* may frequently be interpreted as calling for lower-level cognitive processes—activity consistent with the Knowledge and Comprehension levels in Bloom's Taxonomy. In particular, many *explain* GLEs may be read as asking for students to *state* some mathematics, a class of tasks clearly associated with the Knowledge or Comprehension levels. This central ambiguity about the meaning of *explain* (state vs. explain) becomes more problematic in GLEs that are already troubled by verb concatenation and/or by broad and diverse mathematical predicates. But there are also instances where *explain* does indicate the high cognitive demand of Bloom's Synthesis and Evaluation levels. As we have insisted throughout, however, the verb alone does not generally indicate this demand. Examination of both the verb and its associated mathematical content is required to estimate the level of cognitive demand. Equally important, the mathematical content must be clear and explicit for those estimates to be reliable—and for teachers and students to know what mathematical thinking is expected. As we have seen, many times GLEs fail to achieve this clarity, either in the mathematical content to be explained and/or in how the act of explanation is tied to that content.

DISCUSSION

The central finding of our analysis is that the primary verbs that structure geometry and measurement GLEs are not, by themselves, reliable indices of the cognitive demand of those grade-level expectations. Verb choice in content standards may send important messages about teaching, learning, and assessment, as Achieve (2005) has argued, but verb choice alone does not clarify the cognitive difficulty or demand of grade-level expectations for student learning. As we have seen repeatedly, the same verb can prescribe quite different types of cognitive activity and therefore different levels of cognitive demand, depending on (a) the mathematical predicate coupled with that verb, (b) the meaning attributed to the verb, and (c) the broader mathematical context presented in the grade-level expectation. Therefore we would amend the opening quote from Achieve to say that verbs, as expressions of cognitive processes, coupled with particular mathematical ideas that are the object of those processes are a much better frame for reading, interpreting, and writing grade-level expectations. If so, writers of such standards should attend to verbs, predicates and the broader mathematical context, with equal focus.

In carrying out these analyses, we have found other problems related to verb choice in grade-level expectations. First, we have found a relatively common practice of combining quite different verbs with the same mathematical predicate in a single GLE. Where verb concatenation may shorten the length of standards documents, it also tends to obscure the specific learning objective expressed in GLEs by bundling together quite different cognitive actions. Because each additional verb may hold a different relationship with the target mathematical concept, concatenation makes it more difficult for teachers and supervisors to discern the objective and scope of particular GLEs. We have also frequently seen that verbs have not always been well-chosen to indicate what students must do with the specified mathematical content. In some cases, verbs have called for mastery of a large and diverse set of mathematical relationships (e.g., "Recognize geometric relationships among two-dimensional and three-dimensional objects" [Alabama, Geometry, gr. 7], while in others verbs do not match their predicates in sensible ways (what would it mean exactly to "explain" the Pythagorean Theorem in Grade 7?). We see both as problems of vagueness in coupling verbs and mathematical predicates. Where there are clear limits to the amount of explanatory text that can accompany any GLE, the cost of nontransparent expectations—those that do not clearly specify the desired performance—seems very high for all involved, but particularly for teachers.

Is the failure to find convincing correspondences between the cognitive demand of GLEs structured by verbs and the levels of Bloom's Taxonomy associated with those verbs an indictment of Bloom's analysis? We think not. Instead, we consider Bloom's scheme—a set of verbs associated with fundamentally different levels of cognitive processes, independent of specific subject-matter (mathematics, history, etc.)—is simply too blunt a tool to serve as the sole means of preparing and interpreting grade-level expectations. For example, the verb *explain*, which could describe higher levels of cognitive activity in disciplines such history or medicine, has been used—at least at times—apparently to mean *state* or *define* in K–8 geometry and measurement standards. The lesson we take is that there are clear limits to domain-general tools such as Bloom's Taxonomy in calibrating cognitive demand.

If Bloom's analysis is insufficient, are there other analytic tools, general or specifically mathematical, that educators could appeal to in constructing and interpreting grade-level expectations? We know of none that have withstood the test of examination and varied educational application that Bloom's Taxonomy has. However, there are research teams working to develop frameworks that calibrate the cognitive demand of grade-level expectations and corresponding assessment items in mathematics. For example, Norman Webb and colleagues in the Wisconsin Center for Educational Research have proposed four "depth of knowledge" levels from "recall and reproduction" to "extended thinking" and listed specific verbs associated with some levels (Webb, 1999). This analysis is similar in spirit to Bloom's but informed by significantly deeper understanding of students' mathematical thinking. Until such new analyses are tested and widely available, we think it is prudent for the authors of grade-level expectations to focus on the pairing of verbs and their mathematical predicates in estimating the demands of their GLEs. Authors should give careful attention to this coupling and to the class of mathematical performances (actions or oral or written products) that they expect as evidence of mastery.

The process of matching verbs to mathematical content in GLEs to express specific goals for teaching and learning must be a careful, thoughtful process for any standards writing team. But it is worth remembering how intellectually challenging this work is and how often it is carried out in far less than ideal circumstances. Writers must often complete their work in short periods of time without access to relevant resources, such as mathematical or psychological expertise. In carrying out their work, they must attend to many issues other than those we have emphasized. They must think about the differences between content strands (e.g., does this GLE belong in geometry or in measurement?), identify important connections between topics and strands, and consider and apply trajectories for student learning within content areas—to name only three. And of course they must manage the pressure and responsibility of their power (desired or not) as they establish expectations to which *all* teachers and students in their state will be held accountable.

We honor their work, past, present, and future, as we have worked to identify problems with a sole focus on verb choice and emphasize the importance of matching verbs to target mathematical content. We hope this analysis can serve as a resource for subsequent efforts to improve and strengthen the content and expression of state mathematics standards, in geometry and measurement and more generally. If we are serious about communicating clear expectations for teaching and learning mathematics, we should be equally serious about supporting their continuous improvement.

NOTES

1. More recently, Norman Webb has addressed this relationship with the Depth of Knowledge framework (Webb, 1999).
2. Other less-commonly applied dimensions of Bloom's Taxonomy (at least in mathematics education) are the "effective" and "psychomotor" domains. The cognitive domain was published first, but the term, "Bloom's Taxonomy," generally refers to the three-domain framework. In this paper, we use "Bloom's Taxonomy" to refer only to the cognitive domain.
3. Had the grades levels not been restricted to K–8, we expect that instances of *prove(s)* would very likely have appeared.
4. As in Figure 5.1, the instances of *compare* ($n = 114$) found in state documents that combined geometry and measurement were excluded from this representation.
5. Again, the instances of *explain* in the GLEs of state documents that combined geometry and measurement were excluded from this representation.

CHAPTER 6

THE STATISTICAL PROCESS

A View Across the K–8 State Standards

Jill Newton, Aladar K. Horvath, and Leslie Dietiker

> Our lives are governed by numbers. Every high school graduate should be able to use sound statistical reasoning to intelligently cope with the requirements of citizenship, employment, and family and to be prepared for a healthy, happy, and productive life. (Franklin et al., 2007, p. 1)

Each day people are surrounded by statistics, beginning with information on the breakfast cereal box and continuing through the evening news. Quantitative information is found in all forms of news reports, advertisements, professional journals, research in diverse fields of study, investment reports, on the internet, and even on food labels. The ability to make sense of this quantitative bombardment has become essential for the informed decision making of citizens. As Mooney (2002) stated, "Graphs, charts, tables, averages, and raw data are inescapable in today's information society" (p. 23). The pervasiveness of statistics in everyday life has increased in this age of information and it has not gone unnoticed by educational organizations.

Variability is the Rule: A Companion Analysis of K–8 State Mathematics Standards, pp. 119–159

The National Council of Teachers of Mathematics (NCTM) included a Statistics and Probability strand in both *Curriculum and Evaluation Standards for School Mathematics* (NCTM, 1989) and *Principles and Standards for School Mathematics* (*PSSM*) (NCTM, 2000). The strand title changed slightly from "Statistics and Probability" in the 1989 document to "Data Analysis and Probability" in *PSSM*. Additionally, NCTM chose "Becoming Certain about Uncertainty: Data Analysis and Probability" as their official focal theme of the 2007-08 school year. Mooney (2002) noted that in addition to the mathematics education community highlighting the need for statistics, educational organizations in other fields, have also identified the need for statistical skills (National Assessment Governing Board, 2004; National Council for the Social Studies, 1994; National Council of Teachers of English & International Reading Association, 1996). Given the increasing need for statistical literacy and the growing demand for and attention recently given to statistics education, an analysis of the state mathematics standards that express what students are expected to know and be able to do in statistics is not only needed, but is also quite timely.

The American Statistical Association (ASA) responded to this growing need for statistics literacy in 2005 by endorsing the *Guidelines for Assessment and Instruction in Statistics Education (GAISE) Report: A Pre-K-12 Curriculum Framework* (Franklin et al., 2007).[1] The document's stated purpose was to complement and give further depth and breadth to the statistics strand as detailed in *PSSM*. The *GAISE Report* articulated four components of the statistical process as central to work in statistics and data analysis: (1) formulate questions, (2) collect data, (3) analyze data, and (4) interpret results.

Other documents have put forth four similar components; however, their titles and descriptions have varied slightly. For example Mooney (2002) labeled the four components (1) describing data, (2) organizing and reducing data, (3) representing data, and (4) analyzing and interpreting data, while Friel and Bright (1998) suggested (1) ask a question, (2) collect data, (3) analyze data, and (4) form and communicate conclusions (cited in Konold & Higgins, 2003). Many of the differences between the names and descriptions of these four process components are due to either terminological differences or the complexity and nonlinearity of the statistical process (Wild & Pfannkuch, 1999). This complexity and non-linearity makes it difficult to say exactly where in statistical reasoning one component ends and the next begins. When doing statistics, it is not unusual to move back and forth among these four process components during an investigation.

For our analysis, we chose to use the framework and terminology provided by the *GAISE Report* for three reasons. First, having the components listed in this way steps sequentially through the statistical inquiry process.

Even though the entire process is complex, it would be hard "to analyze data before collecting them or to form conclusions before doing analyses" (Konold & Higgins, 2003, p. 194). Second, the development of the GAISE report involved the participation of many of the leading statisticians and statistics educators who are working in the field today. It can be viewed as representing a summary of the status of the current thinking in this developing field. Finally, the *GAISE Report* provides a benchmark against which to compare current state standards with the most recent recommendations.

METHODS

Our primary goal was to describe what K–8 students in the United States are expected to know and be able to do with respect to the statistical process. To this end, we collected all of the K–8 grade level expectations (GLEs) that address the statistical process from 41 state standards documents that articulate learning expectations on a grade-by-grade basis. The list of states, the name of the document and the year of publication are given in Appendix D. For the majority of states, these documents are identical to those used in the Geometry and Measurement chapters (see Appendix A). For a small number of states the analysis of statistics (this chapter) and probability GLEs (Dingman & Tarr, this volume) examined more recently revised documents since they were undertaken after the corresponding analyses for geometry & measurement were begun. In addition, the standards document from Maine was not included in either the probability or statistics analysis.

As mentioned earlier, we framed our analysis using the recently published *GAISE Report*. We utilized the descriptors for the four components of the statistical process provided in that report (Franklin et al., 2007, p. 11).[2]

I. Formulate Questions

- Clarify the problem at hand
- Formulate one (or more) questions that can be answered with data

II. Collect Data

- Design a plan to collect appropriate data
- Employ the plan to collect the data

III. Analyze Data

- Select appropriate graphical and numerical methods
- Use these methods to analyze the data[3]

IV. Interpret Results

- Interpret the analysis
- Relate the interpretation to the original question

Thus, our initial analysis involved coding each statistics GLE for the applicable process components. In order to be coded into a particular process component, the GLE needed to expect students to do the activity described in at least one of the descriptors for that process component outlined above. Many GLEs were coded as addressing more than one process component. The results of this initial analysis were four subsets of GLEs that corresponded to the four process components. Each decision regarding the collection and coding of a GLE was the result of a discussion between at least two of the authors, and the third author was consulted as necessary to resolve differences. All coding decisions were recorded in order to ensure consistency throughout the analysis.

In addition, we noted that within each process component (i.e., Formulate Questions, Collect Data, Analyze Data, and Interpret Results) were two distinctly different types of GLEs, which we termed Type I and Type II. Type I GLEs expect students to complete some process (e.g., construct a bar graph) and Type II GLEs expect students to evaluate some process (e.g., select the most appropriate representation for a given set of data). Table 6.1 provides several examples of Type I GLEs and how they were coded in our analysis using the descriptors from the *GAISE Report*. The first

Table 6.1. Examples of Type I GLEs Coded for the GAISE Process Components

Example GLE	Formulate Questions	Collect Data	Analyze Data	Interpret Results
Construct and interpret broken line graphs, line plots, bar graphs, picture graphs, glyphs and simple circle graphs. (CT, gr. 4)			x	x
Make conjectures to formulate new questions for future studies. (TN, gr. 6)	x			x
Pose questions and gather data about themselves and their surroundings. (MO, gr. K)	x	x		
Gather data and use information to *complete a scaled and labeled graph.* (SD, gr. 3)		x	x	
Pose information questions; collect data; and *record the results using objects, pictures, and picture graphs.* (CA, gr. K)	x	x	x	

Note: We italicized text in the example GLEs to indicate the phrases that were instrumental in our coding process.

example GLE in Table 6.1 was coded as both Analyze Data and Interpret Results since students are expected to both construct and interpret various types of visual representations. The last example in Table 6.1 was similarly coded as Analyze Data since it expects students to construct visual representations of data. However, it also asks students to formulate questions and collect data so it was coded for these process components as well.

Table 6.2 provides examples of Type II GLEs and the ways in which they were coded in our analysis using the descriptors from the *GAISE Report*. The first Type II example GLE in Table 6.2 does not expect students to formulate a question, but rather to evaluate several questions and determine which is the most appropriate for a given situation. Thus it was coded as a Type II Formulate Question GLE. The last Type II example GLE in Table 6.2 was coded as a Type II Analyze Data GLE since the student is expected to choose the most appropriate statistical measure for a particular situation and justify their choice. Many GLEs were coded as both Type I and Type II. For example,

Example 6.1. Make inferences and formulate and evaluate arguments based on displays and analysis of data. (NJ, gr. 7)

This GLE was coded in Interpret Results as both a Type I and Type II GLE since it expects students to both formulate and evaluate arguments. Type I

Table 6.2. Examples of Type II GLEs Coded for the GAISE Process Components

Example GLE	Formulate Questions	Collect Data	Analyze Data	Interpret Results
Determine which of several questions is most likely to give the desired information. (WA, gr. 4)	x			
Recognize practices of collecting and displaying data that *may bias the presentation or analysis.* (MI, gr. 8)		x	x	
As a class project, *discusses ways to choose a sample representative* of a large group such as a sample representative of the entire school. (FL, gr. 5)		x		
Recognize and analyze faulty interpretation or representation of data. (MD, gr. 7)			x	x
Choose among mean, median, mode, or range to describe a set of data and *justify the choice for a particular situation.* (TX, gr. 7)			x	

Note: We italicized text in the example GLEs to indicate the phrases that were instrumental in our coding process.

and Type II GLEs occur within each of the four process components and will be described further within each appropriate section. In addition to these categories, the sections describing each process component contain more specific categorizations of the GLEs that address particular topics.

The subsequent sections of the paper present our findings. We begin with an overview describing our general findings, followed by sections devoted to each of the four process components: (1) Formulate Questions, (2) Collect Data, (3) Analyze Data, and (4) Interpret Results. The findings are followed by a conclusion where we discuss the implications of the results of this analysis.

RESULTS

General Findings

All 41 states divide their standards document into content strands (e.g., Algebra, Geometry). Statistics and probability topics are found in a joint strand in all states except Maryland which includes two separate strands, *Knowledge of Statistics* and *Knowledge of Probability*. The most common words found in the title of the strand containing the GLEs that address the statistical process in the remaining 40 states are summarized in Table 6.3. It is interesting to note that *Data Analysis and Probability*, the strand title in *Principles and Standards for School Mathematics* (*PSSM*), is also the most common strand title found among the state standards documents (appearing in 16 states). We also note that the Statistics and Probability strand is the last strand listed in 32 of the 41 state standards documents. It is also the last strand mentioned in *PSSM*. In five of the remaining nine states, it is the second to the last strand.

Quantitative summary of the GLEs. There are a total of 1,711 GLEs in the 41 state documents that address the four process components of the statistical process as described in the *GAISE Report*. The minimum, median, and maximum number of GLEs across the states are 17, 32, and 117, respectively. Figure 6.1 illustrates the number of GLEs as they are distributed across grade levels. The number of GLEs is lowest in kindergarten

Table 6.3.   Frequency of Terms in Strand Titles for Statistics and Probability

Terms	Number of States
"Data" or "Data Analysis"	34
"Statistics"	17
"Probability"	38
"Discrete Mathematics"	3

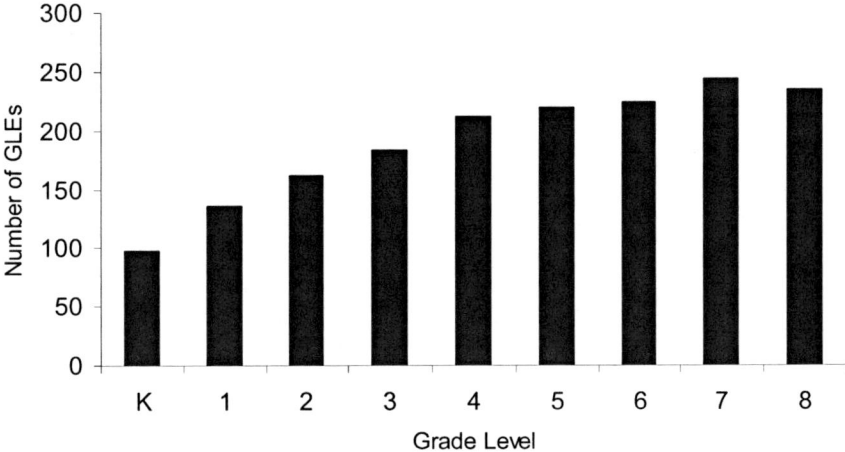

Figure 6.1.   Number of statistics GLEs by grade.

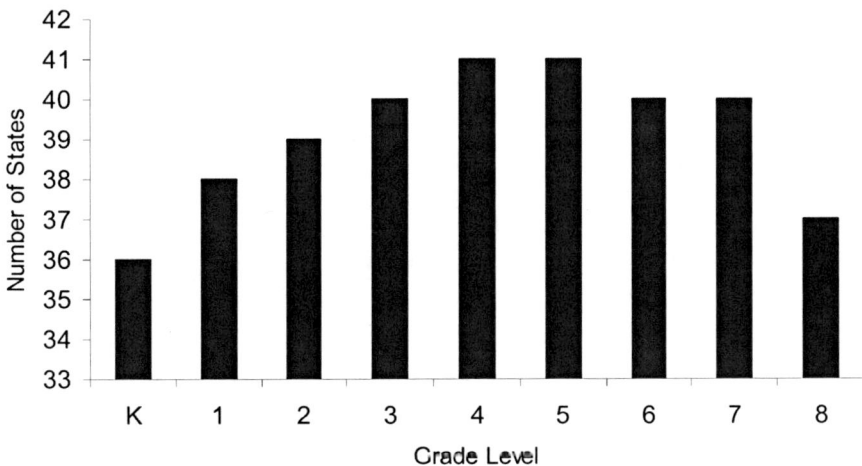

Figure 6.2.   Number of states with statistics GLEs by grade.

(98 GLEs) and reaches its maximum in Grade 7 (244 GLEs). Overall, the quantity of GLEs increases steadily from kindergarten through middle school. Figure 6.2 above highlights different features of this data, showing the number of states that include at least one statistics GLE at each grade level.

Nearly all states have statistics GLEs at every grade level. The minimum number of states with GLEs is represented in kindergarten when 36 of the 41 states (88%) have at least one statistics GLE. The maximum number of states with GLEs is found in Grades 4 and 5 when all 41 states have at least one statistics GLE.

Table 6.4 summarizes several important features of the data collected and coded in our analysis, including the number of GLEs coded into each of the four process components as well as the number of states that contained at least one GLE in each process. In addition, information regarding the number of Type I (*doing* the process) GLEs and Type II (*evaluating* the process) GLEs is included for each process component. Totals for Type I and Type II GLEs are not given because they are not meaningful, due to the large number of GLEs coded for multiple process components. The overall number of GLEs presented in Table 6.4 seems to indicate that states place a greater emphasis on analyzing data and interpreting results than on formulating questions and collecting data. All of the states analyzed expect students to collect data, analyze data, and interpret results, while only 29 states expect students to formulate questions. The number of Type II GLEs is less than Type I in every process component. However, the percentages of Type II GLEs among the process components vary widely, ranging from 8% in Interpret Results to 34% in Analyze Data. All but one of the 41 states analyzed contain at least one Type II GLE.

A closer look at two process components. To provide a preliminary look at the way in which the process component GLEs are distributed across grade levels in individual states, Figures 6.3 and 6.4 show both the grade level in which the first GLE for the process appears in each state and each subsequent grade level that contains at least one GLE addressing the process. Figure 6.3 presents this information for Formulate Questions, illustrating several important points. First, not all states explicitly expect K–8 students to formulate questions for the statistical process. Second, the

**Table 6.4. Frequency of Type I and
Type II GLEs by GAISE Process Component**

Process Component	Overall		Type I		Type II	
	Number of GLEs	Number of States	Number of GLEs	Number of States	Number of GLEs	Number of States
Formulate questions	112	29	110	29	13	5
Collect data	423	41	351	41	119	32
Analyze data	968	41	782	41	325	40
Interpret results	867	41	823	41	66	26
Total	1,711	41				

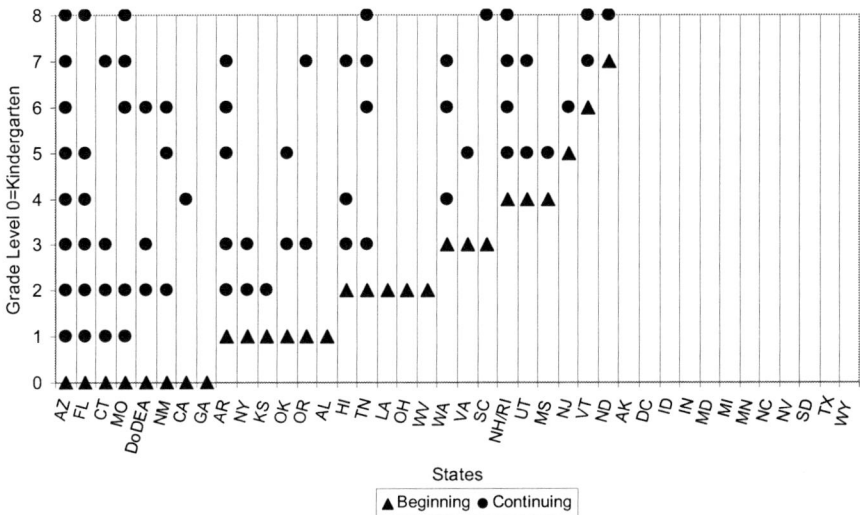

Notes: Not all state documents include standards for all grade levels. New Hampshire and Rhode Island use the same standards document. States are ordered to show trends across the states.

Figure 6.3. Distribution of Formulate questions GLEs by grade and state.

states that contain such a GLE vary greatly in the grade levels in which they expect students to formulate questions. Only one state (Arizona) expects students to formulate questions at every grade level, K–8. The presentation order of the states was chosen to highlight the variation in the grade level at which this process component was introduced.

Figure 6.4 presents the corresponding information for the second process component, Collect Data.[4] It supports the earlier point that many more GLEs address data collection (424 GLEs) than question formulation (112 GLEs). All states address data collection in at least one grade level. Seven states expect students to collect data throughout Grades K–8 and 10 more states expect students to collect data at all but one grade level. The vast majority of states expect students to begin to collect data in either kindergarten, Grade 1, or Grade 2.

Figure 6.3 indicates more variation among states with regard to Formulate Question GLEs than Figure 6.4 does for Collect Data GLEs, both with respect to the grade level at which the state first introduces the process component and the subsequent grade levels at which GLEs are included in the states' standards. More detailed analyses of each process component, both of a qualitative and quantitative nature, will be presented below.

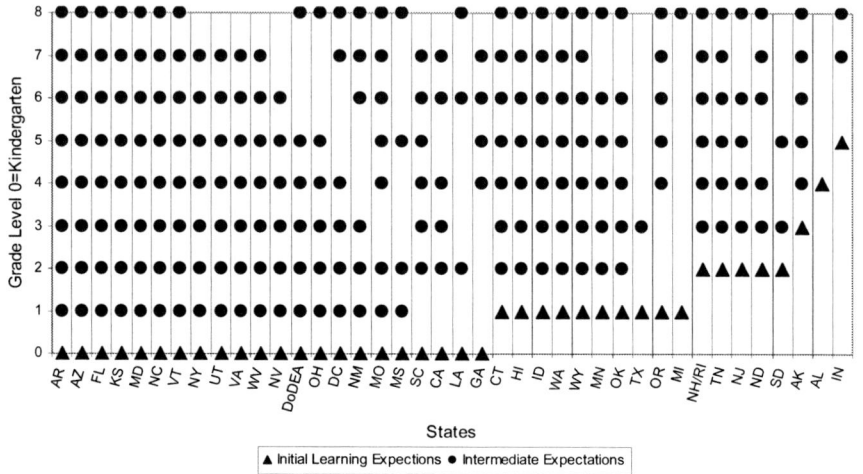

Figure 6.4.   Distribution of Collect data GLEs by grade and state.

Notes: Not all state documents include standards for all grade levels. New Hampshire and Rhode Island use the same standards document. States are ordered to show trends across the states.

GLEs addressing multiple process components. As noted earlier it is common for states to address more than one process component in a single GLE. For example, the following GLE was coded for all four process components:

> *Example 6.2.* Pose questions, collect, record, and interpret data to help answer questions (e.g., Which was the most popular booth at our carnival?). (OK, gr. 3)

In total, 23 GLEs were coded as addressing all four process components and an additional 96 GLEs were coded as addressing three process components. In addition, 41 GLEs, representing 20 states, addressed the statistical process more generally. Example 6.3 exemplifies this sort of broad expectation.

> *Example 6.3.* Design a study that compares two samples, collect data, and select the appropriate representation (e.g., double bar graph, back-to-back stem and leaf plot, parallel box and whisker plots, scatter plot) to compare the sets of data. (HI, gr. 8)

This GLE includes a reference to the overall process of designing a study as well as an emphasis on particular process components. It was coded only for the process components that are mentioned explicitly: Collect Data, Analyze Data, and Interpret Results. This sort of GLE occurs most often in Grades 5–8.

Variation among states in addressing measures of central tendency. In order to illustrate the variation among states with regard to how they address topics across K–8, Tables 6.5, 6.6, and 6.7 present the ways in which three states address measures of central tendency (i.e., mean, median, and mode). These examples are not intended to suggest the right way to address the topic, only to highlight the variation that exists among states. State A (Table 6.5) includes only one GLE that addresses measures of central tendency. This GLE expects students to determine the mean, median and mode, and was therefore coded as Type I. State B (Table 6.6) includes seven GLEs that address measures of central tendency, beginning in Grade 3 and continuing through Grade 8. It expects mode, median, and mean to be introduced in Grades 3, 4, and 5 respectively. This trajectory includes both Type I GLEs, in all Grades 3–8 except Grade 6, and Type II GLEs in all Grades 3–8. State B expects students across Grades 3–8 to be able to both determine and evaluate the measures of central tendency. As in State B, State C (Table 6.7) includes GLEs that address measures of central tendency in Grades 3–8. However, mean, median, and mode are all introduced in Grade 3. In contrast to State A's one GLE and State B's seven GLEs, State C includes 12 GLEs in their sequence. In addition, State C explicitly expects the use of calculators/technology in Grades 4, 5, and 8. The seven GLEs in State C at Grades 3–5 were all coded as Type I, where the five GLEs in Grades 6–8 were coded as both Type I and Type II. This is in contrast to both State A where only Type I was represented and to State B where Types I and II GLEs were included in nearly all Grades 3–8. This comparison of how three states address measures of central tendency serves to illustrate the variation among states with regard to the statistical process. The similarities and differences carry quite different messages to teachers and assessment writers.

Types of data. Twenty-five of the 41 states specify, in at least one of their statistics GLEs, a particular type of data by modifying "data" with a descriptive term. Examples 6.4 and 6.5 are representative.

Example 6.4. Determine which type of graph best represents a given set of *discrete* [italics added] data. (LA, gr. 4)

Table 6.5. State A's Treatment of Measures of Central Tendency

Grade	GLE
7	Determining range, mean, median, or mode.

Table 6.6.   State B's Treatment of Measures of Central Tendency

Grade	GLE
3	Identify the mode of a data set and describe the information it gives about a data set.
4	Identify the median of a set of data and describe what it indicates about the data.
5	Determine and use the range, mean, median and mode, and explain what each does and does not indicate about the set of data.
6	Understand the different information provided by measures of center (mean, mode and median) and measures of spread (range).
7	Analyze a set of data by using and comparing combinations of measures of center (mean, mode, median) and measures of spread (range, quartile, inter-quartile range), and describe how the inclusion or exclusion of outliers affects those measures.
8	Compare two sets of data using measures of center (mean, mode, median) and measures of spread (range, quartiles, interquartile range, percentiles).
	Explain the mean's sensitivity to extremes and its use in comparison with the median and mode.

Table 6.7.   State C's Treatment of Measures of Central Tendency

Grade	GLE
3	Uses concrete materials to determine the mean in a set.
	Identifies the range, median, and mode in a set of numerical data.
4	Identifies the mean, median and mode from a set of data.
	Uses a calculator to determine the range and mean of a set of data.
	Determines appropriate statistical measures for data (range, mean, median, and mode).
5	Uses range and measures of central tendency in real-world situations.
	Uses a calculator to determine the range and mean of a set of data.
6	Finds the range, mean, median, and mode of a set of data.
	Describes real-world data by applying and explaining appropriate procedures for finding measures of central tendency.
7	Applies and analyzes appropriate measures of central tendency (mode, mean, median, range) for a set of data.
8	Determines appropriate measures of central tendency for a given situation or set of data.
	Determines the mean, median, mode, and range of a set of real-world data using appropriate technology.

Example 6.5. Collect and record *categorical* [italics added] data. (MN, gr. 2)

Table 6.8 summarizes the four most commonly contrasted pairs of data types represented in the GLEs and provides both the number of states that explicitly addresses the particular type of data and an example GLE. Categorical and numerical are the types of data most often mentioned in GLEs that address the statistical process. In addition to these common types of data, many other words modify "data" in the GLEs. These words are used to describe a variety of characteristics of data, including the source of the data. We have added emphasis in italics in the eight examples below to highlight the types of data.

Example 6.6. Compare and contrast *survey data* from two groups relative to the same question. (LA, gr. 5)

Example 6.7. Interpret and construct circle graphs from *real-world data*. (MS, gr. 7)

Example 6.8. Identify claims based on *statistical data* and, in simple cases, evaluate the reasonableness of the claims. Design a study to investigate the claim. (IN, gr. 8)

Example 6.9. Given a small ordered data set of *whole number data* points (odd number of points), students will identify the median, mode, and range. (SD, gr. 4)

Example 6.10. Collect and organize *concrete data* using tally mark charts. (LA, gr. K)

Table 6.8.   Four Commonly Contrasted Pairs of Data Types

Data Type	Number of States	Example GLE
Categorical	17	Recognize data as either *categorical or numerical*. (AL, gr. 3)
Numerical	23	
Discrete	4	Differentiate between *discrete and continuous* data and appropriate ways to represent each. (OH, gr. 8)
Continuous	6	
Uni-variate	4	Interpret *one- and two-variable* data graphs to answer questions about a situation. (CA, gr. 4)
Bi-variate	5	
Qualitative	4	Read and interpret *quantitative and qualitative* data. (DoDEA, gr. 5)
Quantitative	4	

Note: We italicized terms for contrasting pairs of data types in the examples above.

Example 6.11. Collect, organize, display, describe, and interpret *simple data* using number lines, pictographs, bar graphs, and frequency tables. (NV, gr. 4)

Example 6.12. Find, use, and interpret measures of center and spread, including mean and interquartile range for *given or derived data.* (OR, gr. 7)

Example 6.13. In response to a teacher- or student-generated question or hypothesis, collects *appropriate data* and makes observations about the data through written or verbal/scribed response. (VT, gr. K)

These examples, along with those in Table 6.8, illustrate the different types of data and the diverse ways that the term "data" is presented in GLEs where students are expected to recognize, differentiate, collect, analyze, and interpret data.

Summary. This section summarized the general findings from our analysis of the 1,711 GLEs in 41 K–8 state standards documents that address at least one of the four process components of the statistical process. The number of GLEs coded for each of the four process components, Formulate Questions ($n = 112$), Collect Data ($n = 423$), Analyze Data ($n = 968$), and Interpret Results ($n = 867$) indicate an emphasis on analyzing data and interpreting results. The number of statistics GLEs per state ranged widely, from 17 to 117 with a median of 32. The total number of GLEs in the 41 states increased steadily across K–8 reaching a maximum in Grade 7.

This section has highlighted both the qualitative and quantitative variation among the states. One example of this variation is the large range (17 to 117) of statistics GLEs across the 41 states. In addition, Figure 6.3 shows the lack of agreement across states regarding if and when K–8 students should be expected to formulate questions for a statistical investigation. Tables 6.5, 6.6, and 6.7 also indicate variation among states, this time regarding the way they address the measures of central tendency in their standards documents. Finally, Table 6.8 illustrates the variation in the types of data targeted in the states' statistics GLEs.

Formulate Questions

According to *PSSM* (NCTM, 2000), all students should be able to "formulate questions that can be addressed with data" by the end of the twelfth grade (p. 47). In addition, the first of the four components of the statistical process presented in the *GAISE Report* (Franklin et al., 2007) is entitled "Formulate Questions," characterized as recognizing and understanding the situation or problem to be studied and formulating questions that can be answered by collecting, analyzing, and interpreting data. With this in mind, we included and analyzed those GLEs that expect the student to formulate a question or state the goal of the statistical investigation. Examples of Formulate Question GLEs are given below.

> *Example 6.14.* Pose questions about personal information, experiences and environment. (CT, gr. K)

> *Example 6.15.* Identify the purpose for *data* collection and collect, organize and display physical objects for describing the results. (AR, gr. 1)

Not all GLEs that mention generating a question were included in this process component. Some GLEs require students to ask questions based on data that is already collected. For example, Grade 1 students in the District of Columbia are expected to "Ask and answer simple questions related to data representations (e.g., Who is the tallest student in the class? What is the favorite fruit of the class?)." Since GLEs like this one involve interpretation of existing data and do not explicitly expect students to start a new statistical investigation, these were coded in the Interpret Results process component, not Formulate Questions.

Surprisingly, for one of the four major statistical process components identified both by *PSSM* and by the *GAISE Report*, only 112 GLEs (about 7% of all statistics GLEs) expect students to formulate a question. These GLEs come from 29 states, which account for approximately 71% of the states in the study. Five states have a single GLE that expects students to formulate a question, while Florida has the maximum number with 11 GLEs.

The Formulate Question GLEs were separated into two categories based on the purpose of the question: those designed to launch or frame an investigation (Launch GLEs) and those that are used to collect data, such as on a survey (Tool Question GLEs). The GLEs were then closely examined to distinguish between Type I and Type II. All of the Launch GLEs expected students to complete the process (i.e., write a question to launch an investigation), and therefore they were all coded as Type I. No Type II GLEs were found among the Launch GLEs. However, some Tool Question GLEs expect students to write the questions for the data collection tool while others expect students to evaluate the questions generated for the data collection tool. Therefore Tool Question GLEs represent both Type I and Type II GLEs. Table 6.9 contains examples of each type of Formulate Question GLE.

**Table 6.9.   Examples of Type I and
Type II Formulate Question GLEs by Category**

Type of Formulate Question GLE	Example GLE	
	Type I	Type II
Launch	Formulate questions, design a study, and evaluate the data to reach a conclusion about characteristics shared by two populations or different characteristics that exist within a population. (DoDEA, gr. 6)	None were found
Tool question	Design a survey question after being given a *topic* and collect, organize, display and describe simple *data* using *frequency tables* or *line plots*, *pic*tographs, and *bar graphs*. (AR, gr. 3)	Explain how the way a question is asked in a survey might influence the results obtained. (NM, gr. 6)

Note: We italicized the text in the Grade 3 GLE from Arkansas to indicate the parts of that GLE that are new in Grade 3.

When it was unclear whether a Formulate Question GLE was a Launch GLE or a Tool Question GLE, such as, "Formulate questions to collect data in contextual situations" (AZ, gr. 4), we used the sentence structure to determine its code. For example, whenever the question was clearly intended to support the collection of data, signaled with a phrase such as, "formulate a question *to* ..." or "formulate a question *for* ...," the GLE was coded as a Tool Question GLE. In contrast, whenever the GLE indicated that formulating the question was only one part of the statistical process, usually indicated with a phrase like, "formulate a question, collect data, *and* ...," then the GLE was categorized as a Launch GLE. In addition, GLEs that signaled that the data collection was intended to answer the question, such as, "Generate questions that can be answered by collecting and analyzing data." (LA, gr. 2), were categorized as Launch GLEs.

Launch GLEs. Of the 112 Formulate Question GLEs, 75 were classified as *Launch GLEs.* All are Type I in that they expect students to formulate a question. They come from 27 states, which represent approximately 66% of the states examined.

While most Launch GLEs intend the question to start a statistical investigation, 20 of the 75 GLEs expect students to formulate a question at the *end* of a statistical investigation in order to start a new investigation. That is, sometimes students are expected to ask a question to initiate an investigation and sometimes to re-launch a subsequent investigation. Therefore, the category was subdivided: the former were labeled Initial Launch GLEs, while the latter were labeled Re-launch GLEs. The Re-launch GLEs only appear in Grades 4 through 8 and are expected by only seven states. Figure 6.5 shows the grade level distribution of both types of Launch GLEs.

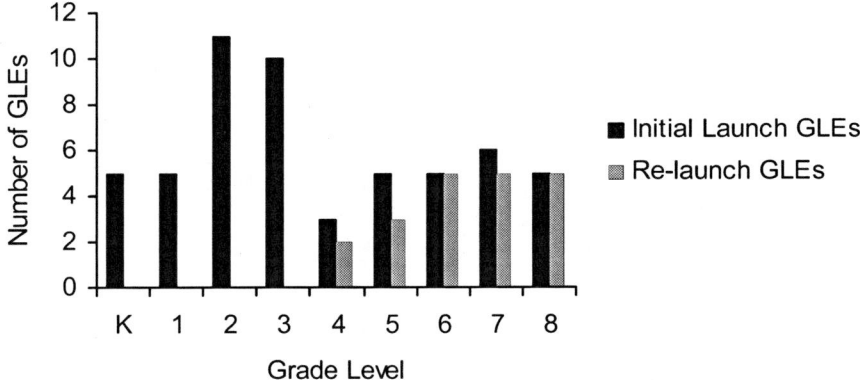

Figure 6.5.   Distribution of Launch GLEs by grade.

Launch GLEs that expect students to formulate a question to start an investigation generally appear in the lower grades, particularly Grades 2 and 3. However, as students enter Grade 4, some states begin to expect students to iterate the statistical process by restarting a statistical investigation from the results of a previous investigation.

Tool Question GLEs. We categorized 39 GLEs out of the 112 Formulate Question GLEs as Tool Question GLEs. Of these, 26 were categorized as strictly Type I, three were categorized as strictly Type II, and ten were categorized as both Type I and Type II. Tool Question GLEs came from 11 states. Of these, Florida and Arizona have the most GLEs with ten and nine, respectively. In fact, these two states represent nearly half the GLEs in this category.

Type II Tool Question GLEs, which require students to go beyond formulating a question and expect the student to recognize if a question is appropriate or to understand how the tool questions affect the collected data, were found in only five states. The grade level distribution of both Type I and Type II Tool Question GLEs is shown in Figure 6.6. While the numbers for Tool Question GLEs are small and slight differences can be misconstrued, the majority of the focus on writing questions for data collection (Type I) exists in Grades 1 through 4, while the Type II Tool Question GLEs are relatively evenly dispersed.

Summary. We were surprised to discover that only 112 (7%) of the 1,711 statistics GLEs expect students to formulate a question. These Formulate Question GLEs came from 29 of the 41 states. Of these 112 GLEs, 75 expect students to formulate a question to launch an investigation, while the rest expect students to formulate or evaluate a question for a data collection tool, such as a survey or interview. We noted that 20 GLEs from

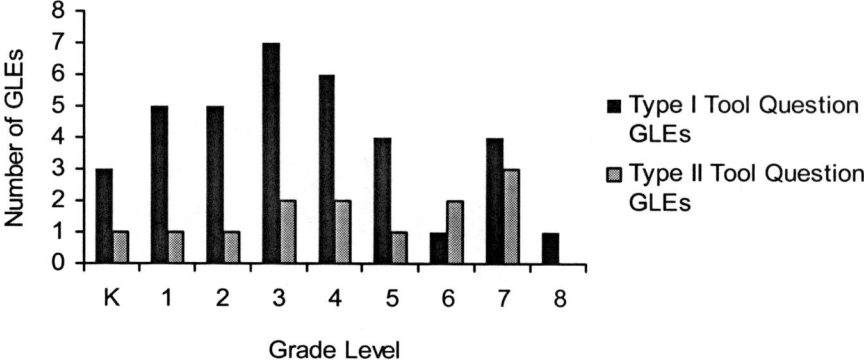

Figure 6.6.   Distribution of Type I and II Tool Question GLEs by grade.

seven states expect students to formulate a question to re-launch the investigative process. Also, most of the GLEs that expect students to initiate a statistical investigation by formulating a question were found in Grades 2 and 3, while those that expect students to formulate a question at the end of an investigation (re-launching a subsequent investigation) were mostly found in Grades 6 through 8.

COLLECT DATA

Once a question is posed, the next stage of the statistical process is to collect data in order to answer that question. Some examples of data collection expectations in the *GAISE Report* include conducting a census, understanding variability, and conducting simple experiments with non-random assignment of treatments (Franklin et al., 2007). Every state in the study has at least one Collect Data GLE, and overall these were found at every grade level, K–8. Of the 1,711 GLEs in this study, 423 (slightly less than 25%) involve data collection. The grade level distribution of Collect Data GLEs is shown in Figure 6.7. The number of Collect Data GLEs generally increases with the grade level. The maximum is found in Grade 6, while the minimum occurs in kindergarten.

The Collect Data GLEs were subdivided into those that expect students to collect data (Type I) and those that expect students to evaluate the effects of the decisions made at this stage (Type II). Type II Collect Data GLEs were further categorized as Type II Evaluating a Characteristic of a Set of Data GLEs and Type II Evaluating a Method of Data Collection GLEs. For

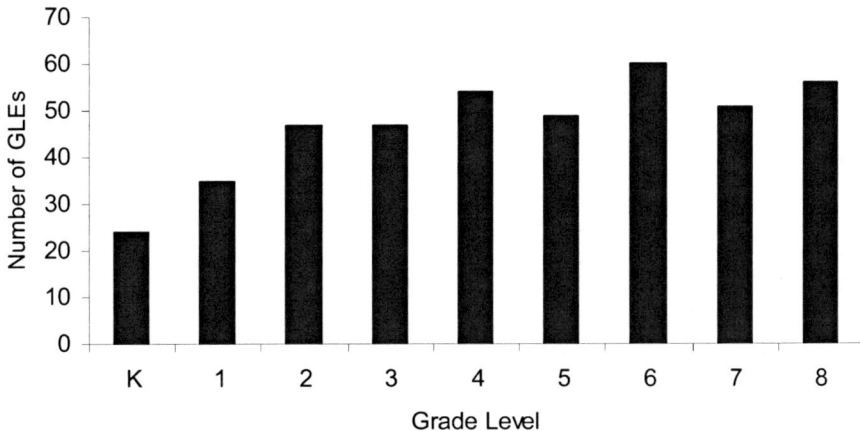

Figure 6.7. Distribution of Collect data GLEs by grade.

Table 6.10. Types and Examples of Collect Data GLEs

Collect Data GLE Type	Number of GLEs	Example GLE
Type I	351	Pose questions about students' selves and their surroundings and gather data by interviewing, surveying, and making observations to answer the questions posed. (NM, gr. 2)
Type II Evaluating a characteristic	28	Distinguish between random and biased samples and identify possible sources of bias in sampling. (OR, gr. 7)
Type II Evaluating a method	48	Selects and justifies the choice of data collection techniques (observations, surveys, or interviews) and sampling techniques (random sampling, samples of convenience, or purposeful sampling) in a given situation. (KS, gr. 7)

brevity, we refer to these categories as Evaluating a Characteristic and Evaluating a Method, respectively, in the balance of the chapter. Examples of each type are given in Table 6.10 above. Of the 423 Collect Data GLEs, 313 specifically contain the word "data," where 253 include the words "collect" or "gather." While "sample" or "sampling" is present in 68 GLEs, "census" does not appear in any of the 1,711 GLEs. One GLE (Example 6.16 below) explicitly expects students to consider a census, although it does not contain the word, "census."

Example 6.16. Compare different samples of a population *with the entire population* [italics added] and determine the appropriateness of using a sample. (NM, gr. 6)

Type I Collect Data GLEs. Of the 423 Collect Data GLEs, 351 of them (approximately 83% of Collect Data GLEs and 21% of all statistics GLEs) explicitly expect students to collect data. The distribution across grade levels for the Type I Collect Data GLEs is shown in Figure 6.8. The number of Type I Collect Data GLEs increases from kindergarten to Grade 2, remains relatively constant until Grade 4, and then generally decreases through Grade 8. In contrast to the overall grade level distribution of all Collect Data GLEs, displayed in Figure 6.7, data collection is emphasized in Grades 2, 3, and 4.

Every state in this study expects students to collect data in at least one grade level. New Mexico has the maximum number of Type I Collect Data GLEs with 20, while Alabama and Michigan have the minimum with only one. Of the 351 GLEs that expect students to collect data, 159 (45%) specify or suggest collection methods. The most common strategy named was experiment, followed by survey, observation, and interview. The distribution across grade levels of these GLEs is shown in Figure 6.9. The results for data collection via a survey, observation or experiment follow a similar trend, and peaks in Grade 4. In contrast, interviews are only mentioned in kindergarten through Grade 4, peaking at Grade 2. Some states also include other forms of data collection, such as, "Collect and record data from a variety of sources (e.g., newspapers, magazines, polls, charts, and surveys)" (NY, gr. 5).

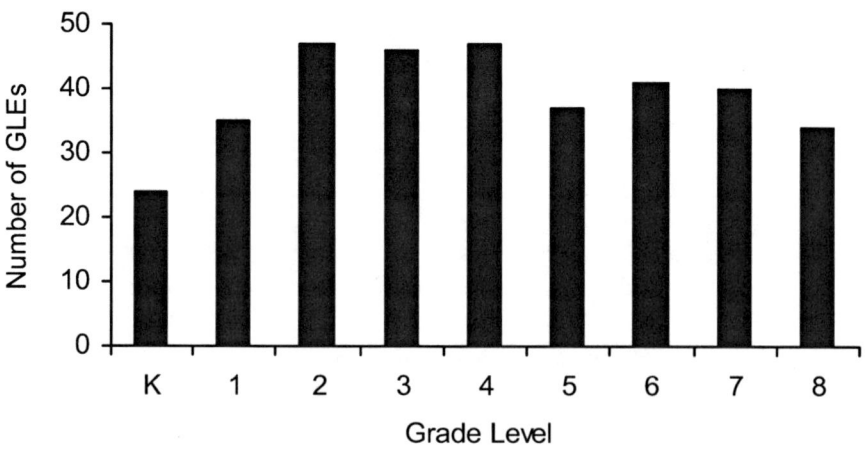

Figure 6.8.   Distribution of Type I Collect data GLEs by grade.

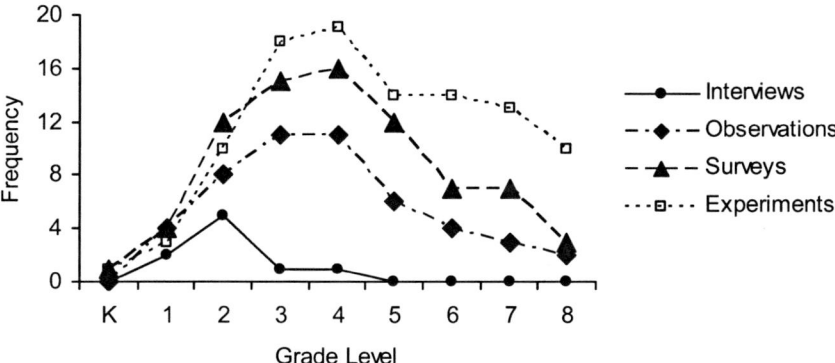

Figure 6.9. Distribution of Collect data GLEs by grade.

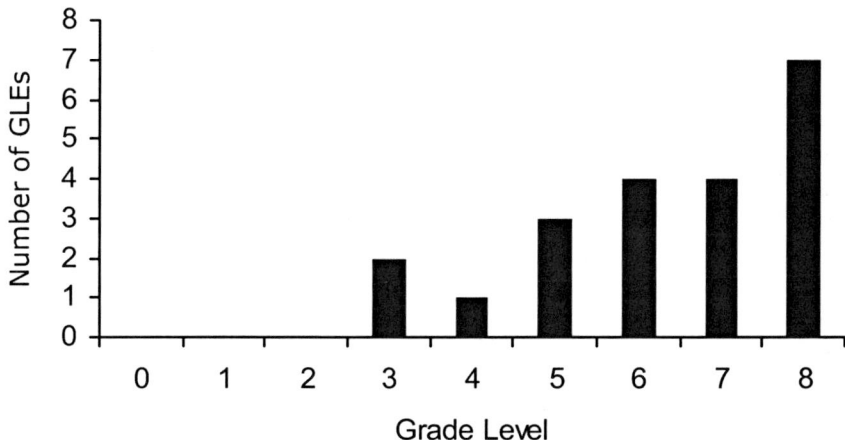

Figure 6.10. Distribution of Collect data GLEs that expect students to collect a sample by grade.

Of the 351 Type I Collect Data GLEs, only 21 explicitly expect students to collect a sample of a population (e.g., "Use data samples of a population and describe the characteristics and limitations of the sample." [NM, gr. 6]). The distribution of these GLEs across grade levels is shown in Figure 6.10 above. As seen in the graph, GLEs that explicitly expect students to collect a sample generally exist in later grades.

Type II Collect Data GLEs. Some Collect Data GLEs expect students to evaluate or understand a data collection method or sample. In total, 119 of the 423 Collect Data GLEs were coded as Type II Collect Data GLEs, and these came from 32 states. Common words found in these GLEs include "explain," "evaluate," "compare," and "describe." As we have explained above, the two most common forms of these Type II GLEs are Evaluating a Characteristic and Evaluating a Method.

We categorized 28 GLEs as Evaluating a Characteristic GLEs and 48 as Evaluating a Method GLEs. Type II Evaluating a Characteristic GLEs occur most frequently in Grade 6, while Type II Evaluating a Method GLEs occur most frequently in Grade 8, as shown in Figure 6.11.

Characteristics of data or a sample that are most often mentioned include random, biased and unbiased, representative (e.g., of the population), and convenience (e.g., data from the classroom). Others require students to identify incorrect data (i.e., error) or missing data. In addition, seven GLEs also include "response" (as in survey response) as a characteristic of data. The distribution of types of characteristics of data or a sample is shown in Figure 6.12.

Summary. Among the 1,711 statistics GLEs, we found 423 that involve data collection or evaluation of either the data collection process or the data itself. Of those, 351 (83%) are Type I GLEs, that expect students to collect data. Type I Collect Data GLEs span kindergarten through Grade 8, with the greatest emphasis in Grades 2 through 4. All 41 states have at least one Type I Collect Data GLE. Also, in spite of the recommendation in the *GAISE Report* (Franklin et al., 2007) for students to take a census, we found only one GLE of the 1,711 that implied that students would need to know about the population. We also noted that some GLEs specify data collection methods, such as experiments, interviews, observations, and surveys. Approximately 28% of the Collect Data GLEs from 28 states

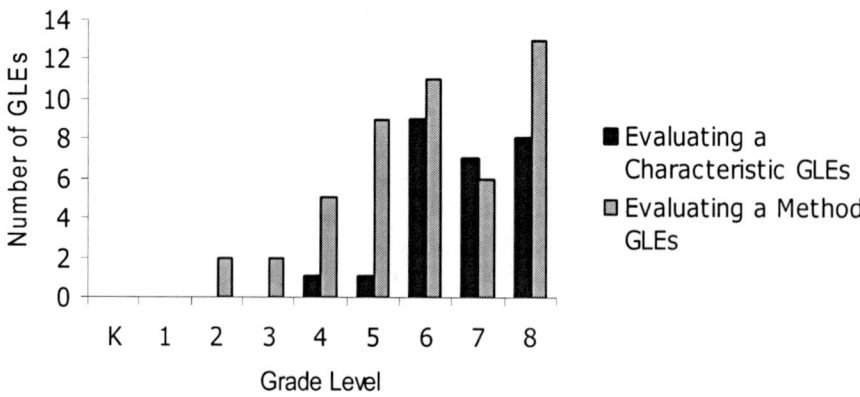

Figure 6.11.   Distribution of Type II Collect data GLEs by grade.

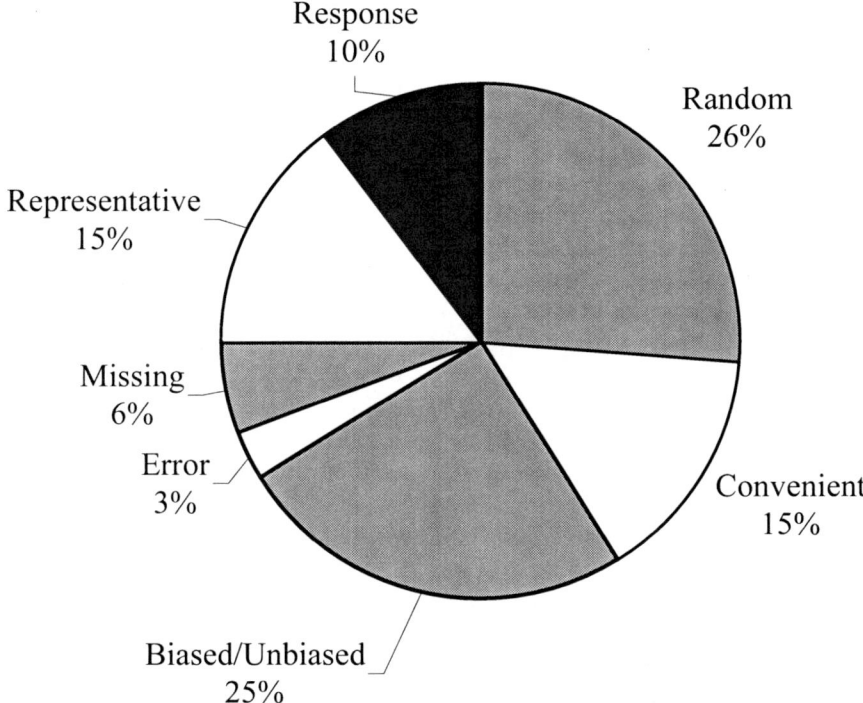

Figure 6.12.   Distribution of characteristics mentioned in Type II Collect data GLEs.

are Type II, which expect students to explain, compare, evaluate, or describe data or data collection methods. The majority are expect students either to evaluate a characteristic of a set of data (28 GLEs) or evaluate a data collection method (48 GLEs). In contrast to Type I Collect Data GLEs, Type II Collect Data GLEs were concentrated in Grades 5 through 8.

Analyze Data

In this section, we report the findings of the third component of the statistical process, Analyze Data. The set of GLEs summarized in this section includes 968 GLEs (57% of all statistics GLEs), making it as the most commonly represented process component in the state standards. Analyze Data GLEs are more than eight times more prevalent than Formulate Question GLEs and twice as prevalent as Collect Data GLEs.

The minimum, median, and maximum number of Analyze Data GLEs across the states are 9, 19, and 61, respectively.

Two categories emerged from our analysis of the Analyze Data GLEs: those addressing Numerical Representations (e.g., mode, range) and those concerning Visual Representations (e.g., picture graphs, scatterplots). Type I and Type II GLEs were found within each category. Type I GLEs expect students to calculate a numerical representation or construct a visual representation. Type II GLEs expect students to understand the meaning of the representation and/or to evaluate in some way the decision to use a specific numerical or visual representation. Of the 968 GLEs coded for this process component, 782 (81%) were categorized as Type I, and 325 (34%) were categorized as Type II. Table 6.11 provides examples of each of these four major types of Analyze Data GLEs.

Many GLEs were coded as both Type I and Type II. Those GLEs typically expect students to be able to both calculate/construct as well as to explain their choice of representation, as illustrated in Example 6.17.

> *Example 6.17.* Determine, with and without appropriate technology, the range, mean, median and mode (whole number data sets) and explain what each indicates about the set of data. (AR, gr. 5)

Type I Numerical Representation GLEs. One hundred and ninety-eight (approximately 20% of the 968 Analyze Data GLEs) were coded as Type I Numerical Representation GLEs. Table 6.12 presents a summary of these GLEs, including an example GLE for each numerical representation and both the total number of GLEs and the number of states that include at least one GLE addressing that particular numerical representation. The Central tendency category is the union of all GLEs in the subsequent three categories (mean, median, and mode) and any GLEs that mention central tendency in general terms (i.e., without reference to a specific measure).

Table 6.11.   Examples of Type I and II Analyze Data GLEs

	Example GLEs	
Analyze Data GLE Type	*Type I*	*Type II*
Numerical	Determine the range, median, mode, and mean for a data set. (HI, gr. 5)	Select the appropriate measure of central tendency or range to describe a set of data and justify the choice for a particular situation. (TX, gr. 8)
Visual	Construct and read line plots and tables. (LA, gr. 2)	Determine the appropriate type of graph to effectively display data. (MD, gr. 5)

The Dispersion category is the union of all GLEs in its subsequent three categories (range, quartiles, and outliers) and any GLEs that mention dispersion generally (i.e., with no mention of a specific measure).

Table 6.12 presents several interesting results. First, all states address at least one measure of central tendency and one measure of dispersion in the standards documents. Second, a similar number of GLEs address central tendency and dispersion (159 and 137 respectively). Third, it is common for a single GLE to address several numerical representations. For example, Virginia includes the following GLE in the Grade 5: "The student will find the mean, median, mode, and range of a set of data." Finally, the vast majority of the states analyzed (at least 95%) address mean, median, mode, and range at least once in their standards document. In contrast, a much smaller number of states address quartiles or outliers in their GLEs (46% and 39%, respectively).

Next, we present the distribution of these GLEs across grade levels. Figure 6.13 summarizes the distribution of the GLEs addressing measures of central tendency (mean, median, and mode).[5] Overall, the trends

Table 6.12.   Numerical Representations in Type I Analyze Data GLEs

Numerical Representation	Example GLE	Number of GLEs	Number of States
Central tendency	Model and then compute measures of central tendency including mean, median, and mode. (NV, gr. 5)	159	41
Mean	Calculate the mean for a given set of data and use to describe a set of data (NY, gr. 5)	106	41
Median	Identify the median of a data set and describe what it indicates about the data set. (DoDEA, gr. 4)	111	40
Mode	Students find and interpret mode for data sets in a problem-solving setting appropriate to grade level. Students communicate their findings. (WY, gr. 5)	118	39
Dispersion	Determines and explains the range, quartiles, and interquartile range for a rational number data set. (KS, gr. 8)	137	41
Range & Minimum/Maximum	Find the range of a set of data using whole numbers. (ID, gr. 5)	114	39
Quartiles & Interquartile range	Compute, describe, and interpret the interquartile range. (SC, gr. 7)	27	19
Outliers	Find the median and possible outliers. (MN, gr. 6)	21	16

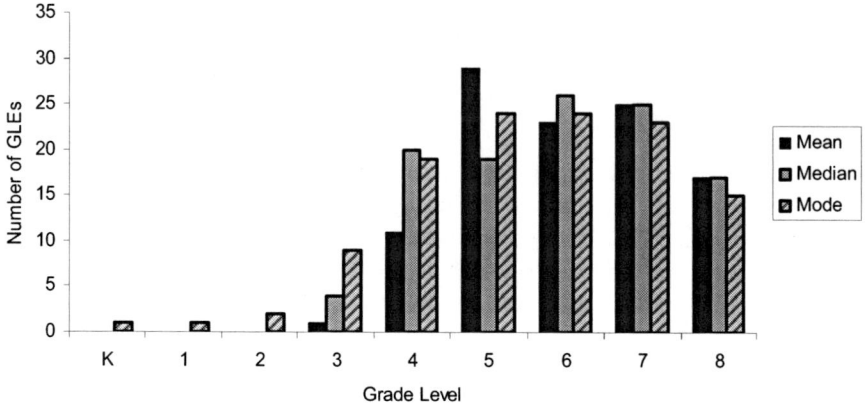

Figure 6.13.   Number of GLEs addressing three measures of central tendency by grade.

across the grade levels for mean, median, and mode are similar. Generally speaking, the focus on these measures occurs in Grades 5–7 with slightly less emphasis in Grades 4 and 8. The number of GLEs addressing mean, median, and mode reach their peaks in Grades 5 and 6. Some minor variations among the representations are indicated. For example, mode is present in kindergarten and Grades 1 and 2 (albeit in small numbers) whereas mean and median do not appear in any of the states analyzed until Grade 3. The largest concentration of any given measure is the mean in Grade 5.

The distribution of GLEs dealing with measures of dispersion (range, quartiles, and outliers) is presented in Figure 6.14. This distribution is much different from the one presented in Figure 6.13, primarily due to the fact that quartiles and outliers receive much less attention than range and the measures of central tendency. The range is present beginning in Grade 1 and increases across the grades until it decreases from Grade 7 to 8. It also experiences a slight dip in Grade 6. The trend indicated for range is similar to those for the measures of central tendency in Figure 6.13. Outliers are mentioned in a few states in Grades 4–6, but the majority occurs in Grades 7 and 8. This middle school focus is also found in the distribution for quartiles whose emphasis is greatest in Grades 7 and 8.

Several other numerical representations (clusters and percentiles) are included in the states' standards, but infrequently, as illustrated in Examples 6.18 and 6.19.

Example 6.18. Identify and distinguish between *clusters* [italics added] and outliers of a data set. (UT, gr. 4)

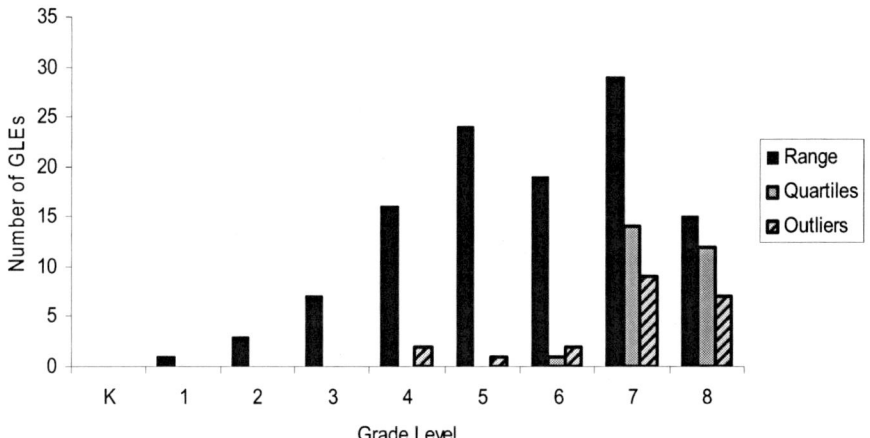

Figure 6.14.   Number of GLEs addressing three measures of dispersion by grade.

Example 6.19. Compare two sets of data using measures of center (mean, mode, median) and measures of spread (range, quartiles, interquartile range, *percentiles* [italics added]). (OH, gr. 8)

Type II Numerical Representation GLEs. One hundred and twenty-one GLEs from 35 states (approximately 13% of the 968 Analyze Data GLEs) were coded as Type II Numerical Representation GLEs. These fall into several subcategories, which are summarized in Table 6.13, with an example GLE and the number of GLEs in each subcategory. The most common Type II GLEs in this process are those in which students are expected to select the appropriate numerical representation in a particular situation and to explain the meaning of the numerical representation. Figure 6.15 provides a picture of the distribution of Type II Numerical Representation GLEs across the grades levels. There are no Type II Numerical Representation GLEs in kindergarten, Grades 1, or 2. The overall trend is an increase from Grades 3 to 8 with the most dramatic increase between Grades 6 and 7. It is interesting to note that nearly 63% occur in Grades 7 and 8. Also of interest is the difference between the number of GLEs and states in Grades 7 and 8. While both Grades 7 and 8 have 38 GLEs, only 24 and 26 states respectively are represented. On the extremes of the range, six states do not include any Type II Numerical Representation GLEs while Washington includes 17.

Type I Visual Representation GLEs. We turn now to a discussion of the Type I Visual Representation GLEs that expect students to construct a variety of graphs and tables. A total of 503 GLEs (52% of all Analyze Data

Table 6.13.   Type II Numerical Representation GLEs

Subcategory	Number of GLEs	Example GLE
Selecting appropriate numerical representations	39	Determining or justifying a choice of range, mean, median, or mode as the best representation of data for a practical situation. (AK, gr. 8)
Explaining the meaning of numerical representations	37	The student will describe the mean, median, and mode as measures of central tendency, describe the range, and determine their meaning for a set of data. (VA, gr. 6)
Determining the effect of additional data on numerical representations (e.g., outliers)	28	Determine how additional values, including outliers, affect mean, median, mode, or range. (MS, gr. 7)
Comparing numerical representations	18	Calculate and compare the measures of central tendency (i.e., mean, median, mode) and spread (i.e., range). (ND, gr. 8)
Recognizing misleading numerical representations	8	Identify and explain misleading statistics and graphs. (NY, gr. 7)

Note: Some GLEs are included in more than one subcategory.

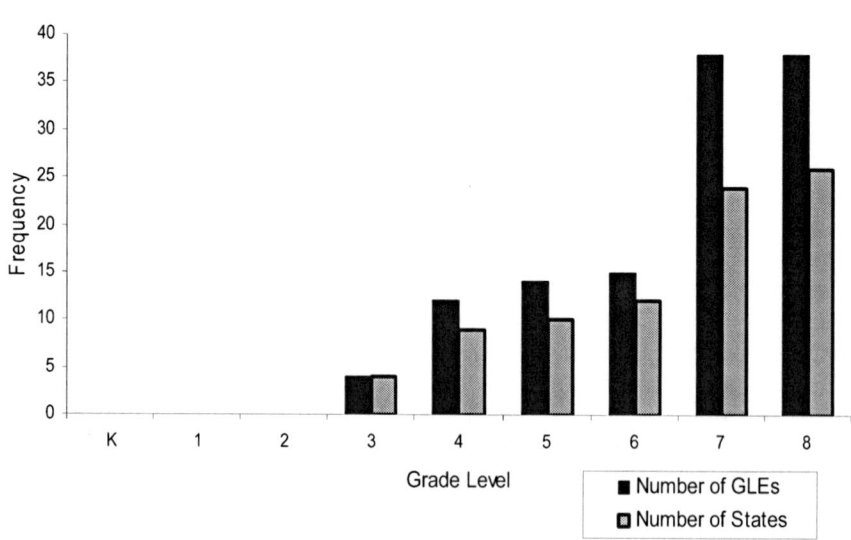

Figure 6.15.   Distribution of Type II Numerical representation GLEs by grade and state.

GLEs) ask students to represent data with visual representations. This kind of expectation is 2.5 times more frequently expressed than Type I Numerical Representations GLEs. Two examples of Type I Visual Representation GLEs are given below.

Example 6.20. Organize and display data in a variety of ways including frequency tables, histograms, and stem-and-leaf plots. (SC, gr. 6)

Example 6.21. Representing the data with the most appropriate graph, including box-and-whisker plot, circle graph, and scatterplot. (AL, gr. 8)

More than 30 different types of visual representations are mentioned in the state standards documents; twelve of which are mentioned in at least 30 GLEs. Table 6.14 presents the distribution of these twelve representations across grade levels indicating the number of GLEs at each grade. The most common visual representations are pictographs, bar graphs, and charts/tables. The use of pictographs is concentrated in Grades K–3, whereas bar graphs and charts/tables appear most often in Grades 1–5 and 2–6, respectively. Five representations (circle graphs, stem-and-leaf plots, histograms, box-and-whisker plots, and scatterplots) are mentioned primarily in Grades 7 and 8. Other visual representations mentioned less

Table 6.14. Distribution of Visual Representations by Grade

Visual representation	Total	K	1	2	3	4	5	6	7	8
Pictograph	137	25	30	29	21	16	8	3	2	3
Tally	54	6	15	16	9	5	2	1	0	0
Venn diagram	37	1	3	11	5	5	3	3	3	3
Bar graph	170	4	20	23	30	30	20	19	14	10
Chart/Table	184	11	16	27	26	29	23	25	14	13
Line plot	55	0	1	2	10	13	12	6	8	3
Line graph	95	0	0	2	2	19	22	22	19	9
Circle graph	67	0	0	0	1	6	14	13	22	11
Stem-and-leaf plot	55	0	0	0	0	0	10	16	21	8
Histogram	32	0	0	0	0	0	3	7	13	9
Box-and-whisker plot	36	0	0	0	0	0	0	1	17	18
Scatterplot	49	0	0	0	0	0	1	6	16	26

Note: The representations are ordered to show trends across grades. Italicized cell entries indicate grades where particular representations are prevalent (i.e., the modal grade and any other grade where the frequency is at least two-thirds of the modal frequency).

frequently include diagrams, lists, frequency distributions, glyphs, number lines, real graphs, matrices, models, timelines, tree diagrams, coordinate graphs, concrete graphs, spreadsheets, data plots, grids, and student-invented representations.

Type II Visual Representation GLEs. Two hundred and twenty-two GLEs from 37 states (approximately 23% of all Analyze Data GLEs) were coded as Type II Visual Representation GLEs. Three closely related subcategories emerged from these GLEs: (a) Comparing visual representations, (b) Selecting the most appropriate visual display for a given set of data (this subcategory assumes the ability to compare visual representations), and (c) Recognizing misuses of visual representations (this subcategory assumes knowledge of both of the previous categories). Table 6.15 provides a summary of these categories, with their total number and an example GLE. The number of GLEs indicates that students are more typically expected to compare representations than to evaluate their use. Figure 6.16 provides an illustration of the distribution of these GLEs across grade levels. Although the overall trend is one of increase across grade levels, the gap between the number of states and the number of GLEs is most pronounced in the upper elementary and middle grades. This pattern, which was mentioned earlier in reference to Type II Numerical Representation GLEs, suggests a wide range in the number of Type II GLEs across states. This is in fact the case. Four states do not include a single Type II Visual Representation GLE, whereas 20 GLEs from the New Mexico standards document were coded as this type.

Summary. Analyze Data GLEs either concerned numerical representations (e.g., median, outlier) or visual representations (e.g., line plot, bar graph). The number of GLEs in this process component is greater than

Table 6.15.   Type II Visual Representation GLEs

Subcategory	Number of GLEs	Example GLE
Comparing visual representations	119	Compare and contrast different representations of the same data; discuss the effectiveness of each representation. (NC, gr. 5)
Recognizing misuse of visual representations	64	Recognize practices of collecting and displaying data that may bias the presentation or analysis. (DC, gr. 8)
Selecting appropriate visual representations	55	Analyze, interpret, and display data in appropriate bar, line, and circle graphs and stem-and-leaf plots and justify the choice of display. (IN, gr. 7)

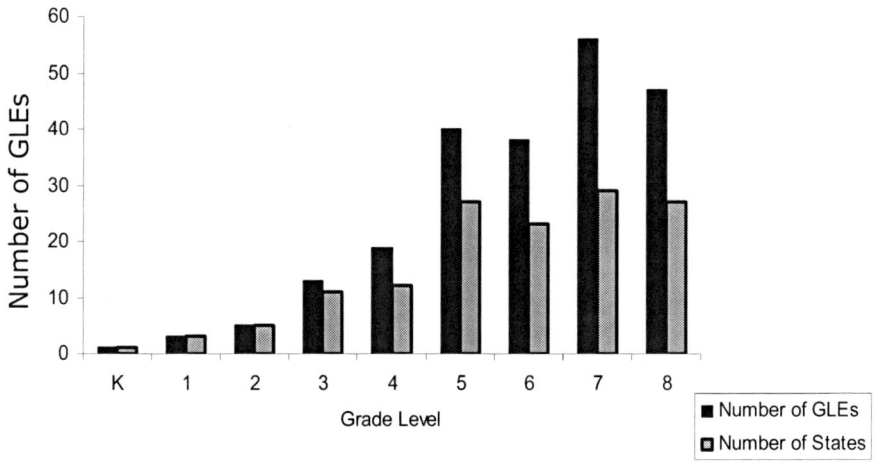

Figure 6.16.   Distribution of Type II Visual representation GLEs by grade.

any other (968 GLEs compared to 112, 423, and 867 for Formulate Questions, Collect Data, and Interpret Results respectively). Both numerical and visual representations are addressed in Type I and Type II GLEs. However, as in the other processes, Type II GLEs are less common than Type I and tend to appear in upper elementary and middle school. Nearly all states include Type I Numerical Representation GLEs that address mean, median, mode, and range, while outliers and quartiles are present much less often. Taken as a whole, the Type I Visual Representation GLEs expect students to construct more than 30 different visual representations. The three most common are charts/tables, bar graphs and pictographs. Type II Analyze Data GLEs most commonly expect students to understand, compare, and select appropriate representations for a particular situation. Overall, GLEs addressing visual representations were 2.5 times more common than those addressing numerical representations.

Interpret Results

The fourth process component in the *GAISE Report* is Interpret Results, which involves (a) interpreting a completed analysis and (b) relating that interpretation to the original question (Franklin et al., 2007). This final component is central to the argument of the importance of statistics and statistics education. Much of the statistical information in today's society is prepared and packaged up to this point. It is up to the individual to be a competent consumer of that information and evaluate numerical and visual representations by either making one's own conclusions, or assessing the validity of another person's existing conclusions.

Of all 1,711 statistics GLEs, 867 (51%) were coded as Interpret Results. All 41 states were represented; the minimum, median, and maximum number of Interpret Results GLEs across the states are 7, 18, and 55, respectively. When the 867 GLEs were considered by grade level, the minimum number of GLEs (49) occurs in kindergarten and the maximum (130) in Grade 8.

As with the other process components, we distinguished between Type I and Type II Interpret Results GLEs. Type I GLEs include those that involve interpreting, comparing, and making conclusions, claims, inferences, and generalizations from data, numerical representations, and visual representations. In contrast, Type II GLEs include those that expect students to evaluate and reflect on the outcomes of Type I Interpret Results GLEs, as well as to understand the uses and misuses of statistics. Table 6.16 summarizes the categories and most common subcategories of Type I and Type II Interpret Results GLEs. The remainder of this section will provide the frequency, examples, and further discussion of each type.

Type I General Interpret Results GLEs. The largest number of Interpret Results GLEs (380, or 44% of the 867 Interpret Results GLEs) is general in nature and therefore labeled General Interpret Results GLEs. All of the GLEs in this category are Type I. They require students to make

Table 6.16.   Categories of Interpret Results GLEs

Type	Category	Subcategory
Type I	General	Interpret from data
		Interpret from visual representation
		Interpret from numerical representations
	Compare	Compare data sets
		Compare information in visual representations
		Compare information in numerical representations
	Outcome	Inference
		Conclusions
		Predictions
Type II	Appropriate use and misuse of statistics	None
	Evaluating conclusions	

Table 6.17.   Type I General Interpret Results GLEs

Subcategory	Number of GLEs	Example GLE
Interpret from data	50	Pose questions, collect, record, and interpret data to help answer questions (e.g., Which was the most popular booth at our carnival?). (OK, gr. 3)
Interpret from visual representations	298	The student will read, construct, and interpret a simple picture and bar graph. (VA, gr. 2)
Interpret from numerical representations	36	Interpret data using mean, median, mode, and range. (WV, gr. 6)

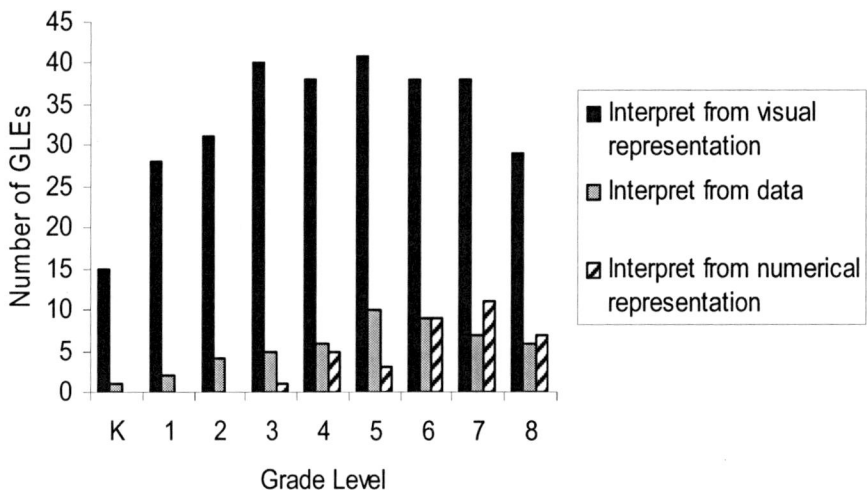

Figure 6.17.   Distribution of Type I Interpret results GLEs by grade.

interpretations (a) from data, (b) visual representations, and/or (c) numerical representations. Table 6.17 above includes the number of General Interpret Results GLEs and an example GLE for each subcategory. Figure 6.17 above further illustrates the frequency of each variety, highlighting the trend across grades and showing the large emphasis placed on interpreting from visual representations at all grade levels.

Type I Compare Interpret Results GLEs. Ninety-nine GLEs from 30 states (11% of the Interpret Results GLEs) focus on comparison. Unlike in previous process components, comparing is categorized here as Type I. This change in classification is due to a change in what information is being compared. In Analyze Data, for instance, multiple visual or numerical representations of data are compared and a choice or evaluation is made about the best representation. However, Compare Interpret Results GLEs involve comparison within the data itself, not an evaluation of an aspect of the statistical process.

Type I Compare Interpret Results GLEs were subcategorized as Comparing data sets, Comparing information in visual representations, and Comparing numerical representations. Table 6.18 includes the number of GLEs in each subcategory and an example of each. As was the case with the General Interpret Results GLEs, the most common form of comparison is based on visual representations. However, unlike the General Interpret Results GLEs, using visual representations was not the most common in all grades. Figure 6.18 indicates that while it is the most typical in Grades K–4, Grades 5–8 become increasingly diverse with respect to the representations of information to be compared. By Grade 8 there are the same number of GLEs from each subcategory.

Type I Outcome Interpret Results GLEs. The last variety of Type I Interpret Results GLEs involves making conclusions, claims, arguments, inferences, generalizations, and predictions. These 245 GLEs from 38 states (28% of all Interpret Results GLEs) were coded as Outcome Interpret Results GLEs. Of these, 53 require students to justify their statements, as shown in Example 6.22.

Example 6.22. Support a conclusion or prediction orally and in writing, using information in a table or graph. (OH, gr. 3)

Fifty of the 53 GLEs that call for justification expect students to both make statements (e.g., draw a conclusion or make an inference) and justify those statements. Example 6.23, where students are expected to both "formulate" conclusions and "justify" those conclusions, is a typical GLE of this sort.

Table 6.18.   Summary of Compare Interpret Results GLEs

Subcategory	Number of GLEs	Example GLE
Compare data sets	33	Compare related data sets. (MO, gr. 5)
Compare information in visual representations	46	Interprets and compares information from picto- and bar graphs including graphs from content-area materials and periodicals. (FL, gr. 3)
Compare information in numerical representations	13	Compare two related sets of data using measures of center (mean, median, and mode) and spread (range) (OR, gr. 5)

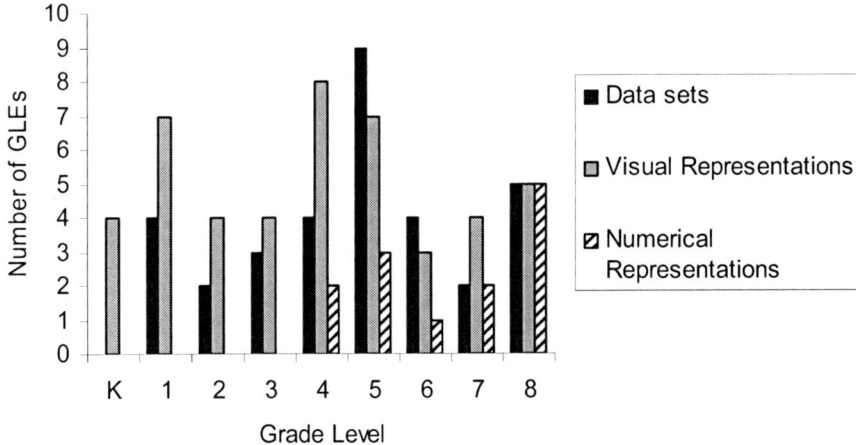

Figure 6.18.   Distribution of Type I Compare Interpret results GLEs by grade.

Example 6.23. Interprets a given representation (line plots, tables, bar graphs, pictographs, or circle graphs) to answer questions related to the data, to analyze the data to formulate or justify conclusions, to make predictions, or to solve problems. (NH/RI, gr. 4)

Since a variety of words in Outcome Interpret Results GLEs reference particular types of statements, the frequency of these words was analyzed. The words included in Table 6.16, inference ($n = 48$), conclusion ($n = 146$), and prediction ($n = 174$), were the most common, both in total number and in the number of grade levels in which they appear. Along with "inference," "conclusion," and "prediction," we also found "generalization," "claim," and "argument." Table 6.19 indicates that the number of Outcome Interpret Results GLEs is most concentrated in the upper grades.

These different types of statements (e.g., generalizations, claims, etc.) were all categorized together even though each has a different and perhaps specific meaning in statistics, because the meanings of each were at times unclear from the context. Examples 6.24 and 6.25 illustrate this ambiguity.

Example 6.24. Use data analysis to make reasonable *inferences/predictions* [italics added] and to develop convincing arguments from data described in a variety of formats (e.g. bar graphs, Venn diagrams, charts, tables, line graphs, and pictographs). (NM, gr. 4)

**Table 6.19.   Distribution of
Outcome Interpret Results Words by Grade**

Word	Total	K	1	2	3	4	5	6	7	8
Generalization	5	1	0	0	1	1	1	0	0	1
Claim	8	0	0	0	0	0	0	4	1	3
Argument	21	0	0	0	0	2	2	1	6	10
Inference	48	0	0	1	6	4	8	9	9	11
Prediction	174	4	5	11	22	25	29	19	27	32
Conclusion	146	5	8	18	18	19	20	19	16	23

Note: The words are ordered to show trends across grades. Italicized cell entries indicate the grades where these words are prevalent (i.e., the modal grade and any other grade where the frequency is at least two-thirds of the modal frequency). Due to the small number of instances of "generalization" at any one grade level, we added no emphasis.

Example 6.25. Formulate *inferences* [italics added] (draw *conclusions* [italics added]) and make educated guesses (conjectures) about a situation based on information gained from data. (DC, gr. 2)

The authors of these GLEs appear to treat conclusions, predictions, and inferences as interchangeable terms with the same meaning. However, an inference refers to an aspect of a population that is statistically valid from the data, while a conclusion or prediction is not as specific in the statistical sense. Because of this ambiguity among the types of statements, what exactly is expected in these GLEs is difficult to determine.

Type II Interpret Results GLEs. GLEs that expect students to evaluate and reflect on the outcomes of Type I GLEs, as well as recognize the uses and misuses of statistics were categorized as Type II Interpret Results GLEs. Of the 867 Interpret Results GLEs, 67 (8%) were categorized as Type II. Two subcategories emerged from our analysis of these GLEs: Appropriate use and misuse of statistics and Evaluating a conclusion. Table 6.20 present the frequencies and examples of each subcategory. The distribution of Type II Interpret Results GLEs across grade levels (see Figure 6.19) is heavily concentrated in Grades 7 and 8. In fact, 61% of Type II Interpret Results GLEs are in these two grades. New Mexico has the maximum number of GLEs ($n = 12$) while 15 states do not have any Type II Interpret Results GLEs.

Summary. Within this process component, Type I GLEs were categorized as General Interpret Results ($n = 380$), Compare Interpret Results ($n = 99$), and Outcome Interpret Results ($n = 245$), while Type II GLEs ($n = 67$) were categorized as Appropriate use and misuse of statistics ($n = 36$) and Evaluating conclusions ($n = 32$). There was an emphasis on visual

Table 6.20.   Type II Interpret Results GLEs

Subcategory	Number of GLEs	Example GLE
Appropriate use and misuse of statistics	36	Understand and reason about the use and misuse of statistics in our society. (WV, gr. 4)
Evaluating a conclusion	32	Develop and evaluate inferences and predictions that are based on data. (TN, gr. 6)

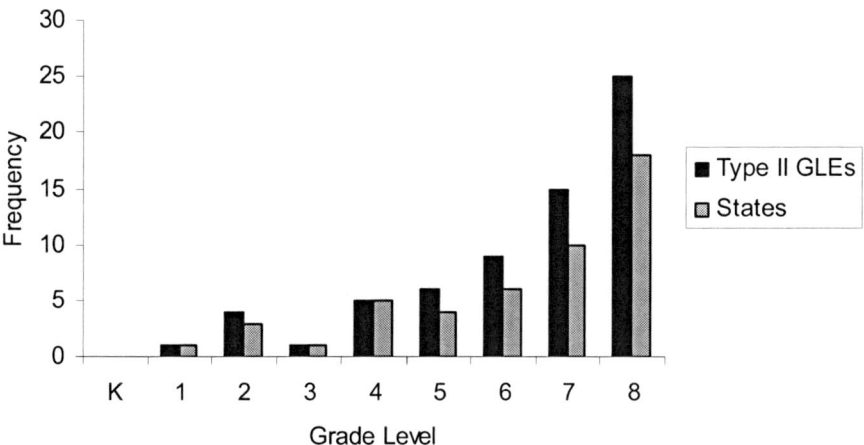

Figure 6.19.   Distribution of Type II Interpret results GLEs by grade and state.

representations in both the General Interpret Results and Compare Interpret Results categories. In these same two categories, interpreting from data ($n = 50$ and 33 GLEs, respectively) was more prevalent than interpreting from numerical representations ($n = 36$ and 13 GLEs, respectively). Finally, similar to the previous process components, Type II GLEs increased in number with increase in grade level.

DISCUSSION

We set out to determine what states expect students to know and be able to do with regard to the statistical process in kindergarten through Grade 8. We used the *GAISE Report* (Franklin et al., 2007) as a framework for our analysis, which enabled us to categorize our data into four process components: Formulate Questions, Collect Data, Analyze Data, and Interpret Results.

In our examination of standards documents from 41 states, we found 1,711 K–8 GLEs that concerned statistical content. An overwhelming majority of these (approximately 87%) were coded in either the Analyze Data or Interpret Results process components or both. Only 351 GLEs (approximately 21%) expect students to collect data, and only 112 (approximately 10%) expect students to formulate a question that can be answered by collecting data.

Another interesting result was that each process component contains some expectation that students to go beyond the procedures associated with statistics, thinking that we have characterized as Type II. Of the 1,711 GLEs analyzed in this study, 475 were classified as Type II. Of these, 80% were found in Grades 5 through 8. The frequency of Type II GLEs increases from kindergarten (4 Type II GLEs) to Grade 8 (113 Type II GLEs). This distribution is shown in Figure 6.20. We found Type II GLEs in 40 of the 41 states, with a median of 8 GLEs per state and a mean of approximately 12 GLEs per state. The state of Washington has the greatest number of Type II GLEs ($n = 59$), followed by New Mexico ($n = 46$).

Table 6.21 shows the number and percentage of the Type II GLEs in each process component. The Collect Data and Analyze Data components have a relatively high proportion of Type II GLEs compared to the Formulate Questions and Interpret Results components. When taken together, Figure 6.20 and Table 6.21 indicate two critical aspects of the distribution of Type II GLEs. First, Type II GLEs are strikingly more common in the middle grades than in early elementary grades. Second, Type II GLEs are much less frequent than Type I GLEs, particularly for the Formulate Question and Interpret Results process components. The evaluation nature of

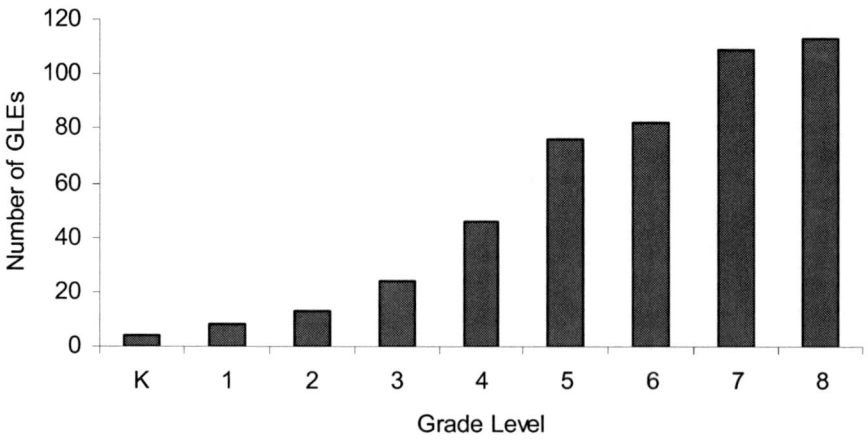

Figure 6.20.   Distribution of Type II GLEs by grade.

Table 6.21. Frequency and Percentage of Type II GLEs by Process Component

Process Component	Formulate Questions	Collect Data	Analyze Data	Interpret Results	Total
Number of Type II GLEs	13	119	325	66	475
Total number of GLEs	112	423	968	867	1,711
Percentage of Type II GLEs	12%	28%	34%	8%	28%

Note: Some GLEs were coded as Type II in more than one process component.

Type II GLEs is essential in all grade levels and all process components in order to prepare individuals to be a competent consumer of statistical information.

One concern that emerged during our analysis was the multiplicity of meanings for many key terms used in the statistics GLEs. The use of the words analyze and interpret were particularly confusing. For example, consider the different uses of "analyze" in each of the GLEs below (Examples 6.26, 6.27, and 6.28).

Example 6.26. Uses technology, such as graphing calculators and computer spreadsheets, to *analyze* [italics added] data and create graphs. (FL, gr. 7)

Example 6.27. Analyze [italics added] data displays and explain why the way in which the question was asked might have influenced the results obtained and why the way in which the results were displayed might have influenced the conclusions reached. (CA, gr. 6)

Example 6.28. The student will read and interpret data represented in line plots, bar graphs, and picture graphs and write a sentence *analyzing* [italics added] the data. (VA, gr. 3)

In the first example, *analyze* may mean performing calculations (such as finding a mean) to summarize the data. However, in the second, the student is expected to examine graphical summaries and make statements that are more interpretive in nature. Finally, the third example uses "analyzing" in a way that suggests drawing a conclusion. Such variation in the use of statistical vocabulary may be problematic for teachers as they try to make sense of these standards.

The four process components of the *GAISE Report* were useful for our analysis. For example, the *GAISE Report* places a heavy emphasis on the need for students to recognize and understand variability. At an introductory level, it expects students to understand and explain "outliers, clusters, and gaps students observe in graphical representations of the data" (Franklin et al., 2007 p. 33) as well as to use the range to analyze the spread of data. During our analysis, we found 137 GLEs from 39 states that expect students to analyze the dispersion of data in general, but were surprised to find that less than 3% of the total involved outliers, clusters, or gaps. Since the *GAISE Report* was developed to orient K–12 statistics education, and since we only analyzed the K–8 GLEs, this difference in grade level focus could account for some of the discrepancy. However, we are still concerned that the lack of emphasis on variability found in the K–8 standards may not prepare students for a more advanced treatment of variability (e.g. standard deviation) in Grades 9–12.

Another discrepancy between the *GAISE Report* and the state standards involves understanding the difference between a census and a sample. For example, when students are introduced to the Collect Data process component, the *GAISE Report* recommends that students "conduct a census of the classroom," while later in the development students should, "address questions involving a group larger than their classroom and begin to recognize the distinction among a population, a census, and a sample" (Franklin et al., 2007, p. 37). However, out of the 1,711 GLEs included in this study, we found only one GLE that requires students to take a census, and no GLE that contains the word "census."

Finally, some unanswered questions remain. While there are 1,711 GLEs from 41 states that addressed statistics, their placement at the end of most standards documents may be a concern. What message does this placement send to teachers and curriculum developers? What is the alignment between these GLEs and state-level standardized assessments? Are the students being assessed on Type II statistics GLEs? And, if so, what do those assessments ask?

Statistics has come to play an increasingly important role in the lives of young people and adults alike (Franklin et al., 2007). As Konold and Higgins (2003) argue, "For those who have traditionally been left out of the political process, probably no skill is more important to acquire in the battle for equity than statistical literacy" (p. 193). To participate fully in society, students need to be able to understand and generate complex statistical representations and recognize when statistical inferences presented by others are valid. While all 41 states analyzed in this study expect basic statistical knowledge and ability, particularly in data analysis, there is great variability among expectations for formulating a question and data collection. This variability is both qualitative and quantitative in nature. In addition, there is also disagreement among states on the importance of evaluative expectations, which often require a deeper understanding of the statistical process. In the future, these differences may matter.

NOTES

1. While the *GAISE Report* was endorsed in 2005, it was not published until 2007.
2. We used only the descriptors corresponding to the process components from the *GAISE Report* since much of the detailed framework did not describe the data that we found in the state standards documents. However, we did use some of the recommendations from GAISE in the framing of our conclusion.
3. We interpreted "use these methods" as including graphical and numerical methods (e.g., calculating the range, constructing a bar graph) based on the examples provided in the *GAISE Report* (Franklin et al., 2007, p. 18).
4. We have not included the corresponding figures for Analyze Data and Interpret Results since nearly every state includes at least one GLE at each grade level K–8 in these two process components.
5. We do not include a corresponding figure comparing the number of states addressing the measures of central tendency because their individual patterns are nearly identical to Figure 6.13.

CHAPTER 7

AN ANALYSIS OF K–8 PROBABILITY STANDARDS

Shannon Dingman and James E. Tarr

Until recently, the study of probability and statistics in the United States was largely restricted to the postsecondary level (Konold & Pollatsek, 2002; Tarr & Shaughnessy, 2007). However, during the past 2 decades, this topic has become an essential component of the school mathematics curriculum with advancements in technology, modern methods of data analysis, and the ubiquity of data in the information age (Franklin et al., 2007). In response to recommendations of the National Council of Teachers of Mathematics' *Curriculum and Evaluation Standards for School Mathematics* (1989) and *Principles and Standards for School Mathematics* (*PSSM*) (2000), probability and statistics now appear in most school mathematics curricular materials. Increased attention to probability and statistics is further evident in the composition of the National Assessment of Educational Progress (NAEP) for mathematics. At Grade 8, items devoted to data analysis, statistics, and probability doubled from 8% in 1986 to 15% in 2003 and, at Grade 12, this strand comprised 25% of the 2005 assessment (National Assessment Governing Board, 2004). More specifically, 47% of the 2003 Grade 4 data analysis, statistics and probability items and

Variability is the Rule: A Companion Analysis of K–8 State Mathematics Standards, pp. 161–191

23% of the Grade 8 items addressed probability and chance (Tarr & Shaughnessy, 2007).

As professional organizations have recommended increased coverage of probability in the school mathematics curriculum, states have heeded the call by developing grade-level learning expectations (GLEs) that address statistics and probability. Of the 44 states with published curriculum frameworks for mathematics, now nearly all offer GLEs for data analysis and probability, spanning kindergarten through secondary school (Center for the Study of Mathematics Curriculum, n.d.). This chapter presents the results from our analysis of the GLEs that address topics in probability in states' Grades K–8 curriculum standards. We focus on probability because it is "an essential tool in applied mathematics and mathematics mathematical modeling ... [and] is also an essential tool in statistics" (Franklin et al., 2007, p. 8). Our chapter begins with a description of the methods and documents used in this analysis, follows with the results of our analyses of the major topics in probability, and concludes with recommendations for the future development of GLEs related to probability.

METHODS FOR ANALYZING PROBABILITY GLEs

Our goals were to present an overview of the content specified in state GLEs as well as to identify grade levels, K–8, where various states articulate GLEs related to probability. Consistent with the bulk of the work reported in this volume, our analysis is not *evaluative* in nature. Instead it is intended to provide rich descriptions of the status of probability in the K–8 mathematics curriculum.

Methods similar to those used in other state standards analyses (Reys, 2006a) informed the design of this research. To begin, GLEs related to probability were extracted from 41 state curriculum documents that articulate standards on a grade-by-grade basis (see Appendix D for listing of those documents). All GLEs were grouped by state and placed in rows of a spreadsheet. In total, 818 GLEs from the 41 states were collected and analyzed. Table 7.1 gives a breakdown of the number of GLEs related to probability by grade level. As shown in this table, more than half (53.3%) of all probability GLEs were located in the middle grades (6–8); 100 of the 818 GLEs (12.2%) were located in the early elementary grades (K–2); and the remaining 35.5% in later elementary grades (3–5).

Previous analyses of concepts related to probability (e.g., Jones, 2004) were used to identify major topics in the teaching and learning of probability, and these served as a coding scheme for analyzing the identified

**Table 7.1.   Number and Percent of
GLEs Pertaining to Probability by Grade**

Grade	Number of GLEs	Percent of Probability GLEs
K	16	1.9
1	34	4.2
2	50	6.1
3	79	9.7
4	98	12.0
5	105	12.8
6	147	18.0
7	143	17.5
8	146	17.8
Total	818	100

GLEs. Our coding scheme, presented in Table 7.2, identifies four major topics: (1) Sample space, (2) Theoretical probability, (3) Experimental probability, and (4) Independence and conditional probability, each of which was specified further into two or more subtopics. These topics and subtopics serve as the organizational structure for presenting our results.

Once the GLEs were collected and the coding scheme specified, we coded a small set of GLEs in order to test and refine the coding scheme and develop consistency in the application of the codes. When the coding scheme was finalized, we individually coded each of the 818 GLEs to one or more of the topics listed in Table 7.2 and then met to discuss and compare our coding. Where discrepancies occurred, we negotiated until we agreed on a consensus code. Overall, agreement was reached on the assignment of 83% of all codes.

The final codes were then entered into the spreadsheet, and the GLEs were sorted by topics and analyzed with respect to trends and major ideas. For some topics, the grade level at which GLEs were found were identified and illustrated in graphs in order to compare two similar ideas (e.g., the placement of GLEs for combinations and for permutations). For other topics, we identified an initial learning expectation (the first GLE specified for the topic in each state), a final learning expectation, and all intermediate learning expectations, and displayed these in state by grade graphs. When a state included only one GLE for a topic, this singular GLE was classified as the initial learning expectation. When two GLEs were given for a topic at different grade levels, we considered these as initial and final learning expectations.

Table 7.2.   Major Themes and Topics Used to Code State GLEs Related to Probability

Themes	Probability Topics
Sample Space	Construct sample space of simple or compound events using organized lists, tree diagrams, etc.
	Use permutations, combinations, Fundamental Counting Principle
Theoretical Probability	Describe the probability of events as certain, impossible, or possible
	Describe the probability of events as more, less, or equally likely
	Calculate theoretical probability of simple or compound events
	Understand that $0 \leq P(E) \leq 1$
	Express probabilities in multiple formats (fractions, decimals, percents, odds)
	Determine or compute the complement of an event
	Use theoretical probability to make predictions
	Determine whether a game is "fair" or if all events are equally likely
Experimental Probability	Design simulations of random phenomena or conduct experiments, collect, record data
	Develop an understanding of randomness or random sampling
	Calculate the experimental probability of simple or compound events
	Compare experimental probability and theoretical probability, or experimental probability with expected values
	Understand the effect of sample size (Law of Large Numbers)
	Use experimental probability to make predictions
Independence & Conditional Probability	Calculate the conditional probability for independent and dependent events
	Distinguish between independent and dependent events

RESULTS

Sample Space

GLEs related to sample space generally focused on determining the possible outcomes or number of outcomes for a particular event. Overall, 211 GLEs (approximately one-fourth of all probability GLEs) were coded in this category. As specified in Table 7.2, these divided into two subtopics: (1) Determining sample space for simple or compound events and (2) Using permutations, combinations, or the Fundamental Counting Principle.

Determining sample spaces. In all, 135 GLEs from 38 states, accounting for 16.5% of all probability GLEs, called for students to determine the sample space of particular events. Figure 7.1 illustrates the grade placement of these GLEs in each of these states, with states being placed from left to right in order of the earliest initial learning expectation that was identified. Arizona and New Jersey included the greatest number of GLEs for this topic with eight each. However, as shown in Example 7.1, Arizona repeated the same GLE for five consecutive grades (2–6).

Example 7.1. Name the possible outcomes of a probability experiment. (AZ, gr. 2–6)

Seven states—Alabama, Georgia, Hawaii, Missouri, Oklahoma, Utah, and Wyoming—stated only one GLE; three states—New Hampshire, Rhode Island, and Idaho—did not include any for this topic.

Initial GLEs were found at a variety of grade levels. Two states (Virginia and Kansas) began in kindergarten, specifying GLEs for the sample space of *simple events*, as shown in Examples 7.2 and 7.3.

Example 7.2. The student recognizes and states whether a simple event in an experiment or simulation including the use of concrete objects can have more than one outcome. (KS, gr. K)

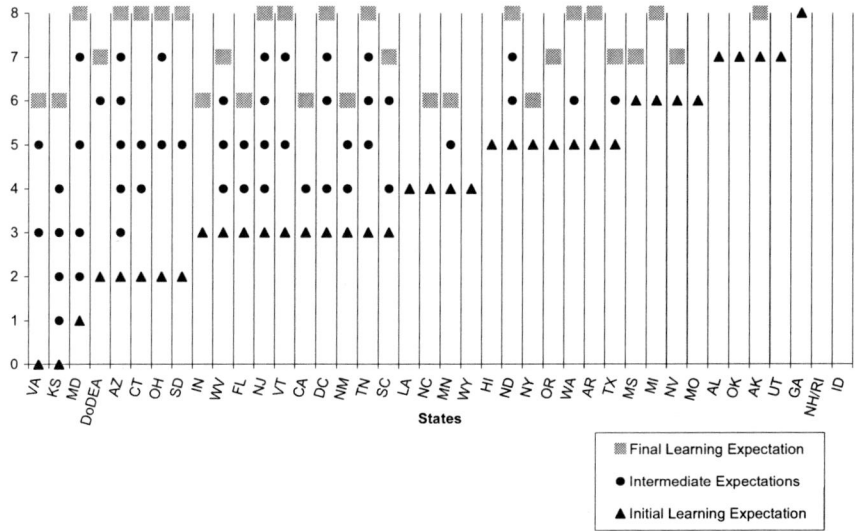

Figure 7.1.   Distribution of GLEs related to determining the sample space of simple or compound events by grade and state.

Example 7.3. Investigate and describe the results of dropping a two-colored counter or using a multicolored spinner. (VA, gr. K)

By contrast, Georgia offered only one GLE related to sample space (Example 7.4) and articulated it for Grade 8 students.

Example 7.4. Use tree diagrams to find the number of outcomes. (GA, gr. 8)

As shown in Figure 7.1, ten states initiated this topic in Grade 3, with seven more states doing so in Grade 5.

GLEs presented in the elementary grades typically asked students to determine the possible outcomes of simple events, in some cases using models or concrete materials. Examples 7.5 and 7.6 illustrate these expectations.

Example 7.5. Record the possible outcomes for a simple event (e.g., tossing a coin) and systematically keep track of the outcomes when the event is repeated many times. (CA & SC, gr. 3)

Example 7.6. Model simple probabilities by displaying the outcomes for real-world and mathematical problems. (MN, gr. 4)

In later grades, students are asked to use tree diagrams or other organized lists to determine sample spaces of simple or compound events. Examples 7.7 and 7.8 are typical instances.

Example 7.7. Determine all possible outcomes of a particular event or all possible arrangements of objects in a given set by applying various methods including tree diagrams and systematic lists. (OR, gr. 7)

Example 7.8. Determine the number of possible outcomes for a compound event by using the fundamental counting principle and use this to determine the probabilities of events when the outcomes have equal probability. (NY, gr. 6)

Overall, the most frequent placement for these GLEs for this topic was Grades 5–7, as 23 states specify GLEs for determining sample space at Grade 6, 20 states articulate these GLEs at Grade 5, and 19 states offer these at Grade 7. Table 7.3 presents the grade placement of all 135 GLEs pertaining to determining the sample space of a simple or compound event. As shown, the greatest frequency for this topic was found in Grades 5 and 6 (41.5%).

Table 7.3. Number and Percent of GLEs Pertaining to Determining the Sample Space of an Event by Grade

Grade	Number of GLEs (From 38 states)	Percent of Probability GLEs
K	2	1.5
1	2	1.5
2	7	5.2
3	16	11.9
4	17	12.6
5	26	19.3
6	30	22.2
7	19	14.1
8	16	11.9
Total	135	100

Note: Percents do not sum to 100% due to rounding.

Permutations, combinations, and the Fundamental Counting Principle. A topic closely associated with determining the sample space is the use of permutations, combinations, and the Fundamental Counting Principle to do so. In many cases, GLEs pertaining to determining the sample space were double-coded as using permutations, combinations, and the Fundamental Counting Principle. Permutations and combinations were found much more frequently than the Fundamental Counting Principle.

Figure 7.2 presents the grade placement of GLEs related to determining the number of combinations and permutations of particular sets of objects by state. In all, 88 GLEs from 31 states (about 11% of all probability GLEs) required students to work with permutations and combinations. Arizona recorded the greatest number with nine. It was also was the only state to provide a GLE for this topic in *each* grade level, K–8, using larger sets of objects with each successive grade. Arizona's sequence of ten GLEs is given in Table 7.4. In contrast to Arizona, eight states offer only one GLE related to this topic, while 11 states did not include *any* GLE that specifically referenced combinations and/or permutations.

As Figure 7.2 shows, states did not consistently include GLEs for *both* permutations and combinations. Fifteen states offered GLEs for finding both permutations and combinations, but seven states—Alaska, Arkansas, District of Columbia, Florida, New Mexico, Texas, and Washington—articulate GLEs for only combinations. Four states—Indiana, Minnesota, North Dakota, and Virginia—use the term "arrangements" when

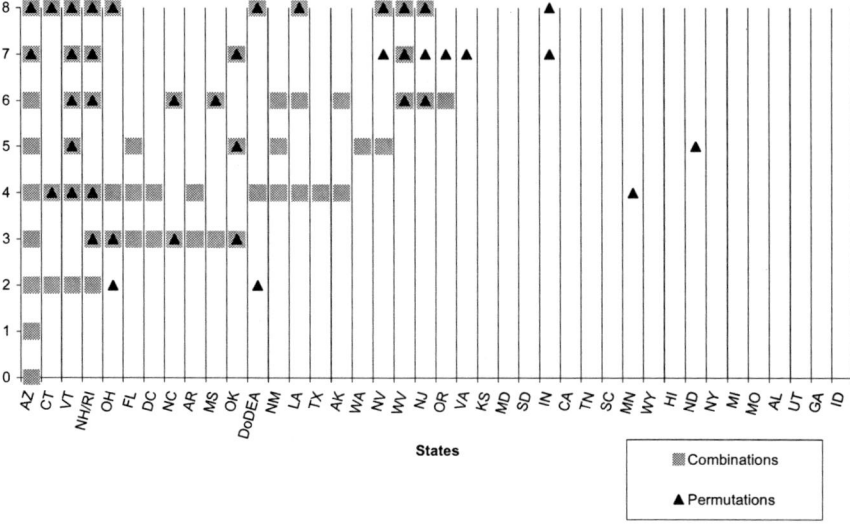

Figure 7.2.   Distribution of GLEs related to determining combinations or permutations of objects by grade and state.

Table 7.4.   Arizona's Sequence of GLEs related to Permutations, Combinations, and the Fundamental Counting Principle

Grade(s)	GLE
K, 1, & 2	Make arrangements that represent the number of combinations that can be formed by pairing items taken from two sets, using manipulatives.
3	Make a diagram to represent the number of combinations available when one item is selected from each of three sets of two items.
4	Find all possible combinations when one item is selected from each of two sets containing up to three objects.
5	Find all possible combinations when one item is selected from each of two sets of different items, using a systematic approach.
6	Determine all possible outcomes involving a combination of three sets of three items, using a systematic approach.
6	Determine all possible arrangements given a set with four or few objects using a systematic list, table or tree diagram when order is not important.
7	Determine all possible arrangements of a given set, using a systematic list, table, tree diagram, or other representation.
7	Determine all possible outcomes involving the combination of up to three sets of objects.
8	Determine all possible outcomes involving the combination of two or more sets of objects.
8	Determine all possible arrangements given a set.

discussing permutations. Overall, 14 states place GLEs related to permutations and combinations at Grade 4, while 11 states defer such GLEs until in Grades 6 and 8. Table 7.5 presents the distribution of GLEs related to permutations or combinations by states and grade.

Along with permutations and combinations, several states made explicit reference to use of the Fundamental Counting Principle or basic counting principles as tools for determining the complete sample space. In all, 24 GLEs from 16 states specify use of the Fundamental Counting Principle. New Jersey and Vermont each offered four GLEs focusing on this topic, while New Jersey provided the earliest placement, at Grade 5. On the other hand, Grade 8 was the most common level at which this topic was mentioned; eight states—District of Columbia, Georgia, Indiana, New Hampshire, New Jersey, North Dakota, Rhode Island, and Vermont—included a Fundamental Counting Principle GLE at this grade. Seven other states did so at Grade 7, and six others at Grade 6.

Summary. The grade placement of GLEs related to determining sample spaces, combinations, and permutations varied markedly across states. Some states recommend the study of these topics in early grade levels with elementary concepts, developing this idea with increasing sophistication across subsequent grade levels. Other states provide a more narrow set of GLEs for these topics, focusing attention at only one or two grades.

Table 7.5.   Number and Percent of GLEs Pertaining to Determining Combinations or Permutations of Objects by Grade

Grade	Number of GLEs (From 31 States)	Percent of Probability GLEs
K	1	1.1
1	1	1.1
2	7	8.0
3	13	14.8
4	16	18.2
5	9	10.2
6	14	15.9
7	11	12.5
8	16	18.2
Total	88	100

Note: Percents do not sum to 100% due to rounding.

Theoretical Probability

GLEs coded for the broad topic of theoretical probability included a number of subtopics related to the procedural and conceptual understanding of theoretical probability and its applications. Overall, an astonishing 414 GLEs—*more than half of all probability GLEs*—were coded into the following subtopics: (1) Describe the probability of events as certain, impossible, or possible, (2) Describe the probability of events as more, less, or equally likely, (3) Calculate theoretical probability of simple or compound events, (4) Understand that $0 \leq P(E) \leq 1$, (5) Express probabilities in multiple formats (fractions, decimals, percents, odds), (6) Determine or compute the complement of an event, (7) Use theoretical probability to make predictions, and (8) Determine whether a game is "fair" or if all events are equally likely.

Describing the probability of event. Many states begin the study of probability by asking students to describe the likelihood of an event using relatively informal terminology such as "impossible," "never," "possible," "always," or "certain." Closely related to simple description is the comparison of the likelihood of two events, describing whether one event is more or less likely in relation to another event, or if the two events are equally likely. Figure 7.3 shows the grade placement of GLEs related to describing the probability of an event or events using these terms. In total, 148 GLEs pertaining to this concept were located in 40 of the 41 state documents. New Mexico and Florida possessed the greatest number of GLEs with 12 and ten, respectively, while Georgia did not address the topic at all.

As indicated in Figure 7.3, eight states expect students to classify events as certain, impossible, or possible beginning in kindergarten. These early GLEs are illustrated in Examples 7.9–7.11.

> *Example 7.9.* Explore, discuss and demonstrate an understanding of the terms "always," "maybe," and "never" events. (MS, gr. K)
>
> *Example 7.10.* Describe the probability of an event as being possible or not possible. (AR, gr. K)
>
> *Example 7.11.* Describe the likelihood of events related to personal experiences. (CT, gr. K)

Fifteen states included similar GLEs at Grade 1, while 12 states used the language of "more," "less," or "equally likely." Example GLEs in this latter category are given below (Examples 7.12 and 7.13).

> *Example 7.12.* Describe events related to student's experiences as more likely or less likely to happen. (DoDEA, gr. 1)

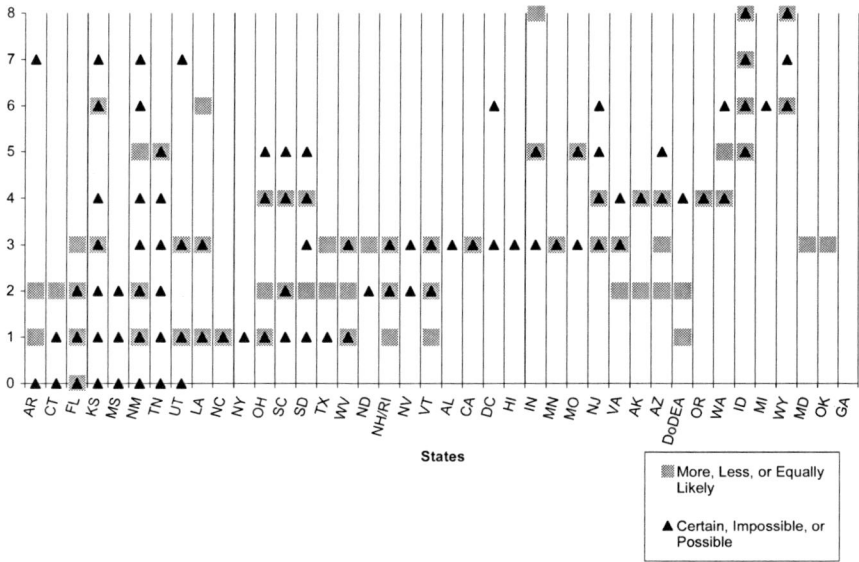

Figure 7.3.   Distribution of GLEs related to describing the probability of events as certain, impossible or possible, or as more, less or equally likely, by grade and state.

Example 7.13. Knows if a given event is more likely, equally likely, or less likely to occur. (FL, gr. K & 1)

Several states included terms for both types of comparisons in the same GLE, as shown below in Example 7.14.

Example 7.14. Appropriately use basic probability vocabulary (e.g., more likely to happen/less likely to happen, always/never, same as). (LA, gr. 1)

Expectations addressing this topic generally decrease in the upper elementary and middle grades. GLEs found at these grade levels generally extend concepts from earlier grade levels or extend the expression of likelihood from qualitative to quantitative terms. Michigan, for example, expects its Grade 6 students to express theoretical probabilities in all three numerical representations of rational numbers (Example 7.15).

Example 7.15. Express probabilities as fractions, decimals, or percentages between 0 and 1; know that 0 probability means an event will not occur and that probability 1 means an event will occur. (MI, gr. 6)

Table 7.6 presents the number of states that include GLEs using the two types of qualitative descriptions of probability distinguished above at each grade level.

As depicted in Table 7.6, the number of states generally increases through the primary grades, reaching a maximum at Grade 3, where 20 states include GLEs using the certain, impossible, or possible terminology while 17 include GLEs using the more, less, or equally likely language. After Grade 3, the frequency of states generally decreases.

Computing theoretical probabilities. Once students have learned to describe the likelihood of events qualitatively, more precise methods assign numerical probabilities, commonly referred to as the "theoretical probability of the event." In this section, our analysis combines GLEs focused on the computation of the theoretical probability of both *simple* and *compound events.* Overall, 154 GLEs from over 40 states were identified as relating to this subtopic. New Mexico and Washington expressed the greatest number of GLEs with nine each, with Maryland and New Jersey each stating eight. Conversely, *no* GLE for this topic was found in the Idaho document, while six states—Hawaii, Michigan, Missouri, Texas, Utah, and Wyoming—included only one.

Theoretical probability GLEs of this sort varied markedly across states. Some states ask students to compute probabilities of specific events (e.g., simple, compound) (as in Example 7.16) or to use particular methods for determining those probabilities (as in Examples 7.17 and 7.18).

Example 7.16. Determine the probability that a specific event will occur in a single stage probability experiment. (AZ, gr. 7)

Table 7.6. Number of States With GLEs Related to Describing Events as Certain, Impossible, or Possible, or More, Less, or Equally Likely by Grade

Grade	Number of States With GLEs Pertaining to Describing Events as Certain, Impossible, or Possible	Number of States With GLEs Pertaining to Describing Events as More, Less, or Equally Likely
K	8	1
1	15	12
2	11	16
3	20	17
4	13	8
5	9	6
6	8	4
7	6	1
8	2	3

Example 7.17. Finds the probability of a simple event in an experiment or simulation using geometric models. (KS, gr. 7)

Example 7.18. Represent all possible outcomes for compound events in an organized way (e.g., tables, grids, tree diagrams) and express the theoretical probability of each outcome. (NM, gr. 6)

In contrast, other states offer no such guidance (Example 7.19).

Example 7.19. Calculate probability for an event. (WA, gr. 6)

Figure 7.4 displays the grade placement and sequence of GLEs related to computing theoretical probabilities for each state. Six states—Alabama, Arkansas, Florida, Maryland, Mississippi, and New Mexico—initiate the topic in Grade 3, while 12 states do so in Grade 4. Nine other states state their first GLEs in Grades 5 or 6. Overall, 28 of the 40 states that include GLEs for this topic place these GLEs in Grade 6, while 26 states articulate this GLE in Grade 7 and 24 in Grade 5.

Understanding $0 \leq P(E) \leq 1$. Closely related to the computation of theoretical probabilities is understanding the range of possible numerical probabilities. Several states may implicitly subsume this concept in their computation of theoretical probability GLEs because they do not mention

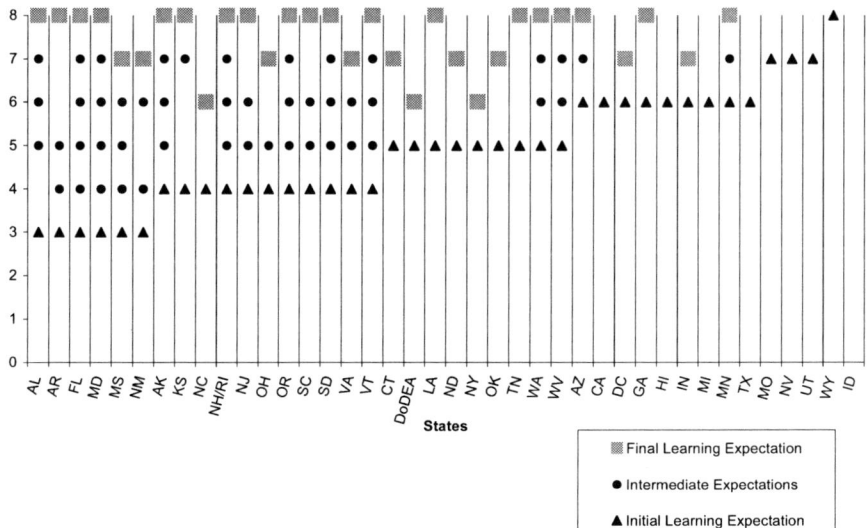

Figure 7.4.   Distribution of GLEs related to the theoretical probability of simple or compound events by grade and state.

the numerical range explicitly. However, 21 states did address this concept in their standards.

In all, 37 GLEs were identified as addressing the fact that theoretical probabilities must fall between zero and one, inclusive. Ten states each place GLEs related to this concept in Grades 5 and 6, and four states—Indiana, New Jersey, Utah, and Washington—do so at both grades. These GLEs span Grades 4 through 8, with six states articulating this topic at Grade 4 while only one state (Idaho) specifying this GLE at Grade 8. Examples 7.20 and 7.21 are typical GLEs in this category.

> *Example 7.20.* Understand that the probability of an event can be represented by a number from 0 (impossible) to 1 (certain). (OR, gr. 4)

> *Example 7.21.* Explain that probability ranges from 0% to 100% and identify a situation as having high or low probability. (ID, gr. 8)

Expressing probabilities in multiple formats. Another topic related to the computation of theoretical probabilities concerns their expression in multiple numerical formats, such as fractions, decimals, percents, or odds. Twenty-six states offer GLEs pertaining to expressing probabilities in multiple formats. In all, 54 GLEs across these 26 states were coded as relating to this topic.

Given that students need to develop proficiency with converting between these number formats, many of these GLEs were found in the later grade levels. In fact, 53 of the 54 GLEs were found in Grades 5 through 8. The greatest number of GLEs for this concept was located at Grade 6, where 17 states stipulate GLEs requiring students to express probabilities in multiple formats. Eleven states provide GLEs for this topic at Grade 7, while ten states place these GLEs in Grade 8. Three typical examples of these GLEs are given below (Examples 7.22–7.24).

> *Example 7.22.* Express probabilities as fractions, ratios, decimals, and percents. (CT, gr. 6)

> *Example 7.23.* Explain the relationship between probability and odds and calculate the odds of a desired outcome in a simple experiment. (NM, gr. 8)

> *Example 7.24.* Express probabilities as fractions or decimals between 0 and 1 and percents between 0 and 100. (WA, gr. 6)

Determining the Complement of an Event. Only 19 GLEs from 13 states ask students to understand the complement of an event and determine the probability of the event and its complement. These GLEs were primarily found in Grades 6 through 8, with seven states placing GLEs for this idea in Grade 6 and five states doing so in Grade 7. Examples 7.25 and 7.26 are typical expectations for this topic.

> *Example 7.25.* Find the probabilities of a simple event and its complement and describe the relationship between the two. (TX, gr. 6)

> *Example 7.26.* Know that if P is the probability of an event occurring, then 1-P is the probability of that event not occurring. (IN, gr. 7; MN, gr. 8)

Using Theoretical Probability to Make Predictions. An important product of determining the theoretical probability, either by calculation or by description (e.g., impossible, certain), is interpreting what that number means and how it can be used to make predictions. Overall, 86 GLEs from 26 states were identified for this category. Figure 7.5 shows the grade placement of GLEs pertaining to using the theoretical probability of an event to make predictions. As shown in Figure 7.5, states vary greatly regarding when they initiate this topic and where they place their GLEs. Six states state their first GLE in Grade 3, while five states each do so in Grades 5 and 6. The most frequent grade placement is in Grade 5, where 17 states offer GLEs. Arizona specified the greatest number of GLEs for

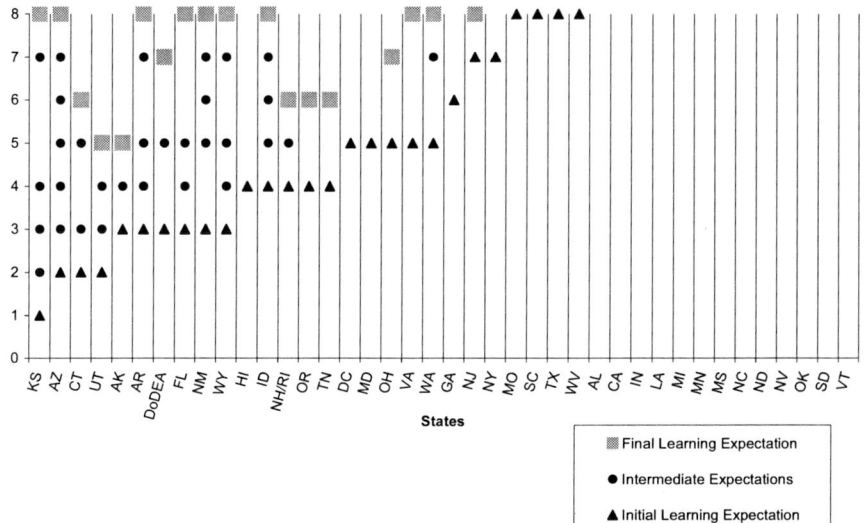

Figure 7.5.   Dsitribution of GLEs related to using theoretical probabilities to make predictions by grade and state.

this topic. However, seven of their nine GLEs are the same expectation repeated from Grade 2 to 8 (see Example 7.27 below).

> *Example 7.27.* Predict the outcome of a grade-level appropriate probability experiment. (AZ, gr. 2, 3, 4, 5, 6, 7, & 8)

New Mexico followed Arizona with seven GLEs for this topic. Conversely, 13 states did not offer any, and nine states include only one.

Expectations in this category increase in sophistication by grade level. Elementary grade GLEs generally focus on making predictions based upon experiments or on student experiences, as illustrated in Examples 7.28 and 7.29.

> *Example 7.28.* Predict the most likely or least likely outcome in probability experiments (e.g., predict the chance of spinning one of the 2 colors on a 2-colored spinner). (AZ, gr. 2)

> *Example 7.29.* Discuss the likelihood of various events, state possibilities, make predictions, and test them in practical situations. (CT, gr. 2)

But in later grades, students are subsequently expected to use theoretical probabilities, and in some instances experimental probabilities, to make predictions about future events. Examples 7.30 and 7.31 are typical expectations of this sort.

> *Example 7.30.* Estimate the probabilities and make predictions based on experimental and theoretical probabilities. (NJ, gr. 7)

> *Example 7.31.* Make predictions based on theoretical probabilities, design and conduct an experiment to test the predictions, compare actual results to predicted results, and explain differences. (AR, gr. 8)

Determining whether games are fair. The final subtopic is the application of theoretical probabilities to determine whether games or contests are fair. It should be noted that games are defined to be "fair" when either (a) for a single player, there is an equally likely chance of winning or losing, or (b) for more than one players, there is an equal probability of winning associated with each player. Ten states state a total 26 GLEs related to determining whether games of chance are fair, and the three states (Washington, New Hampshire, and Rhode Island) account for 14 of these 26. The expectations span Grades 3 through 8, with six states placing GLEs in Grade 6 and four states each offering them in Grades 5 and 8. Three typical examples are given below (Examples 7.32–7.34).

Example 7.32. Explore the fairness of games involving spinners and dice of various kinds. (CT, gr. 3)

Example 7.33. Given a fair game, create an advantage for one of the players (e.g., if the game selecting marbles include more marbles of one color than the other). (WA, gr. 5)

Example 7.34. Apply theoretical probability to determine if an event or game is fair or unfair and pose and evaluate modifications to change the fairness. (OR, gr. 8)

Summary. As was the case for GLEs pertaining to sample space, permutations, and combinations, the GLEs for theoretical probability vary markedly across states with respect to both the grade placement and the content articulated in the GLEs. As seen with topics such as determining the complement of an event or determining whether games are fair, some topics pertaining to probability are commonly absent from state standards. Similarly, the grade level at which students are expected to be able to compute theoretical probabilities varies across grades, while other topics exhibit the same lack of consensus.

Experimental Probability

Grade-level expectations addressing experimental probability concerned topics related to conducting and examining trials of simulations in order to develop and test conjectures as well as to interpret outcomes of the experiments. Some of the subtopics pertaining to experimental probability closely mirror those for theoretical probability, while others are specific to conducting simulations and experiments to examine probabilistic concepts. In total, 319 GLEs—39% of the all probability GLEs—were coded into the following six subtopics: (1) Design simulations or conduct experiments to collect and record data, (2) Develop an understanding of randomness or random sampling, (3) Calculate the experimental probability of simple or compound events, (4) Compare experimental probability to theoretical probability or expected values, (5) Understand the effect of sample size (Law of Large Numbers), and (6) Use experimental probability to make predictions.

Design simulations or conducting experiments to collect and record data. In many states, one of the earliest topics concerning experimental probability is the concept of collecting and recording of data from experiments and simulations. This idea provides the foundation for data analysis and interpretation as well as a link to the probability of different outcomes. Overall, 168 GLEs address this topic. Figure 7.6 shows the grade placement of

GLEs from 38 states related to designing and conducting experiments to collect and record data. Kansas included the largest number with 11, followed by Arizona and New Jersey with 10 and Connecticut with 9. Surprisingly, no GLE related to this topic was found in the Michigan, Missouri, and South Dakota standards.

Three states—Florida, Kansas, and Virginia—place their initial GLE in kindergarten. As the examples below indicate (7.35 and 7.36). These GLEs ask students to record the results of simple experiments.

> *Example 7.35*. The student conducts an experiment or simulation with a simple event and records the results in a graph using concrete objects or frequency tables (tally marks). (KS, gr. K)

> *Example 7.36*. Investigate and describe the results of dropping a two-colored counter or using a multicolored spinner. (VA, gr. K)

The use of concrete materials is a common theme throughout the early grades GLEs, as students are asked to use various manipulative devices to collect data. The following examples from California and Arkansas are typical.

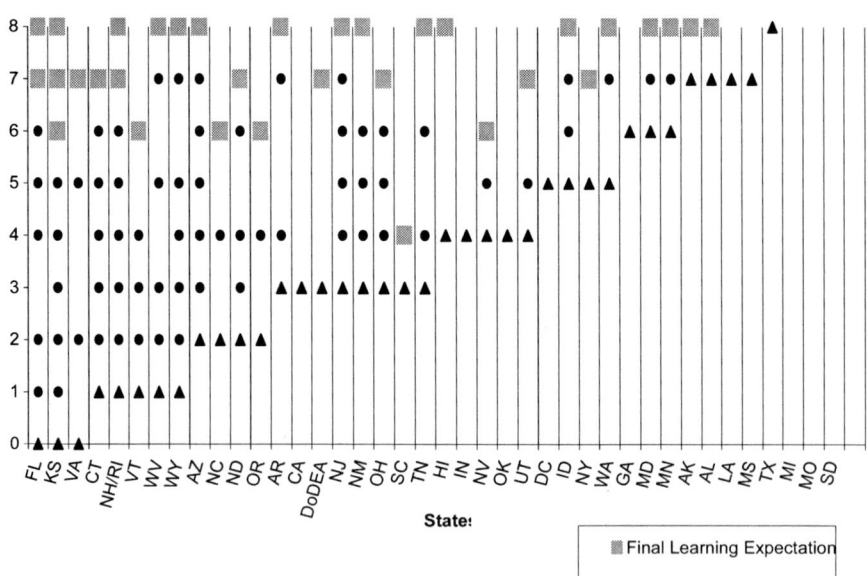

Figure 7.6.   Distribution of GLEs related to designing simulations and conducting experiments to collect and record data by grade and state.

Example 7.37. Record the possible outcomes for a simple event (e.g., tossing a coin) and systematically keep track of the outcomes when the event is repeated many times. (CA, gr. 3)

Example 7.38. Conduct simple probability experiments, record the data and draw conclusions about the likelihood of possible outcomes (roll number cubes, pull tiles from a bag, spin a spinner, or determine the fairness of games). (AR, gr. 3 & 4)

States also varied considerably in the level of specificity expressed in their GLEs for this topic. As illustrated in Example 7.39, some states provided extensive detail about what students should know and be able to do.

Example 7.39. Conducts an experiment or simulation with a compound event composed of two independent events including the use of concrete objects; records the results in a chart, table, or graph; and uses the results to draw conclusions and make predictions about future events. (KS, gr. 7)

In contrast, other states specified succinct, general statements without specifying the device, number of outcomes, or number of trials to be carried out, as shown in Example 7.40.

Example 7.40. Design and conduct an experiment to test predictions. (NY, gr. 7)

The grade placement of GLEs for conducting experiments and simulations varied considerably across the 38 states that included them. With respect to their initial GLE, states ranged across *all* grades (K–8) with three states beginning this concept in kindergarten, with four states not offering a GLE for conducting experiments and simulations until Grade 7. One state (Texas) delayed the topic until Grade 8. As shown in Figure 7.6, the distribution of the placement of initial GLEs was roughly uniform across the grades, and once initiated, most states continued some focus on the topic.

Develop an understanding randomness or random sampling. As students design and conduct experiments or simulations and examine the results, the concept of randomness becomes relevant. Although randomness and random sampling are commonly associated with statistics and data analysis, they are also important in understanding the outcomes of experiments. In all, 37 GLEs from 23 states were identified as relating to randomness. Kansas and Oregon each specified four GLEs pertaining to this concept. With respect to grade placement, the overwhelming majority of randomness GLEs related were located in Grades 6–8. Only three GLEs were stated prior to Grade 6. Example 7.41 is a typical GLE that addresses random sampling.

> *Example 7.41.* Recognize and understand the connections among the concepts of independent outcomes, picking at random, and fairness. (NJ & OR, gr. 6)

Calculate the experimental probability of simple or compound events. In designing and conducting experiments and simulations of random phenomena, students collect data that allow them to compute the experimental probability (or relative frequency) of an event. In total, 76 GLEs from 32 states concerned the calculation of experimental probability. Figure 7.7 presents the grade placement of those GLEs across the 32 states. Oregon had the largest number of GLEs pertaining to this topic with 6 GLEs in Grades 4, 6, and 7, while Kansas, New Mexico, and Utah each included five. Conversely, we found no GLE related to this topic in nine states, while 13 states provide a single GLE. As depicted in Figure 7.7, the earliest placement was at Grade 4, where nine states initiate this topic. Ten states delay addressing this topic until Grade 5, while five states each place their initial GLE at Grades 6 and 7. Overall, most of the GLEs for

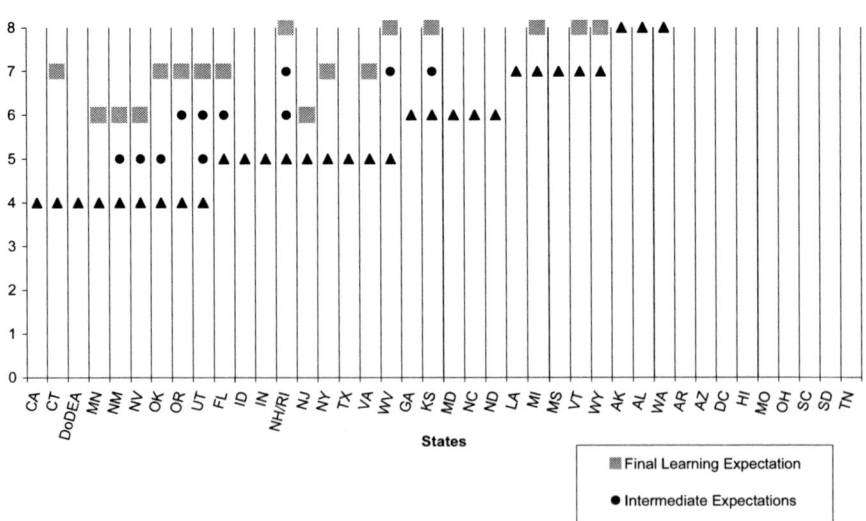

Figure 7.7.   Distribution of GLEs related to determining experimental probability of simple and compound events by grade and state.

this topic appear in Grades 5–7, with 21 GLEs at Grade 6, 18 in Grade 7, and 17 in Grade 5.

Several states require students to be able to compute experimental probabilities for simple and/or compound events. In fact, 16 of the 76 total GLEs specifically call for students to examine compound events when calculating experimental probabilities. Some GLEs, like Example 7.42 below, exclusively focus on compound events.

Example 7.42. Finds the probability of a compound event composed of two independent events in an experiment, simulation, or situation. (KS, gr. 8)

Other states, however, combine compound and simple events in their treatment of experimental probability, as Mississippi did in Example 7.43.

Example 7.43. Determine the probability of simple and compound events through experimentation, simulation, or calculation. (MS, gr. 7)

But many states fail to specify simple or compound events when they ask students to determine experimental probabilities (see Example 7.44 below).

Example 7.44. Determining the probability of an event through simulation. (AL, gr. 8)

Compare experimental probability to theoretical probability or expected values. An important concept concerns how experimental probability values compare to the expected values or theoretical probability of possible outcomes. Figure 7.8 illustrates the grade placement of 93 GLEs from 31 states that address this topic. Arizona specifies the greatest number of GLEs with 14. However, as we have seen before with this state, these 14 GLEs are actually two different GLEs repeated across seven grades. These are given in Examples 7.45 and 7.46 below.

Example 7.45. Compare the outcome of an experiment to predictions made prior to performing the experiment. (AZ, gr. 2, 3, 4, 5, 6, 7, & 8)

Example 7.46. Compare the results of two repetitions of the same grade-level appropriate probability experiment. (AZ, gr. 2, 3, 4, 5, 6, 7, & 8)

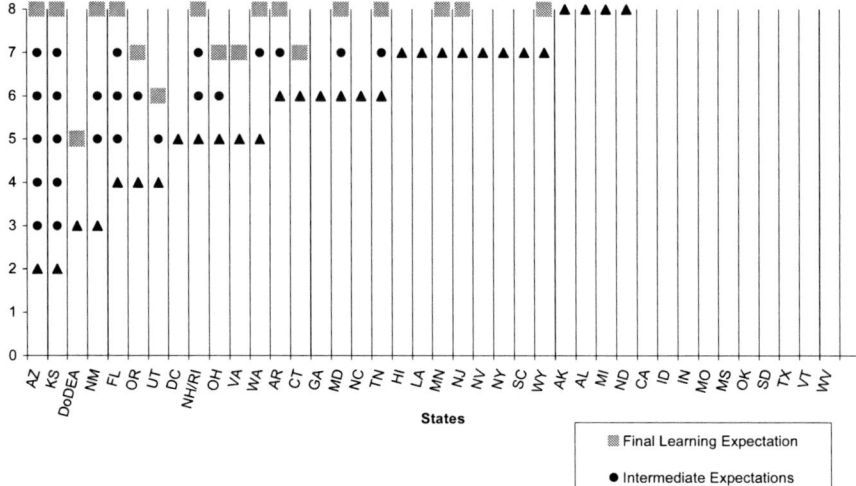

Figure 7.8.   Distribution of GLEs related to comparing experimental probabilities to theoretical probabilities or expected values by grade and state.

By contrast, Kansas provides eight unique GLEs spanning Grades 2–8. Conversely, 10 states include no GLE for this topic, while 10 others specify only one.

In addition to Arizona and Kansas that initiate this topic in Grade 2, two others states begin these comparisons in Grade 3. Although experimental probabilities are not specifically mentioned at these grade levels, students are expected to use the results of experiments to compare and judge earlier predictions, as is the case in Example 7.47.

> *Example 7.47.* Makes a prediction about a simple event in an experiment or simulation; conducts the experiment or simulation including the use of concrete objects; records the results in a chart, table, or graphs; and makes an accurate statement about the results. (KS, gr. 2)

In later grades, GLEs explicitly ask students to use probabilities or expected values in their comparisons. Examples 7.48 and 7.49 are typical illustrations of these expectations.

> *Example 7.48.* Use a variety of experiments to explore the relationship between experimental and theoretical probabilities. (MN, gr. 7)

> *Example 7.49.* Compares and explains the results of an experiment with the mathematically expected outcomes. (FL, gr. 8)

Overall, 21 states include GLEs for comparing experimental and theoretical probabilities in Grade 7, while 15 states do so in Grades 6 and 8. In fact, nearly 70% (65 of 93) of the GLEs related to this topic are located in Grades 6–8.

Understand the effects of sample size (Law of Large Numbers). A concept closely related to the comparison of experimental and theoretical probabilities is the Law of Large Numbers: As the number of trials increases without bound, the percentage difference between the experimental and theoretical probability approaches zero. In analyzing the GLEs addressing this concept, we found that many were also coded under the topic of comparing experimental and theoretical probabilities. In total, only 14 GLEs from eight states address the idea that as the sample size increases, the experimental and theoretical probabilities converge. These 14 GLEs were found across Grades 5–8; six were located in Grade 6. Oregon presents three GLEs for this topic spanning Grades 5–6, while Georgia, Kansas, Tennessee, and Utah offer two GLEs each. Two example GLEs for this topic are given below (Examples 7.50 and 7.51). Note the difference in the level of specificity in how the Law of Large Numbers is expressed.

Example 7.50. Understand that experimental probability approaches theoretical probability as the number of trials increases. (OR, gr. 6)

Example 7.51. Explore the relationships between the number of trials in an experiment and the predicted outcomes. (CT, gr. 6)

Use experimental probabilities to make predictions. The final subtopic related to experimental probability concerning using experimental results to make predictions. A total of 73 GLEs from 29 states address this topic. Figure 7.9 displays their grade placement. Kansas stated the largest number of GLEs pertaining to this topic, with eight GLEs from Grades 4 to 8. Vermont and New Mexico both specify six GLEs. Conversely, 12 states do not identify any GLE with this topic, while ten states include only one GLE.

As Figure 7.9 reveals, GLEs for this topic span Grades 1 to 8. The greatest number of expectations ($n = 15$ from 12 states) was found in Grade 8. Eleven states address this idea in Grade 6, while nine states do so at Grade 7. Eight states state these GLEs at each grade from 2 to 5.

As we found with the comparison of experimental and theoretical probabilities, GLEs in the early grades that concern making predictions address the results of probability experiments without explicitly mentioning experimental probability (see Examples 7.52 and 7.53 on next page).

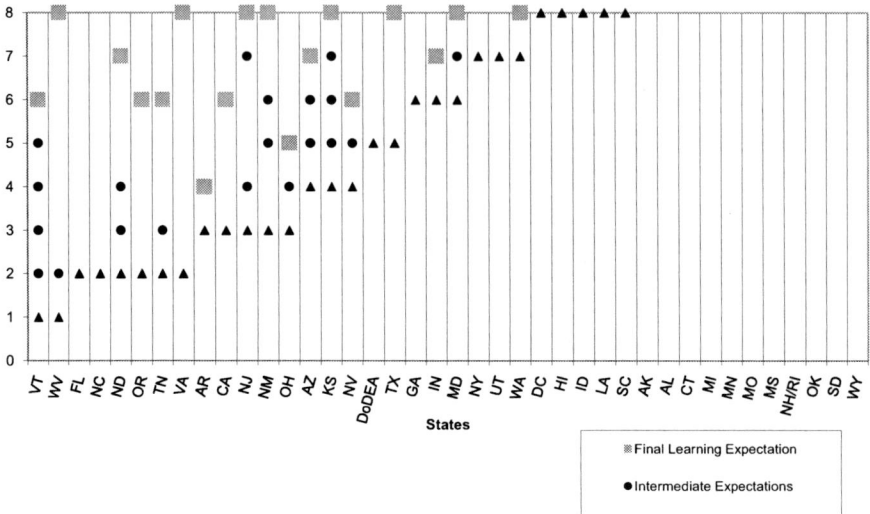

Figure 7.9.   Distribution of GLEs related to using experimental probability to make predictions by grade and state.

Example 7.52. Conduct simple experiments with more than two outcomes and use the data to predict which event is more, less, or equally likely to occur if the experiment is repeated. (WV, gr. 1)

Example 7.53. Predict outcomes of events based on data gathered and displayed. (TN, gr. 2)

At the later grades, however, GLEs are more explicit about students using the actual experimental probability in developing predictions. Examples 7.54 and 7.55 are representative of this shift.

Example 7.54. Predict the probability of a given event through trials/simulations (experimental probability), and represent the probability as a ratio. (GA, gr. 6)

Example 7.55. Analyzes the results of an experiment or simulation of two independent events to generate convincing arguments, draw conclusions, and make predictions and decisions in a variety of real-world situations. (KS, gr. 8)

Summary. The GLEs concerning experimental probability illustrate many of the same patterns we have seen in our analysis of previous topics (sample space and theoretical probability). Here as before, there was little consensus across states about the grade placement of GLEs, the grade level at which topics are introduced, and in some cases the topics that are covered. GLEs related to determining experimental probabilities span five grade levels (Grades 4–8), while GLEs concerning the comparison of experimental and theoretical probabilities span seven grades (Grades 2–8) and GLEs for using experimental probability to make predictions extend across eight grade levels. There were also dramatic differences regarding the emphasis of studying experimental results, with states such as Kansas, Oregon, and New Mexico providing extensive coverage of topics in experimental probability while Missouri and South Dakota did not include a single GLE under the theme of experimental probability.

Independence and Conditional Probability

The final section concerns GLEs related to independent and dependent events as well as the determination of conditional probability. As above, some GLEs pertaining to these topics were also coded with other topics such as determining theoretical or experimental probabilities. Some, however, are specific to the determination of independent and dependent events. In all, 57 GLEs (approximately 7% of all probability GLEs) coded in two subtopics: (1) Calculate the conditional probability for independent and dependent events, and (2) Distinguish between independent and dependent events.

Calculate the conditional probabilities for independent and dependent events. In all, 40 GLEs from 23 states address this subtopic. Many were also coded in the categories of determining theoretical and/or experimental probabilities. Figure 7.10 illustrates the grade placement of 40 GLEs across the 23 states.

More than half of the GLEs ($n = 21$) appeared in Grade 8, while 13 others were placed in Grade 7. Only one GLE was found before Grade 6, and it focused only on the idea that the preceding outcomes of independent events do not affect probabilities of later outcomes (Example 7.56 below).

> *Example 7.56.* Use everyday events and chance devices, such as dice coins, and unevenly divided spinners, to explore concepts of probability. Likely, unlikely, certain, impossible, improbable, fair, unfair. More likely, less likely, equally likely. Probability of tossing "heads" does not depend on outcomes of previous tosses. (NJ, gr. 4)

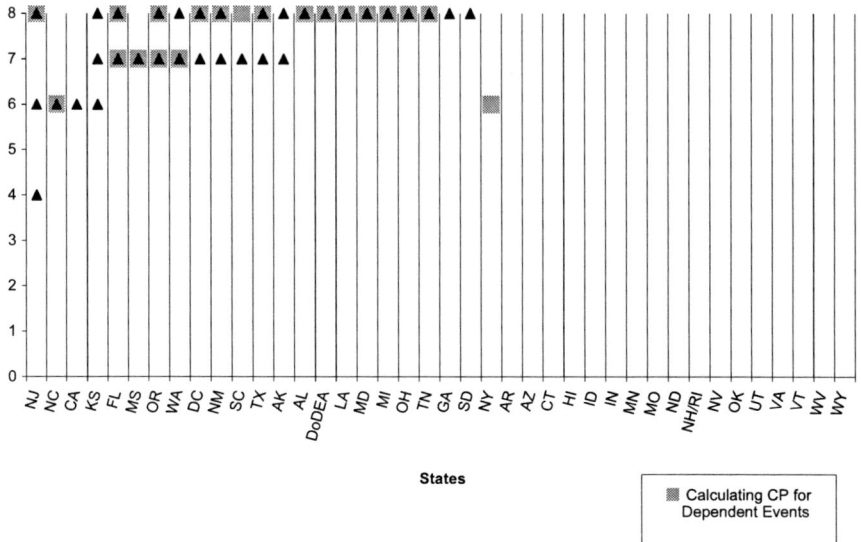

Figure 7.10.   The distribution of GLEs related to calculating conditional probabilities for independent and dependent events by grade and state.

Kansas outlined the most GLEs concerning this topic with four from Grades 6 to 8, while New Jersey, New Mexico, and Washington include three. Eighteen states did not devote explicit attention to conditional probability in their probability standards.

One feature of the distribution depicted in Figure 7.10 is the emphasis placed on finding probability of independent events over finding the probability of dependent events. Exactly half of the GLEs (20 of 40) in this category focused specifically on finding the probability of independent events. In fact, five of the 23 states that had GLEs addressing this subtopic—Alaska, California, Georgia, Kansas, and South Dakota—only focused on finding probabilities of independent events, with simple or compound. Only 4 of the 40 GLEs focused solely on dependent events; one state—New York—specified GLEs for this subtopic only for dependent events. In the remaining 16 GLEs, both independent and dependent events are referenced. In all, 90% of the GLEs (36 of 40) analyzed in this category focused attention on finding the probability of independent events, while 50% of these GLEs (20 of 40) dealt with dependent events.

Distinguish between independent and dependent events. Closely related to determining the probability of independent and dependent events is the ability to distinguish between these two types of events. Overall, 20 GLEs across 15 states focused attention on describing the differences between independent and dependent events; the other 26 states do not explicitly focus on this idea. All but one of the 20 GLEs lie within the 6–8 grade band, with half of the GLEs in this category placed at Grade 8. Five states place GLEs for distinguishing between independent and dependent events at Grade 6. These five states include the populous states of California, Texas, and New Jersey, all of which specify their only GLE pertaining to this topic at Grade 6. Examples 7.57 and 7.58 are representative of this set of 20 GLEs.

> *Example 7.57.* Understand the difference between independent and dependent events. (CA, gr. 6)

> *Example 7.58.* Determine and explain when events are mutually exclusive. (WA, gr. 7)

Summary. Our analysis of GLEs pertaining to independent and dependent events and conditional probability reveals that states have given relatively minimal attention to this topic. In fact, 16 of the 41 states' standards did not contain a GLE related to independent and dependent events, and ten others included only one. For this small number of GLEs, there was general consensus among the states about the grade placement of these topics. Most states placed GLEs for determining the probability for independent and dependent events as well as distinguishing between independent and dependent events in the 6–8 grade band.

DISCUSSION

In the final section, we highlight some general themes in our analysis of the K–8 probability grade-level expectations. Across the 41 state documents, the 818 GLEs related to probability provide evidence that this content area has indeed emerged as an essential component of the school mathematics curriculum. However, despite an average of 20 GLEs per state, the study of probability receives significantly less attention than its statistics counterpart, for which 1,711 GLEs were analyzed (Newton, Horvath, & Dietiker, this volume). This disparity is not surprising given that three of four probability and statistics standards in *PSSM* deal with data analysis and only one addresses probability. Throughout our analysis, we have found one recurring top-level feature of states' GLEs: There was little consistency with regard to the grade-level placement of probability topics. Beyond that general point, we draw attention to some additional problematic aspects of GLEs in states' probability standards.

One finding is that, while many states articulate numerous GLEs for probability, few state standards represent a coherent treatment of the content area. In particular, connections between related probability concepts are largely absent as most states "pigeonhole" topics into separate and discrete GLEs, often placing related concepts in different, even nonconsecutive grades. Consider sample space, which is fundamental to understanding probability (e.g., Jones, 2004; Tarr, 2002). Determining the total number of elements in the sample space is essential in making part-whole comparisons and computing the theoretical probability of an event (Piaget & Inhelder, 1975), and yet—astonishingly—not all states include a GLE explicitly related to sample space. Various counting techniques using permutations, combinations, and/or the Fundamental Counting Principle are available to determine complete sample spaces. Such tools are invaluable to solving probability problems, and yet 11 states do not consider counting strategies worthy enough to include in their standards documents; eight more states have only one GLE for this subtopic.

Although permutations, combinations, and the Fundamental Counting Principle are inherently related, such interconnectedness is not apparent in most state standards documents. For example, while 15 states offer GLEs for permutations *and* combinations, most states do not advocate the simultaneous study of these topics in any given grade. This troubling result might begin to explain why students typically struggle to distinguish between contexts where the order matters (permutations) from those when it does not (combinations). Moreover, it is disconcerting to learn that many states treat the Fundamental Counting Principle as a topic to be studied *separately* from permutations and combinations, when in fact, they are merely applications of the that Principle. This separation of these topics threatens the coherence of the curriculum and likely erodes the potential for sense-making.

Similarly, the relationship between experimental and theoretical probability is foundational to understanding probability because probability represents the relative frequency of an event over the long run. Although several states explicitly address experimental and theoretical probability within a single GLE, most do not. When experimental and theoretical probabilities are addressed in a single GLE, there is little consistency in how their relationship is characterized. Consider the following contrasting pair of GLEs (Examples 7.59 and 7.60).

Example 7.59. Comparing experimental and theoretical probability. (AL, gr. 8)

Example 7.60. Compares expected results (theoretical probability) with experimental results (empirical probability) in an experiment or situation with a compound event composed of two simple independent events and understands that the larger the sample size, the greater the likelihood that the experimental results will equal the theoretical probability. (KS, gr. 7)

In the succinctly stated, five-word GLE, Alabama students are expected to simply compare experimental and theoretical probabilities. In the more robust, 46-word GLE, what Kansas students should know is made quite clear and specific, namely that the law of large numbers explains the relationship between theoretical and experimental probabilities.

The relationship between experimental and theoretical probabilities underscores the inherent nature of the subject, namely that data and chance are companion elements in the development of probabilistic reasoning. Historically, curricular materials have given preference for a *classical* approach to probability in which probabilities are determined by counting the number of favorable outcomes, the number of total outcomes, and expressing the probability as a ratio of these two numbers (Jones, 2004). Consistent with this notion, more than half of all GLEs addressed theoretical probability. However, current recommendations (e.g., Jones, Langrall, & Mooney, 2007; Shaughnessy, 2003) call for teaching probability through, and in conjunction with, data collection and analysis—that is, using a *frequentist* approach to probability.

Our analysis indicates that states are indeed heeding the call to examine probability from a frequentist approach, with approximately 39% of all GLEs coded as experimental probability. However, this result warrants caution because more than half of the 319 experimental probability GLEs ($n = 168$) were coded as *Designing simulations or conducting experiments to collect and record data*. Although 38 of 41 states expect students to collect and record data from experiments, many states do not specify *what students are to do* with their experimental data. For example, in Maryland, students in Grades 6, 7, and 8 are expected to "conduct a probability experiment." But what happens after data are collected? What are students expected to learn from their experiments? Ideally, students should predict the outcome of an experiment, collect data, and compare results to their predictions, or alternatively, compare results to an expected value or to the theoretical probability of an event. However, many states do not make explicit the connections students are to make between data and chance. This lack of specificity places the onus on the classroom teacher to promote connections between data and chance. Without such connections, students could easily learn that probability and statistics are largely unrelated branches of school mathematics.

The lack of specificity in probability GLEs evident in some state standards is problematic in at least three ways. First, students themselves may be understand what they are expected to learn. Consider the following terse GLE (Example 7.61).

Example 7.61. Uses the language of probability. (ID, gr. 5–8)

Precisely what "language of probability" are students expected to learn to use each year for 4 years? Is there an increase in the sophistication of vocabulary students should use as they progress from Grade 5 to Grade 8? If not, then why should this GLE be repeated for four consecutive years?

Second, teachers likely will struggle to develop and present instruction to address such ambiguous GLEs. In addition to Example 7.61, consider the GLE in Example 7.62.

Example 7.62. Investigate experimental probability. (DoDEA, gr. 4)

What instructional task (or for that matter, set of tasks) addresses this GLE? An experiment in which students roll a number cube seems plausible, but precisely what does such an investigation entail? Who is responsible for deciding the number of trials to carry out, the students or teacher? How should instruction proceed within such a lesson? What is the ultimate "goal" of the investigation? How will the teacher know that students are progressing toward that goal?

Third, test developers will find it difficult to write items or assessment tasks to measure student performance in relation to broad, terse, or poorly-worded GLEs. Recall the following multi-grade GLE from Arizona (Example 7.27 above and 7.63 below).

Example 7.63. Predict the outcome of a grade-level appropriate probability experiment. (AZ, gr. 2, 3, 4, 5, 6, 7, & 8)

Before writing an test item, a test developer will need to decide what makes an experiment "grade-level appropriate" and how will the assessment task(s) vary from Grade 2 to Grade 8? GLEs that are repeated *verbatim* seem to reflect problematic features of a U.S. curriculum criticized for being highly repetitive and superficial in its treatment of mathematical topics. Moreover, the repeated GLEs fail to convey developmental trajectories over the K–8 school mathematics curriculum.

Notwithstanding the aforementioned shortcomings in state standards for probability, our analysis uncovered 818 GLEs, a number seemingly unimaginable a generation ago. Consistent with recent recommendations of the American Statistical Association, probability now has "its own place in the curriculum" (Franklin et al., 2007, p. 9). However, states give markedly different emphasis on this essential content with regard to topic placement, depth of coverage, clarity, and coherence. Additional studies are needed to learn how teachers interpret GLEs, plan instruction, and assess student learning in relation to how content is specified in GLEs.

CHAPTER 8

MAJOR LESSONS FROM THE SECOND ROUND OF STANDARDS ANALYSES

John P. Smith III, Glenda T. Lappan, and James E. Tarr

In the work reported in this volume, graduate students and faculty working in the Center for the Study of Mathematics Curriculum at Michigan State University, the University of Missouri, Columbia, and Western Michigan University carefully sorted, examined, and analyzed the K–8 grade level expectations (GLEs) from more than 40 states in two focal areas of school mathematics, geometry & measurement and probability & statistics. The primary goals of these analyses were to (a) assess the level of consensus/variability in what, when, and how the states currently expect students to learn in these content areas, and (b) offer recommendations for writing, organizing, and revising GLEs to be clearer and more effective guides for teaching, learning, and assessment. We hope our work encourages all involved in the development of standards and expectations—policymakers, state and district curriculum coordinators, school boards, and administrators—to work together with teachers to produce standards with the quality and clarity that will stimulate and support excellent school mathematics programs. Certainly, our teachers and students deserve no less.

In this final chapter, we look briefly across the reports in previous chapters to emphasize some broad and central lessons for all who wish to raise

Variability is the Rule: A Companion Analysis of K–8 State Mathematics Standards, pp. 193–204

our national capacity in school mathematics. As the chapter authors have argued and we underline again here, clear, coherent, and high-quality standards are not easy to achieve. But since our purpose has not solely been to *describe* the current form and content of state K–8 standards but also to support their continuous improvement, it is important to clarify what the challenges inherent in writing high-quality standards and, where possible, offer general suggestions for those who prepare and revise them. The lessons we present are relatively content-free; they concern our current GLEs and the task of writing them in any content area of mathematics.

This volume describes some patterns similar to those reported in the first (Reys, 2006a). On the one hand, the analyses reported here have shown some commonality across states. Frequently, we have seen substantial agreement on what to teach, when to introduce it, and how that content can be developed over a series of grades. On the other, we have also seen substantial variation between the states along those same dimensions. In closing, we have chosen to focus on the general theme of variation across the states primarily because it is the single clearest common pattern in these analyses. But in addition, variation leads to the analysis of the dimensions of differences and in turn, we hope, the thoughtful review and revision of standards documents. In this chapter we summarize five main types of variation evident in this volume's analyses: *grade placement & continuity, linguistic complexity, specific language, cognitive demand*, and *development across grades*. To ground the presentation of each type, we draw on examples from the previous chapters (though examples also exist in the first volume). Though we cannot offer detailed prescriptions for high-quality expectations (or standards more generally), we do suggest broad principles of good practice when it is warranted.

It is important to note that we are not the only analysts of state standards who have reported variability across state documents. The Committee on State Standards in Education has also seen variability as an important top-level result in their recent review of standards documents from all 50 states (National Research Council, 2008). What distinguishes this analysis, however, is our focus on specific mathematical topics and content areas and the detail of the analysis from mathematical, cognitive, and pedagogical perspectives.

FIVE DIMENSIONS OF VARIABILITY

Grade Placement & Continuity

Perhaps the simplest type of variation reported in this volume (e.g., Kasten & Newton; Wang & Smith; and Dingman & Tarr) and the previous (Reys, 2006a) concerns when mathematical topics are introduced and for how long they are taught. States differ significantly in the grade level of introduction (as indicated by the first GLE for a specific topic), the grade level of termination (as indicated by the last GLE for that topic), and the how continuously the topic is developed in the intermediate grades (as indicated the presence of related GLEs in those grades). Figure 8.1, which shows the distribution of congruence GLEs by grades and states, is a typical example of a general pattern we have seen for many topics in this volume.

States vary widely in the grade chosen to first introduce the topic of congruence (from kindergarten to Grade 5); they similarly terminate that topic at different points (from Grade 3 to Grade 8); and most important, they differ substantially in how continuously they develop the topic (as judged by the many large "holes" in the columns). The only commonality evident in Figure 8.1 is that every state includes at least one GLE dealing with congruence in its standards document. But by measures of timing and importance (total number of GLEs across states for this topic), the dominant message of Figure 8.1 is variability, not consensus.

Figure 8.1 also exemplifies two other considerations of location and continuity. With respect to the first, the grade where particular topics are introduced should not be an arbitrary choice. Standards authors should make thoughtful judgments about when to introduce a topic drawing on the best available evidence at hand from curricula, relevant theory and

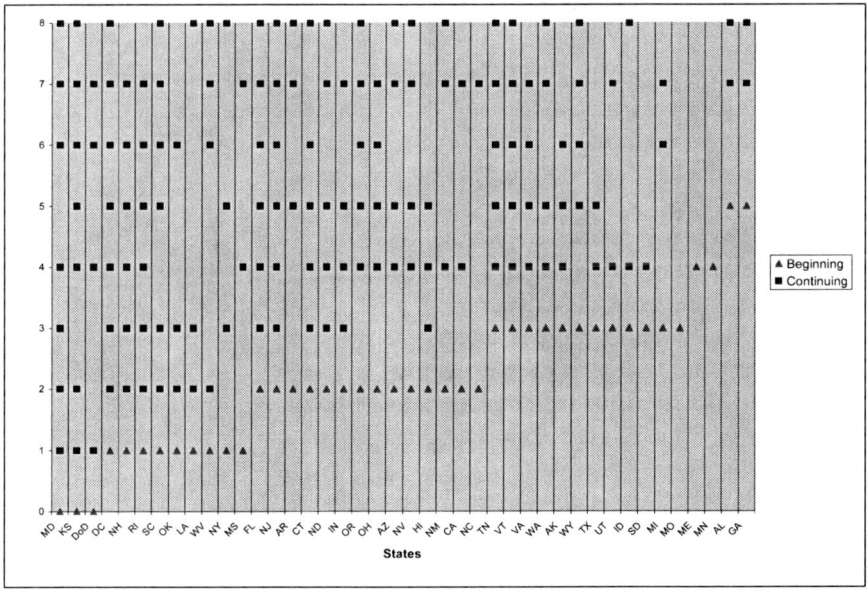

Figure 8.1. Distribution of congruence GLEs by state and grade.

empirical research, and classroom practice. With respect to the second, multigrade gaps in topic development are problematic for teaching and learning for many reasons. To name two, topics with "gaps" may be perceived as less important than those that are continuously developed, and more continuous development supports learning and retention and so limits re-teaching. Whenever possible, topics should be developed continuously to desired level of sophistication before they are terminated.

Linguistic Complexity

A second important dimension of variation is the sheer number of words (and attendant grammatical structures) that standards authors have used to express individual expectations. Put simply, some state authors express multiple topically-related but quite different expectations in the same GLE, where others have come closer to stating each GLE in a single sentence. For example, on the topic of data display (Newton, Horvath, Dietiker, this volume), Kansas combined different cognitive processes (e.g., constructing and reading data displays), different types of data (quantitative and qualitative), and different types of representation in the same Grade 2 expectation (Example 8.1 below). In contrast, New York distributed similar expectations over eight distinct GLEs from kindergarten to Grade 3 (Table 8.1), each expressing a narrower and more specific expectation with simpler wording.

> *Example 8.1.* Organizes, displays, and reads numerical (quantitative) and non-numerical (qualitative) data in a clear, organized, and accurate manner including a title, labels, categories, and whole number intervals using these data displays:

(a) graphs using concrete objects;
(b) pictographs with a whole symbol or picture representing 1, 2, or 10 (no partial symbols or pictures);
(c) frequency tables (tally marks);
(d) horizontal and vertical bar graphs;
(e) Venn diagrams or other pictorial displays, e.g., glyphs;
(f) line plots. (KS, gr. 2, Data)

It seems less important whether the topic of displays of data is introduced in kindergarten or Grade 1. Indeed, these states have agreed to introduce the topic of data displays early—in the primary grades. Rather, the issue in this contrast is how the linguistic expression of expectations helps or hinders their comprehension. Where the Kansas

**Table 8.1.   GLEs Related to Data Display From
New York's Statistics and Probability Standards**

Grade	GLE
K	Represent data using manipulatives.
1	Display data in simple pictographs for quantities up to 20 with units of one.
1	Display data in bar graphs using concrete objects with intervals of one.
1	Use Venn diagrams to sort and describe data.
2	Display data in pictographs and bar graphs using concrete objects or a representation of the object.
3	Construct a frequency table to represent a collection of data.
3	Identify the parts of pictographs and bar graphs.
3	Display data in pictographs and bar graphs.
3	State the relationships between pictographs and bar graphs.

expectation has the virtue of collecting together related content in the same GLE at one grade level, the comprehension demands on the reader of that long and complex statement are quite high. By contrast, New York expects much less in comprehension at each grade level, so there is less danger that important content will be overlooked. Where it is difficult to argue against simplicity of expression, well-formed GLEs must balance clarity and simplicity of expression with sufficient mathematical detail and specificity.

Specific Language

The third important dimension of variation concerns the specific words and associated meanings that are used to articulate expectations. One important class of specific words is the verbs that describe the cognitive and/or physical actions expected of students—what Larnell & Smith (this volume) have called "primary verbs." A second kind is the predicates of those verbs: The mathematics objects that students are supposed to act upon. These objects include concepts, relationships, properties, or procedures. For a simple example, an expectation that asks students to "state the Pythagorean Theorem" is a different expectation—as indicated by its specific language—than one that asks students to "use (or apply) the Pythagorean Theorem." Success on one expectation does not necessarily mean that a student can competently fulfill the other. Similarly, stating the meaning or definition of length is a quite different expectation than stating the Pythagorean Theorem.

Issues of specific language (over and above the more general issue of linguistic complexity) have been explored in some detail, but in different ways in different chapters. The Larnell & Smith chapter, which focused on the role of primary verbs as measures of the cognitive demand of expectations, reports two important features of current standards: (a) Verbs designating lower levels of cognitive demand (as analyzed by Bloom) remain dominant, even when some, like *explain*, would otherwise be associated with higher levels of cognitive activity, and (b) verbs alone are poor single indicators of cognitive demand, when their mathematical predicates are not also considered. Those authors argue that standards writers need to pay close attention to the key verbs and nouns that structure specific expectations. Careful choices of verbs and nouns will go a long way toward providing expectations that clearly communicate what students (and teachers) are expected to know and do.

Newton's analysis of geometry expectations using the van Hiele framework emphasized similar issues, at a slightly larger grain-size. Recall that (a) the van Hiele levels distinguish the recognition of whole figures, from isolated properties of figures, relationships between properties and figures, and finally proof and deductive reasoning and (b) expectations at Levels 1 and 2 (figures and isolated properties) dominate state geometry standards, and Level 3 expectations are quite scarce. If we want to prepare students for deductive reasoning in geometry more effectively, additional expectations must clearly articulate how we expect students to reason about relationships between properties and figures. To do so, we need the appropriate verbs to indicate what we expect students to do with those relationships (e.g., *state* or *explain*) and nouns to name clearly the relationships we want them to master.

Third, one of the principal lessons of the statistics chapter (Newton, Horvath, & Dietiker, this volume) also concerned issues of specific language. Their analysis showed how frequently statistics expectations ask students to *do* something with data and how infrequently they are asked to *evaluate* a representation of data or product of statistical reasoning. This result for statistics is broadly consistent with other chapters in this volume and in its predecessor (Reys, 2006a).

Cognitive Demand

In some sense, this dimension of variation has already been considered, principally with respect to specific language. The cognitive demand of expectations is strongly influenced by the choice of primary verbs and nouns specifying the mathematical concepts that are the objects of those actions. But the measurement of cognitive demand is a highly approximate and interpretive enterprise. As Larnell and Smith (this volume) have argued, cognitive demand is strongly shaped by the character of primary verbs and sophistications of their mathematical predicates. But this two-element scheme, while it is superior to focusing verbs alone, remains an approximate measure. Even before they are paired, neither verbs nor their mathematical predicates carry any absolute level of cognitive demand or difficulty. Nor should we expect that any framework or rubric will make the judgment of cognitive demand of expectations a simple and reliable process. Standards authors can and should attend to word choice, conceptual frameworks (those general, like Bloom's and those more mathematically specific, like van Hiele's), and relevant empirical research on students' learning of mathematics in estimating cognitive demand. But ultimately, those judgments will be interpretive and should be revisited when performance data (and additional research) is available.

Development Across Grades

This final dimension of variation may be the most difficult of the six to articulate and constitutes the most serious challenge for standards' authors to resolve. Because of its importance, we allot more space to sketching some of the developmental issues that emerge from the analyses in this volume. Development across grades concerns how states treat broader topic areas, like congruence, similarity, function, and proportionality, whose importance and complexity require development across grades. Unlike most of the other dimensions, it is a feature of sequences of expectations, not individual GLEs. Development across grades is more than "continuity," as initially discussed above. Where continuity demands some continuous attention over a number of grades, development concerns *the content, not just the presence* of related grade level expectations. As with the preceding dimensions, we see a relatively wide variety of practices across states and topics with respect to development. The following examples illustrate some of the different patterns we have seen in how authors have addressed the issue. Because we appreciate the difficulty of articulating sensible learning trajectories, our discussion is intended more to illustrate the challenge of coherent development than to critique any author team's work or endorse any particular approach. In no cases are the examples given below a state's complete treatment of the topic.

Some states simply repeat the same GLE over two or more grade levels. As we have seen a number of times in the probability analysis (Dingman & Tarr, this volume, Arizona frequently restated the same GLE over two or more years. Example 8.2 below (also Example 7.63 in the previous chapter), that addresses the use of theoretical probabilities to make predictions, was repeated every year from Grade 2 to 8.

Example 8.2. Predict the outcome of a grade-level appropriate probability experiment. (AZ)

Where repetition does underline the importance of particular competencies, it does not help teachers understand the path that students' learning may follow within the designated content area. The Arizona GLE clearly identifies an appropriate starting point for reconciling predictions and outcomes in a probability experiment, but it does not help middle school mathematics teachers see what more might be expected of students who have already mastered this idea in the elementary grades.

A slightly different pattern combines the repetition of expectations with some conceptual progression across grades. Tennessee's treatment of congruence in their Geometry strand in the upper elementary grades is a good illustration (Table 8.2 below). Tennessee's expectations that elementary students recognize congruent figures and describe a motion or motions that will show the congruence of two figures are repeated in two consecutive grades. But that sequence of seven GLEs also gradually increases the complexity of the reasoning expected of students in the latter grades. First, the expectation of identifying a single motion in Grade 4 expands to include a series of motions thereafter. Second, the expected cognitive processes—recognition, compare/contrast, and describe (presumably in general terms)— are different across grades and sensibly ordered.

A third pattern is yet more ambitious, sequencing both changes in the cognitive processes expected of students and in the kind of mathematical

Table 8.2.   A Sequence of GLEs Addressing Congruence From Tennessee's Geometry Standards

Grade	GLE
3	Recognize congruent geometric figures.
4	Recognize congruent geometric figures.
4	Describe a motion that will show that two shapes are congruent.
5	Compare and contrast congruent and symmetrical geometric figures.
5	Describe a motion or a series of motions that will show that two shapes are congruent.
6	Describe similarity and congruence.
6	Describe a motion or a series of motions that will show that two shapes are congruent.

objects those processes operate on. In their Geometry & Measurement strand, New Hampshire and Rhode Island outline the expected development of students' conceptual understanding of similarity across the elementary grades by varying both process verbs and mathematical predicates. Table 8.3 presents their sequence of four GLEs that concern similarity and span Grades 3 to 6. The sequence begins with the simple recognition/identification of similar shapes and then as Tennessee does, steps up the targeted cognitive process to application and problem solving and then to the description of results. But in addition, the objects of those actions change from the shapes alone, to the shapes related by map scales, to the shapes related by specific numerical proportions, and understanding of similarity and proportional change was expected for simpler figures (triangles and rectangles) before more complex ones (polygons and circles).

Ideally, a developmental sequence of expectations will describe a learning trajectory for an important concept where each successive GLE builds sensibly on its predecessor in a manner consistent with research on students' learning and performance. But this ideal may not be achievable in the actual working contexts where standards are written because (a) useable forms of research (i.e., summaries that are comprehensive and accessible for teachers) are scarce and (b) deciding the appropriate

Table 8.3. A Sequence of GLEs Addressing Similarity From New Hampshire and Rhode Island's Geometry & Measurement Standards

Grade	GLE
3	Demonstrates conceptual understanding of similarity by identifying similar shapes.
4	Demonstrates conceptual understanding of similarity by applying scales on maps, or applying characteristics of similar figures (same shape but not necessarily the same size) to identify similar figures, or to solve problems involving similar figures. Describes relationships using models or explanations.
5	Demonstrates conceptual understanding of similarity by describing the proportional effect on the linear dimensions of triangles and rectangles when scaling up or down while preserving angle measures, or by solving related problems (including applying scales on maps). Describes effects using models or explanations.
6	Demonstrates conceptual understanding of similarity by describing the proportional effect on the linear dimensions of polygons or circles when scaling up or down while preserving the angles of polygons, or by solving related problems (including applying scales on maps). Describes effects using models or explanations.

mathematical advance for each grade level and describing that step in words are challenging tasks, even with a solid and accessible research base. As the last example above shows, managing the sequence of expected cognitive processes expressed by verbs AND the different mathematical objects involved in those processes is a challenging enterprise. Getting it even close to "right" will require both resources devoted to considered expectations and cyclical review of their communicative effect and students' performance on relevant assessment items.

CONSEQUENCES OF VARIABILITY

Two significant consequences of the variation among states in how, when, and for how long states express their expectations for learning mathematics K–8 are the negative influence on development of high quality mathematics curriculum materials and the increased difficulty of assessment of student learning on a national scale. With respect to the first issue, content differences among states in the content and form of their expectations, sequences of expectations, and standards (e.g., Geometry vs. Geometry & Measurement) make it difficult, if not impossible to bring curricula to the market that address those expectations in a serious and comprehensive manner. A single textbook series will not suffice, and state-by-state adjustments in content—our current practice—may "meet" each state's standards but with consequent damage to conceptual coherence. Similarly, large-scale assessments of student learning, on annual or grade-band basis, cannot be carried out on a national scale without asking students to demonstrate learning of content that, according to their state standards, their teachers may not have been expected to teach and they have not been expected to learn. The more such assessments are aligned carefully to one or another state's standards (perhaps to a large and/or influential state), the more they undermine the goals of other states' standards.

The "simple" solution to both difficulties might be to develop a set truly national standards and a series of national tests. Indeed, the National Assessment of Educational Progress (NAEP) already represents such a candidate national test at Grades 4, 8, and 12. On the other hand, one could also argue that national standards necessarily bring national uniformity, thereby stifling the possibility of productive innovation that requires variation—such as the state-by-state variation that currently exists. Underlying our current system of articulating expectations at each grade and testing for the achievement of those expectations annually from Grades 3 to 8 is the implicit assumption that all children to mature mathematically at a uniform rate. But if mathematical development and learning is not uniform, testing all children at each grade makes little sense. If this argument were taken seriously, grade-band GLEs (e.g., Grades 3 & 4, 5 & 6, and 7 & 8) and testing at the end of each grade band would be a sensible alternative to current practice. It would allow students longer periods of time to learn and demonstrate target competencies without significant sacrifice in resolution, for example, items assessing the mastery of higher level competencies by faster learners could still be included.

We will not endorse any of these alternatives, as our principal task in this context is to provide accurate and detailed descriptions of our current state mathematics standards to inform a broader policy discussion among many more players. In short, our job has been to describe the nature of state-by-state variability and suggest some possibilities to consider in response. That said, within the current regime of grade-by-grade expectations and annual grade-level tests, we offer three broad recommendations that we believe can improve our national and state-level teaching and learning performance—at least to some degree.

RECOMMENDATIONS

The results of this volume and the preceding one (Reys, 2006a) suggest the following three priorities for producing high-quality standards and expectations: (1) Identify major mathematical goals at each grade, K–8, and build learning trajectories to achieve these goals, within and across those grades, (2) collaborate, within and across states, to promote clarity, communicability, and consensus, and (3) support the work of authors who write and revise expectations.

The first recommendation is a plea for more careful specification of the growth of mathematical ideas over adjacent grade levels—the issue that we have discussed as *development across grades* above. We have seen many examples in the chapters of this volume where collections of GLEs have outlined students' engagement with important mathematical ideas over several grades. That anticipated engagement develops along multiple dimensions—size and kind of numbers or figures involved, complexity of problem situations, connections to other mathematics ideas, and in the growth of complexity of mathematical thinking. This kind of careful development of sequences of GLEs can support more focused and productive discussions among educators about the development of the mathematical thinking and competence across grade levels. Such cross-grade discussions can have very positive consequences for both teachers and students. Knowing what students have learned in a prior grade and what they need to know to be successful in the next grade can have a powerful influence on teachers' planning, classroom teaching, and assessment.

Second, if we truly believe that mathematics standards can support more effective teaching and learning, composing them in state "silos" makes little sense. For many reasons, American families—and therefore American children—are very mobile. Movement between states means we subject our students to the differences in learning expectations documented in these chapters. Imagine if educators in nearby states worked together to articulate more common standards, as New Hampshire and Rhode Island have done. Even increased *regional* coherence would be a worthy step forward. We should collaborate to seek the best of educational innovation in teaching and learning mathematics and use these ideas to create next generations of standards that are clear and understandable to teachers, students, parents, and other stakeholders.

Third, where it has been relatively easy to find and describe differences among states and critique current practice in writing standards for our teachers and students, articulating high-quality standards is difficult work. This is particularly true when (and if) it involves serious *collaboration* with colleagues from other states; a focus on *trajectories of learning*, rather than narrow and particular competencies; attention to the lessons of *relevant research*, and cycles of *revision*. If we truly care about setting "high standards," we should get serious about providing the modest resources—principally time and intellectual resources for authors—necessary to produce and revise them. The same is true for high-quality assessment items to test the achievement of those standards. Continuous improvement, even at the state-level only, is not only needed, it is achievable. But national improvement will require more than simply saying that we care about education and want to hold our teachers and students to high standards. It requires us to sustain our focus and commitment.

APPENDICES

Appendix A

Standards Documents Used in the Analysis of Geometry & Measurement GLEs (*N* = 42 States)

State	Document Title	Year	Grades	Strands
Alabama	Alabama Course of Study: Mathematics (Bulletin 2003, No. 4)	2003	K–8	G, M
Alaska	Performance Standards (Grade Level Expectations) For Grades 3–10	2005	3–8	G, M
Arizona	Arizona Academic Content Standards, Mathematics	2003	K–8	G & M
Arkansas	K-8 Mathematics Curriculum Framework	2004	K–8	G, M
California	Mathematics Framework for California Public Schools (K–12) (Draft Document)	2004	K–7	G & M
Connecticut	Mathematics Curriculum Framework (Draft)	2005	K–8	G & M
Department of Defense	Mathematics Curriculum Content Standards	2004	K–8	G, M
District of Columbia	District of Columbia Mathematics pre-K through Grade 12 Standards	2005	K–8	G, M
Florida	Sunshine State Standards: Grade Level Expectations	1999	K–8	G, M
Georgia	Georgia Mathematics Curriculum	2004	K–8	G, M
Hawaii	Grade Level Performance Indicator Progression for Mathematics	2004	K–8	G, M
Idaho	Power Standards by Grade	2005	K–8	G, M

Appendix A continues on next page.

Appendix A Continued

State	Document Title	Year	Grades	Strands
Indiana	Indiana's Academic Standards for Mathematics	2000	K–8	G, M
Kansas	Kansas Curricular Standards for Mathematics	2003	K–8	G
Louisiana	Mathematics Grade Level Expectations	2004	K–8	G, M
Maine	State of Maine Grade Level Expectations for Mathematics Grades 3–8	2004	3–8	G, M
Maryland	Maryland Voluntary State Curriculum	2004	K–8	G, M
Michigan	Michigan Grade Level Content Expectations (GLCE)	2004	K–8	G, M
Minnesota	Minnesota Academic Standards-Mathematics K–12	2003	K–8	G & M
Mississippi	Mississippi Mathematics Framework 2000	2000	K–8	G, M
Missouri	Mathematics Grade-Level Expectations	2004	K–8	G, M
Nevada	Nevada Mathematics Content Standards for kindergarten and Grades 1 through 8 and 12	2003	K–8	G, M
New Hampshire	Draft K - 8 New Hampshire and Rhode Island Local and NECAP Grade Level Expectations	2004	K–8	G & M
New Jersey	New Jersey Core Curriculum Content Standards for Mathematics	2002	2–8	G & M
New Mexico	Mathematics Content Standards, Benchmarks, and Performance Standards	2002	K–8	G, M
New York	Mathematics Core Curriculum MST Standard 3, pre-kindergarten–Grade 12	2005	K–8	G, M
North Carolina	Mathematics Standard Course of Study and Grade Level Competencies K–12	2003	K–8	G, M
North Dakota	North Dakota Mathematics Content and Achievement Standards Grades K–12	2005	K–8	G, M
Ohio	Academic Content Standards K–12 Mathematics	2001	K–8	G, M
Oklahoma	Priority Academic Student Skills	2002	K–8	G & M
Oregon	Oregon Grade Level Standards and K–2 Foundations	2002	K–8	G, M
Rhode Island	Draft K–8 New Hampshire and Rhode Island Local and NECAP Grade Level Expectations	2004	K–8	G & M
South Carolina	South Carolina Mathematics Curriculum Standards 2000	2001	K–8	G, M

South Dakota	South Dakota Mathematics Content Standards	2004	K–8	G, M
Tennessee	Mathematics Curriculum Standards	2001	K–8	G, M
Texas	Texas Essential Knowledge and Skills for Mathematics (Grades 6–8 and HS updated in 2005)	1998/2005	K–8	G, M
Utah	Mathematics Core Curriculum	2003	K–7	G, M
Vermont	Grade Expectations for Vermont's Framework of Standards and Learning Opportunities	2004	K–8	G & M
Virginia	Mathematics Standards of Learning Curriculum Framework	2002	K–8	G, M
Washington	Mathematics K–10 Grade Level Expectations: A New Level of Specificity	2004	K–8	G, M
West Virginia	Mathematics Content Standards and Objectives for West Virginia Schools	2003	K–8	G, M
Wyoming	Wyoming Mathematics Content and Performance Standards	2003	K–8	G, M

Note: G" or "M" indicates states that have separate geometry and measurement strands where "G & M" denote states that combine their geometry and measurement expectations into a single strand.

Note: Oklahoma's Grade K standards separated Geometry and Measurement.

Appendix B

Framework for Analyzing Measurement GLEs (Adapted From the Clarke et al., 2003)

1. The child shows awareness of the attribute and its descriptive language (may include words such as "know," "identify," "recognize," or "understand")

  1.1. Awareness of the attribute

    1.1.1. Meaning of the attribute

    1.1.2. Definition of the attribute

    1.1.3. Representation of the attribute

    1.1.4. Awareness of the units and tools associated with the attribute

  1.2. Awareness of the descriptive language of the attribute

2. The child compares, orders, and matches objects by the attribute

  2.1. Compares/Sorts objects by attributes

  2.2. Orders objects by attributes

  2.3. Matches objects by attributes

3. The child chooses and uses nonstandard units and tools for estimating and measuring

  3.1. Chooses nonstandard units/tools

Appendix B continues on next page.

Appendix B Continued

3.2. Measures with nonstandard units

3.3. Estimates with nonstandard units

4. The child chooses and uses standard units and tools for estimating and measuring, with accuracy

4.1. Chooses units

4.1.1. No system mentioned

4.1.2. Customary

4.1.3. Metric

4.2. Chooses tools

4.3. Precision/Accuracy (measures to the nearest…)

4.4. Measures (using tools)

4.4.1. No system mentioned

4.4.2. Customary

4.4.3. Metric

4.5. Estimates

4.5.1. No system mentioned

4.5.2. Customary

4.5.3. Metric

5. The child solves a range of problems involving important concepts and skills

5.1. Unit relationships

5.1.1. No mention of standard or nonstandard units

5.1.2. Standard units

5.1.3. Customary units

5.1.4. Metric units

5.1.5. Between measurement systems

5.2. Formulae (rules)

5.2.1. Develops formulae

5.2.2. Understands formulae

5.2.3. Uses/Applies formulae

5.2.4. Knows formulae

5.2.5. Selects formulae

5.3. Applications

5.3.1. Congruence, similarity, and scale factors

5.3.2. Transformations

5.3.3. Pythagorean Theorem

5.3.4. Solves problems/real-world problems

5.3.5. Coordinate geometry and number line

5.4. Relationships between one-, two- and three-dimensional measures

5.4.1. Meanings of relationships

5.4.2. Relationships among units (distinguish)

5.4.3. Changes

5.5. Miscellaneous Problem Solving

5.5.1. Develops strategies

5.5.2. Investigates/Explores

5.5.3. Compares, estimates, and measures

5.5.4. Draws/Constructs/Builds/Sketches

5.5.5. Composite figures (combining or subdividing irregular figures)

5.5.6. Adds and subtracts measurements

APPENDIX C

Brief Analysis of High School Geometry Standards

Eighteen states had produced high school geometry standards at the time of this analysis: Alabama, Arkansas, California, District of Columbia, Florida, Hawaii, Indiana, Maryland, Mississippi, New York, North Carolina, Oklahoma, South Carolina, Tennessee, Texas, Utah, Virginia, and West Virginia. These standards were analyzed only to determine how often and what type of formal deductive reasoning (van Hiele Level 4) is required of students. Fourteen of the 18 states analyzed explicitly require formal deduction. Examples C.1 and C.2 are typical expectations.

Example C.1. Writes a proof (two column or paragraph) to defend conjectures. (Hawaii)

Example C.2. Construct logical arguments in formal and informal methods with direct and indirect reasoning. (West Virginia)

Six states expect students to recognize the need for a counterexample to disprove a statement, as illustrated in Example C.3.

Example C.3. Devise ways to verify results or use counterexamples to refute incorrect statements. (New York)

Utah's document includes an expectation that requires students to understand what does not count as proof (Example C.4)

Example C.4. Realize that observing a pattern and stating a conjecture related to the pattern does not constitute a proof. (Utah)

Two states, Texas and West Virginia, expect students to compare and contrast Euclidean and non-Euclidean geometries (see Examples C.5 and C.6)

Example C.5. Compare and contrast the structures and implications of Euclidean and non-Euclidean geometries. (Texas)

Example C.6. Compare and contrast other geometry to Euclidean geometry. (West Virginia)

The relationship between inductive and deductive reasoning is also included in several documents. Table C.1 summarizes the number of states that explicitly address induction, deduction, and those that expect students to contrast these two types of reasoning. It was interesting to find that all of the states that address inductive reasoning also address deductive reasoning; however, two states (North Carolina and Virginia) only explicitly mention deductive reasoning.

Tables C.2, C.3, and C.4 summarize in three different ways how requirements for proof are expressed in the 14 states whose standards address formal deduction. Table C.2 presents two-dimensional figures that are explicitly mentioned as the objects of the proofs. When states specify the object of proof, triangles and quadrilaterals are the most frequently mentioned. Three states, California, Indiana, and North Carolina, explicitly mention polygon and circle proofs as well as proofs addressing triangles and quadrilaterals. Table C.3 summarizes the particular types of proofs required in the states where type is explicitly specified. Indirect proofs (or proof by contradiction) and coordinate geometry proofs were surprisingly most frequently mentioned—perhaps reflecting only their distinct nature. Three states (New York, Utah, and Virginia) do not specify particular types of proof, specifying instead that students should be able to construct a variety of proofs (see Example C.7).

Example C.7. Select and use various types of reasoning and methods of proof, as appropriate. (Virginia)

Finally, Table C.4 summarizes the particular mathematical topics addressed in the proofs (at various levels of specificity) explicitly mentioned by the states. The most common proofs concern congruence and similarity relationships and the Pythagorean Theorem.

Table C.1. Number of States With Level 4 GLEs That Specify Inductive and Deductive Reasoning

Type of Reasoning	Number of States
Deductive	14
Inductive	12
Contrast Inductive and Deductive	3

Table C.2. Number of States With Level 4 GLEs That Address Particular Objects of Proof

Proof Object	Number of States
Triangle	5
Quadrilateral	4
Polygon	3
Circle	3
Parallel/Perpendicular lines	2

Table C.3. Number of States With Level 4 GLEs That Address Particular Types of Proof

Proof Type	Number of States
Indirect/Contradiction	3
Coordinate	3
Two-column	2
Paragraph	2
Construction	2
Flowchart	1
Analytic	1
Algebraic	1
Transformational	1

Table C.4.   Number of States With Level 4 GLEs That Address Proof of Particular Mathematical Content

Mathematical Content	Number of States
Similarity	6
Congruence	5
Pythagorean Theorem	4
Angle Relationships	2
Segment Division	2
Regularity of Polygons	1
Distance Formula	1
Inequality	1
Hinge Theorem	1

Appendix D

State Standards Documents Used in the Analysis of Statistics and Probability GLEs (*N* = 41 states)

State	Document Title	Date
Alabama	Alabama Course of Study: Mathematics	2003
Alaska	Math Performance Standards (Grade Level Expectations) for Grades 3–10	2005
Arizona	Arizona Academic Content Standards–Mathematics (Grade Level Expectations)	2003
Arkansas	Arkansas Mathematics Curriculum Frameworks K–12	2004
California	Mathematics Framework for California Public Schools: K–12	2005
Connecticut	Mathematics Curriculum Framework	2005
Department of Defense	Mathematics Curriculum Content Standards	2004
District of Columbia	Mathematics pre-K-Grade 12 Standards	2005
Florida	Sunshine State Standards with Grade Level Expectations	1999
Georgia	Georgia Performance Standards	2004
Hawaii	Hawaii Content & Performance Standards III (Mathematics Content Standards)	2005
Idaho	Idaho Content Standards	2006
Indiana	Indiana's Academic Standards for Mathematics	2000
Kansas	Kansas Curricular Standards for Mathematics	2003
Louisiana	Grade Level Expectations	2004
Maryland	Maryland Voluntary State Curriculum	2004

Michigan	Michigan Grade Level Content Expectations (GLCE)	2004
Minnesota	Minnesota Academic Standards for Mathematics	2003
Mississippi	Mississippi Mathematics Framework 2007	2006
Missouri	Mathematics Grade Level Expectations	2004
Nevada	Nevada Mathematics Standards	2006
New Hampshire	New Hampshire K-8 Mathematics Grade Level Expectations (K–8) (with Rhode Island)	2006
New Jersey	New Jersey Core Curriculum Content Standards for Mathematics	2002
New Mexico	Mathematics Content Standards, Benchmarks, and Performance Standards	2002
New York	New York Learning Standards for Mathematics	2005
North Carolina	Mathematics Standard Course of Study and Grade Level Competencies K–12	2003
North Dakota	Mathematics Content and Achievement Standards	2005
Ohio	Academic Content Standards	2001
Oklahoma	Priority Academic Student Skills	2002
Oregon	Oregon Grade Level Standards and K–2 Foundations	2002
Rhode Island	NECAP and Local Mathematics Grade Level Expectations (K–8) (with New Hampshire)	2004
South Carolina	South Carolina Mathematics Curriculum Standards 2000	2001
South Dakota	South Dakota Mathematics Content Standards	2004
Tennessee	Mathematics Curriculum Standards	2001
Texas	Texas Essential Knowledge and Skills for Mathematics	2005
Utah	Mathematics Core Curriculum	2003
Vermont	Grade Expectations for Vermont's Framework of Standards and Learning Opportunities	2004
Virginia	Virginia Mathematics Standards of Learning Curriculum Framework	2002
Washington	Mathematics K–10 Grade Level Expectations: A New Level of Specificity	2004
West Virginia	Mathematics Content Standards and Objectives for West Virginia Schools	2003
Wyoming	Wyoming Mathematics Content and Performance Standards	2003

REFERENCES

Achieve. (2005). *Maryland State Department of Education: Analysis of the voluntary state curriculum (VCS) in science grades pre-K–8*. Retrieved on May 8, 2007, from http://www.achieve.org/files/MDscience.pdf

Achieve. (2006). *Our goal*. Retrieved September 17, 2006, from www.achieve.org

Achieve. (2007). *Mathematics benchmarks*. Retrieved February 18, 2007, from http://www.achieve.org/node/187

Bloom, B. S. (1956). *Taxonomy of educational objectives: Handbook of cognitive domain.* New York: McKay.

Bloom, B. S. (1984). *Taxonomy of educational objectives.* Boston: Allyn & Bacon.

Burger, W. F., & Shaughnessy, J. M. (1986). Characterizing the van Hiele levels of development in geometry. *Journal for Research in Mathematics Education, 17,* 31–48.

Center for the Study of Mathematics Curriculum. (n.d.). *State mathematics content standards.* Columbia: University of Missouri. Retrieved November 7, 2005, from http://matheddb.missouri.edu/states.php

Clark, D. (1999). *Learning domains or Bloom's Taxonomy.* Retrieved July 9, 2006, from http://www.nwlink.com/~donclark/hrd/bloom.html

Clarke, D., Cheeseman, J., McDonough, A., & Clarke, B. (2003). Assessing and developing measurement with young children. In D. H. Clements (Ed.), *Learning and teaching measurement* (pp. 68–79). Reston, VA: National Council of Teachers of Mathematics.

Clements, D. H. (1999). Geometric and spatial thinking in young children. In J. V. Copley (Ed.), *Mathematics in the early years* (pp. 66–79). Reston, VA: National Council of Teachers of Mathematics.

Clements, D. H. (2003). Teaching and learning geometry. In J. Kilpatrick (Ed.), *A research companion to principles and standards for school mathematics* (pp. 151–178). Reston, VA: National Council of Teachers of Mathematics.

Clements, D. H., & Battista, M. T. (1992). Geometry and spatial reasoning. In D. A. Grouws (Ed.), *Handbook of research on mathematics teaching and learning* (pp. 420–464). New York: MacMillan.

Clements, D. H., Swaminathan, S., Hannibal, M. A. Z., & Sarama, J. (1999). Young children's concepts of shape. *Journal for Research in Mathematics Education, 30,* 192–212.

The College Board. (2006). *College Board standards for college success: Mathematics and statistics.* New York: Author.

Coxford, A. L., & Usiskin, Z. (1971). *Geometry: A transformational approach.* River Forest, IL: Laidlaw Bros.

Crowley, M. (1987). The van Hiele model of the development of geometric thought. In M. Lindquist (Ed.), *Learning and teaching geometry, K–12* (pp. 1–16). Reston, VA: National Council of Teachers of Mathematics.

Finn, C. E., Julian, L., & Petrilli, M. J. (2006). *The state of state standards 2006.* Washington, DC: Thomas B. Fordham Foundation.

Franklin, C., Kader, G., Mewborn, D., Moreno, J., Peck, R., Perry, M., et al. (2007). *Guidelines for assessment and instruction in statistics education (GAISE) report: A pre-K–12 curriculum framework.* Alexandria, VA: American Statistical Association.

Friel, S. N., & Bright, G. W. (1998). Teach-Stat: A model for professional development in data analysis and statistics for teachers K–6. In S. P. Lajoie (Ed.), *Reflections on statistics: Learning, teaching, and assessment in grades K-12* (pp. 89–117). Mahwah, NJ: Erlbaum.

Fuys, D., Geddes, D., & Tischler, R. (1988). *The van Hiele model of thinking in geometry among adolescents.* Reston, VA: National Council of Teachers of Mathematics.

Govender, R., & de Villiers, M. (2002, July). *Constructive evaluation of definitions in a sketchpad context.* Paper presented at the meeting of the Association for Mathematics Education of South Africa, Durban, South Africa.

Groth, R. E. (2005). Linking theory and practice in teaching geometry. *Mathematics Teacher, 99*(1), 27–30.

Gutierrez, A. (1996). Visualization in 3-dimensional geometry: In search of a framework. In L. Puig & A. Gutierrez (Eds.), *Proceedings of the twentieth annual meeting of the International Group for the Psychology of Mathematics Education, Vol 1* (pp. 3–19). Valencia, Spain: Universidad de Valencia.

Gutierrez, A., & Jaime, A. (1988). *Globality versus locality of the van Hiele levels of geometric reasoning.* Unpublished manuscript, Universitat De Valencia, Valencia, Spain.

Gutierrez, A., Jaime, A., & Fortuny, J. M. (1991). An alternative paradigm to evaluate the acquisition of the van Hiele levels. *Journal for Research in Mathematics Education, 22,* 237–251.

Gutierrez, A., Pegg, J., & Lawrie, C. (2004). Characterization of students' reasoning and proof abilities in 3-dimensional geometry. In M. J. Hoines & A. B. Fuglestad (Eds.), *Proceedings of the twenty-eighth annual meeting of the International Group for the Psychology of Mathematics Education, Vol 2* (pp. 511–518). Bergen, Norway: Bergen University College.

Hartweg, K. (2005). Solutions to the triangular bicycle flags problem. *Teaching Children Mathematics, 11,* 466–471.

Henderson, K. B. (Ed.). (1973). *Geometry in the mathematics curriculum: 1973 Yearbook*. Reston, VA: National Council of Teachers of Mathematics.

Hoffer, A. (1983). Van Hiele-based research. In R. Lesh & M. Landau (Eds.), *Acquisition of mathematics concepts and processes* (pp. 205–228). New York: Academic Press.

Howe, K. (2006). *Review* [Review of the report *The state of state standards 2006*]. Great Lakes Center for Educational Research and Practice. Retrieved September 12, 2006, from http://greatlakescenter.org/docs/Think_Twice/TT_Fordham%20State%20Standards%20Review%202006.pdf

James, I. (2002). *Remarkable mathematicians: from Euler to von Neumann*. Washington, DC: Mathematical Association of America.

Jones, D. L. (2004). *Probability in middle grades mathematics textbooks: An examination of historical trends, 1957–2004*. Unpublished doctoral dissertation, University of Missouri-Columbia.

Jones, G. A., & Bishop, A. (Eds.). (2005). *Exploring probability in school: Challenges for teaching and learning*. Dordrecht, The Netherlands: Kluwer Academic Press.

Jones, G. A., Langrall, C. W., & Mooney, E. S. (2007). Research in probability. Responding to classroom realities. In F. Lester (Ed.), *Second handbook of research on mathematics teaching and learning* (pp. 909–956). Charlotte, NC: Information Age Publishing.

Kastberg, S. E. (2003). Using Bloom's Taxonomy as a framework for classroom assessment. *Mathematics Teacher, 96*(6), 402–405.

Kilpatrick, J., Swafford, J., & Findell, B. (Eds.). (2001). *Adding it up: Helping children learn mathematics*. Washington, DC: National Academy Press.

Konold, C., & Higgins, T. L. (2003). Reasoning about data. In J. Kilpatrick, W. G. Martin, & D. Schifter (Eds.), *A research companion to Principles and Standards for School Mathematics* (pp. 193–215). Reston, VA: National Council of Teachers of Mathematics.

Konold, C., & Pollatsek, A. (2002). Data analysis as the search for signals in noisy processes. *Journal for Research in Mathematics Education, 33*, 259–289.

Lehrer, R. (2003). Developing understanding of measurement. In J. Kilpatrick, W. G. Martin & D. Schifter (Eds.), *A research companion to Principles and Standards for School Mathematics* (pp. 179–192). Reston, VA: National Council of Teachers of Mathematics.

Lehrer, R., Jacobson, C., Kemeny, V., & Strom, D. (1999). Building on children's intuitions to develop mathematical understanding of space. In E. Fennema & T. A. Romberg (Eds.), *Mathematics classrooms that promote understanding* (pp. 63–87). Mahwah, NJ: Lawrence Erlbaum.

Lehrer, R., Jaslow, L., & Curtis, C. (2003). Developing an understanding of measurement in the elementary grades. In D. H. Clements (Ed.), *Learning and teaching measurement* (pp. 100–121). Reston, VA: National Council of Teachers of Mathematics.

Lindquist, M.M. (Ed.). (1987). *Learning and teaching geometry, K–12: 1987 Yearbook*. Reston, VA: National Council of Teachers of Mathematics.

Llorens Fuster, J.-L., & Perez Carreras, P. (1997). An extension of van Hiele's model to the study of local approximation. *International Journal of Mathematical Education in Science and Technology, 28*, 713–726.

Lott, J., & Nishimura, K. (Eds.). (2004). *Standards and curriculum: A view from the nation.* National Council of Teachers of Mathematics: Reston, VA.

Malloy, C. E. (1999). Perimeter and area through the van Hiele model. *Mathematics Teaching in the Middle School, 5*, 87–90.

Mason, M. M. (1989, April). *Geometric understanding and misconceptions among gifted fourth-eighth graders.* Paper presented at the meeting of the American Educational Research Association, San Francisco, CA.

Mayberry, J. (1983). The van Hiele levels of geometric thought in undergraduate preservice teachers. *Journal for Research in Mathematics Education, 14*, 58–69.

Mistretta, R. M. (2000). Enhancing geometric reasoning. *Adolescence, 35*, 365–379.

Monaghan, F. (2000). What difference does it make? Children's view of the differences between some quadrilaterals. *Educational Studies in Mathematics, 42*, 179–196.

Mooney, E. S. (2002). A framework for characterizing middle school students' statistical thinking. *Mathematical Thinking and Learning, 4*, 23–63.

Mumford, D., Series, C., & Wright, D. (2002). *Indra's pearls: The vision of Felix Klein.* Cambridge, UK: Cambridge University Press.

National Assessment Governing Board. (2004). *Mathematics framework for the 2005 National Assessment of Educational Progress.* Retrieved January 16, 2008, from http://www.nagb.org/pubs/m_framework_05/toc.html

National Council for the Social Studies. (1994). *Expectation of excellence: Curriculum standards for social studies.* Washington, DC: Author.

National Council of Teachers of English, & International Reading Association. (1996). *Standards for the English language arts.* Urbana, IL: National Council of Teachers of English.

National Council of Teachers of Mathematics. (1989). *Curriculum and evaluation standards for school mathematics.* Reston, VA: Author.

National Council of Teachers of Mathematics. (1991). *Professional standards for teaching mathematics.* Reston, VA: Author.

National Council of Teachers of Mathematics. (1995). *Assessment standards for school mathematics.* Reston, VA: Author.

National Council of Teachers of Mathematics. (2000). *Principles and standards for school mathematics.* Reston, VA: Author.

National Council of Teachers of Mathematics. (2006). *About NCTM: Mission.* Retrieved September 17, 2006, from http://www.nctm.org/about/

National Council of Teachers of Mathematics. (2006). *Curriculum focal points for pre-kindergarten through grade 8 mathematics: A quest for coherence.* Reston, VA: Author.

National Mathematics Advisory Panel. (2008). *Foundations for success.* Washington, DC: U.S. Department of Education.

National Research Council (1989). *Everybody counts: A report to the nation on the future of mathematics education.* Washington, DC: National Academy Press.

National Research Council. (2008). *Assessing the role of K–12 academic standards in states.* Washington, DC: National Academy Press.

Newton, J., Larnell, G., & Lappan, G. (2006). Analysis of K-8 Algebra Grade-Level Learning Expectations. In B. J. Reys (Ed.), *The intended mathematics curriculum as represented in state-level curriculum standards: Consensus or confusion?* (pp. 59-87). Charlotte, NC: Information Age Publishing.

Nixon, E. (2005). Creating and learning abstract algebra: Historical phases and conceptual levels. Doctoral dissertation, University of South Africa, 2005. *Dissertations Abstracts International, 68,* 05.

Pegg, J. (1997). *Broadening the descriptors of van hiele levels 2 & 3.* In F. Biddulph, & K. Carr (Eds.), *People in Mathematics Education, Proceedings of the twentieth annual conference of the Mathematics Education Group of Australasia* (pp 391–396). Rotorua, New Zealand: University of Waikata.

Piaget, J., & Inhelder, B. (1975). *The origin of the idea of chance in children.* New York: Norton.

Piaget, J., Inhelder, B., & Szeminska, A. (1960). *The child's conception of geometry.* New York: W. W. Norton.

Price, M. (1997). Book Review. [Review of the book *What's happening in math class? Vol 2: Reconstructing Professional Identities*]. *Zentralblatt für Didaktik der Mathematik. 29,* 191–193.

Reys, B. J. (Ed.). (2006a). *The intended mathematics curriculum as represented in state-level curriculum standards: Consensus or confusion?* Charlotte, NC: Information Age Publishing.

Reys, B. J. (2006b). State-level curriculum standards: Growth in authority and specificity. In B. J. Reys (Ed.), *The intended mathematics curriculum as represented in state-level curriculum standards: Consensus or confusion?* (pp. 1–13). Charlotte, NC: Information Age Publishing.

Reys, B. J., Dingman, S., Olson, T., Sutter, A., Teuscher, D., & Chval, K. (2006). Analysis of K-8 Number and Operation Grade-Level Learning Expectations. In B. J. Reys (Ed.), *The intended mathematics curriculum as represented in state-level curriculum standards: Consensus or confusion?* (pp. 15–57). Charlotte, NC: Information Age Publishing.

Schmidt, W. H., McKnight, C. C., Valverde, G. A., Houang, R. T., & Wiley, D. (1997). *Many visions, many aims: A cross-national investigation of curriculuar intentions in school mathematics* (Vol. 1). Boston: Kluwer.

Senk, S. (1989). Van Hiele levels and achievement in writing geometry proofs. *Journal for Research in Mathematics Education, 20,* 309–321.

Sharp, J. M., & Hoiberg, K. B. (2001). And then there was Luke: The geometric thinking of a young mathematician. *Teaching Children Mathematics, 7,* 432–439.

Shaughnessy, M. (2003). Research on students' understandings of probability. In J. Kilpatrick, W. G. Martin, & D. Schifter, (Eds.), *A research companion to Principles and Standards for School Mathematics* (pp. 216–226). Reston, VA: National Council of Teachers of Mathematics.

Sinclair, N. (2008). *A history of the geometry curriculum in the United States.* Charlotte, NC: Information Age Publishing.

South Dakota Department of Education. (2004). *South Dakota mathematics content standards.* Retrieved October 25, 2006, from http://doe.sd.gov /contentstandards/math/standards.asp

Stephan, M., & Clements, D. H. (2003). Linear and area measurement in prekindergarten to grade 2. In D. H. Clements (Ed.), *Learning and teaching measurement* (pp. 3–15). Reston, VA: National Council of Teachers of Mathematics.

Strom, D., Kemeny, V., Lehrer, R., & Forman, E. (2001). Visualizing the emergent structure of children's mathematical argument. *Cognitive Science, 25*, 733–773.

Swadener, M. (1987). Pictures, graphs, and transformations a distorted view of plane figures for middle grades. In J. M. Hill (Ed.), *Geometry for grade K–6: Readings from the Arithmetic Teacher* (pp. 76–82). Reston, VA: National Council of Teachers of Mathematics.

Tarr, J. E. (2002). Principles and Standards: Providing opportunities to learn probability concepts. *Teaching Children Mathematics, 8*(8), 482–487.

Tarr, J. E., & Shaughnessy, J. M. (2007). Data analysis, statistics, and probability. In F. Lester & P. Kloosterman (Eds.), *Results from the 2003 National Assessment of Educational Progress*. Reston, VA: National Council of Teachers of Mathematics.

University of Illinois Committee on School Mathematics. (n.d.). *Stretchers and shrinkers*. Urbana, IL: University of Illinois Press.

Usiskin, Z. (1982). *Van Hiele levels and achievement in secondary school geometry* (Final report of the Cognitive Development and Achievement in Secondary School Geometry Project: ERIC Document Reproduction Service No. ED 220 288). Chicago: University of Chicago.

Van de Walle, J. A. (2000). *Elementary and middle school mathematics: Teaching developmentally*. New York: Longman.

Van Hiele, P. M. (1957). *The problem of insight in connection with schoolchildren's insight into the subject matter of geometry*. University of Utrecht.

Van Hiele, P. M. (1959). *Development and learning process: A study of some aspects of Piaget's psychology in relation with the didactics of mathematics*. Groningen, The Netherlands: J. B. Wolters.

Van Hiele, P. M. (1986). *Structure and insight: A theory of mathematics education*. Orlando, FL: Academic Press.

Van Hiele, P. M. (1988). The child's thought and geometry. In D. Fuys, D. Geddes & R. Tischler (Eds.), *English translation of selected writings of Dina van Hiele-Geldof and Pierre M. Van Hiele* (pp. 243–252). New York: Brooklyn College.

Van Hiele, P. M. (1999). Developing geometric thinking through activities that begin with play. *Teaching Children Mathematics, 5*, 310–315.

Van Hiele, P. M., & Van Hiele-Geldof, D. (1958). A method of initiation into geometry at secondary school. In H. Freudenthal (Ed.), *Report on methods of initiation into geometry* (pp. 67–80). Groningen, The Netherlands: J. B. Wolters.

Van Hiele-Geldof, D. (1957). *The didactics of geometry in the lowest class of the secondary school*. University of Utrecht, The Netherlands.

Vidakovic, D., Bevis, J., & Alexander, M. (2003). Bloom's Taxonomy in developing assessment items. *Journal of Online Mathematics and Its Applications. 3.* Retrieved November 1, 2006, from http://mathdl.maa.org/mathDL/4/?pa=content&sa=viewDocument&nodeId=504&pf=1

Webb, N. L. (1999). *Alignment of science and mathematics standards and assessments in four states*. Washington, DC: Council of Chief State School Officers.

Whitman, N. C., Nohda, N., Lai, M. K., Hashimoto, Y., Iijima, Y., Isoda, M., et al. (1997). Mathematics education: A cross-cultural study. *Peabody Journal of Education, 72*, 215–232.

Wild, C. J., & Pfannkuch, M. (1999). Statistical thinking in empirical enquiry. *International Statistics Review, 67*(3), 223–265.

Wirszup, I. (1974). *Some breakthroughs in the psychology of learning and teaching geometry.* Paper presented at the Annual Meeting of the National Council of Teachers of Mathematics, Atlantic City, NJ.

Wirszup, I. (1976). Breakthroughs in the psychology of learning and teaching geometry. In J. L. Martin & D. A. Bradbard (Eds.), *Space and geometry. Papers from a research workshop* (pp. 75–97). Athens, GA: University of Georgia, Georgia Center for the Study of Learning and Teaching Mathematics. (ERIC Document Reproduction Service No. ED 132 033)

ABOUT THE AUTHORS

Leslie Dietiker is a mathematics education doctoral student at Michigan State University. Her primary interest is in finding ways to improve written curricula to increase aesthetic appeal, student accessibility, and learning opportunities.

Shannon Dingman is assistant professor in the Department of Mathematical Sciences at the University of Arkansas. His research interests concern issues of alignment and nonalignment between mathematics curricula and state standards.

Aladar K. Horvath is a mathematics education doctoral student at Michigan State University. His interests focus on teaching and learning collegiate mathematics and in assisting teachers at all levels understand the mathematics in the curriculum for the benefit of their students.

Sarah E. Kasten is assistant professor in mathematics education at Northern Kentucky University. She works with middle grades preservice and practicing mathematics teachers, and her research focuses on preservice mathematics teachers' experiences in teacher education programs.

Glenda T. Lappan is a University distinguished professor in the Department of Mathematics at Michigan State University. Her interests in mathematics standards comes from her decades of work on curriculum research and development and teachers' learning and teaching, particularly at the middle school level.

Gregory V. Larnell is a mathematics education doctoral student at Michigan State University. His interests concern mathematics curriculum and more centrally, equity and identity in mathematics education, particularly the success and failure of African American students in remedial college mathematics courses.

Jill Newton is assistant professor in mathematics education at Purdue University. She taught high school mathematics and science for 12 years in six countries and currently oversees Purdue's secondary mathematics program. Her research examines written curricula, including textbooks, standards documents, and syllabi, and their enactment in mathematics classrooms.

John P. Smith III, "Jack" to his colleagues, is associate professor in the Department of Counseling, Educational Psychology, and Special Education in the College of Education at Michigan State University. His interests concern the nature of people's understanding and learning of mathematics across the lifespan.

James E. Tarr is associate professor in the Department of Learning, Teaching & Curriculum in the College of Education at the University of Missouri. His research interests include the development of students' probabilistic reasoning, teachers' use of curricular materials, and the impact of curriculum on student learning.

Sasha Wang is a mathematics education doctoral student at Michigan State University. Her research interests stem from a commitment to understanding students' mathematical thinking and reasoning, and its implications for teaching and learning, particularly in the area of geometry.

LaVergne, TN USA
27 December 2010
210083LV00003B/4/P